RAISING SPIRIT IN BLACKFOOT TERRITORY

Collaborative Design and Ethnographic Refusal

Jan Newberry

Raising Spirit in Blackfoot Territory examines the ethnographic dilemmas that arose across the run of the Raising Spirit project. This book asks what ethnography can be in the era of reconciliation based on this multi-year, multimodal, collaborative project to articulate child-rearing values in Blackfoot Territory.

Collaborative work between a university and Indigenous community organization to build a digital storytelling library brought together researchers young and old, Indigenous and settler, university and community-based. This book centrally concerns ethnography as a form of expertise and its need for a decolonizing fix. Young researchers were positioned as para-ethnographers and tasked with identifying cultural values for the digital library. Their design-influenced innovations to code collaboratively were an inspired answer to the political and ethical questions of knowledge production in a time of Indigenous resurgence and racial reckoning. Yet, when asked to serve as culture experts, young Indigenous researchers refused. The generative power of their refusals revealed the possibility for new imaginaries that exceed ethnographic recognition.

Anthropologist Jan Newberry probes deeply into important questions on how to produce knowledge in a system that was designed to erase the voices it now is trying to bring to the fore. This work contributes to the reimagining of ethnographic methods in anthropology and productively expands attention to issues of expertise and ethnographic collaboration with Indigenous peoples.

JAN NEWBERRY is a professor emeritus of anthropology at University of Lethbridge. An award-winning teacher whose research has been recognized internationally, she also helped co-found the Institute for Child and Youth Research and the Community Bridge Lab at the university.

Raising Spirit in Blackfoot Territory

Collaborative Design and Ethnographic Refusal

JAN NEWBERRY

In collaboration with
Tanya Pace Crosschild
Amy Mack
Erin Spring
With contributions from
Hudson Eagle Bear
Tesla Heavy Runner
Mikey Lewis
Taylor Little Mustache

UNIVERSITY OF TORONTO PRESS
Toronto Buffalo London

Toronto Buffalo London
utppublishing.com
Printed in Canada

ISBN 978-1-4875-6001-0 (cloth)
ISBN 978-1-4875-6002-7 (paper)
ISBN 978-1-4875-6003-4 (uPDF)
ISBN 978-1-4875-6004-1 (ePUB)

Library and Archives Canada Cataloguing in Publication

Title: Raising Spirit in Blackfoot territory : collaborative design and ethnographic refusal / Jan Newberry ; in collaboration with Tanya Pace Crosschild, Amy Mack, Erin Spring ; with contributions from Hudson Eagle Bear, Tesla Heavy Runner, Mikey Lewis, Taylor Little Mustache.
Names: Newberry, Janice C., author
Description: Includes bibliographical references and index.
Identifiers: Canadiana (print) 20250284340 | Canadiana (ebook) 20250284944 | ISBN 9781487560010 (hardcover) | ISBN 9781487560027 (softcover) | ISBN 9781487560034 (PDF) | ISBN 9781487560041 (EPUB)
Subjects: LCSH: Ethnology—Methodology. | LCSH: Anthropology—Methodology. | LCSH: Ethnology—Moral and ethical aspects. | LCSH: Anthropological ethics. | LCSH: Community-based research. | CSH: Blackfoot—Social life and customs.
Classification: LCC GN345 .N49 2025 | DDC 305.897/352—dc23

Cover design: Val Cooke
Cover image: Courtesy of author Jan Newberry

We wish to acknowledge the land on which the University of Toronto Press operates. This land is the traditional territory of the Wendat, the Anishnaabeg, the Haudenosaunee, the Métis, and the Mississaugas of the Credit First Nation.

This book has been published with the help of a grant from the Federation for the Humanities and Social Sciences, through the Awards to Scholarly Publications Program, using funds provided by the Social Sciences and Humanities Research Council of Canada.

University of Toronto Press acknowledges the financial support of the Government of Canada, the Canada Council for the Arts, and the Ontario Arts Council, an agency of the Government of Ontario, for its publishing activities.

Canada Council for the Arts Conseil des Arts du Canada

ONTARIO ARTS COUNCIL
CONSEIL DES ARTS DE L'ONTARIO
an Ontario government agency
un organisme du gouvernement de l'Ontario

Funded by the Government of Canada Financé par le gouvernement du Canada

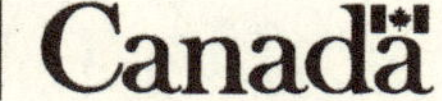

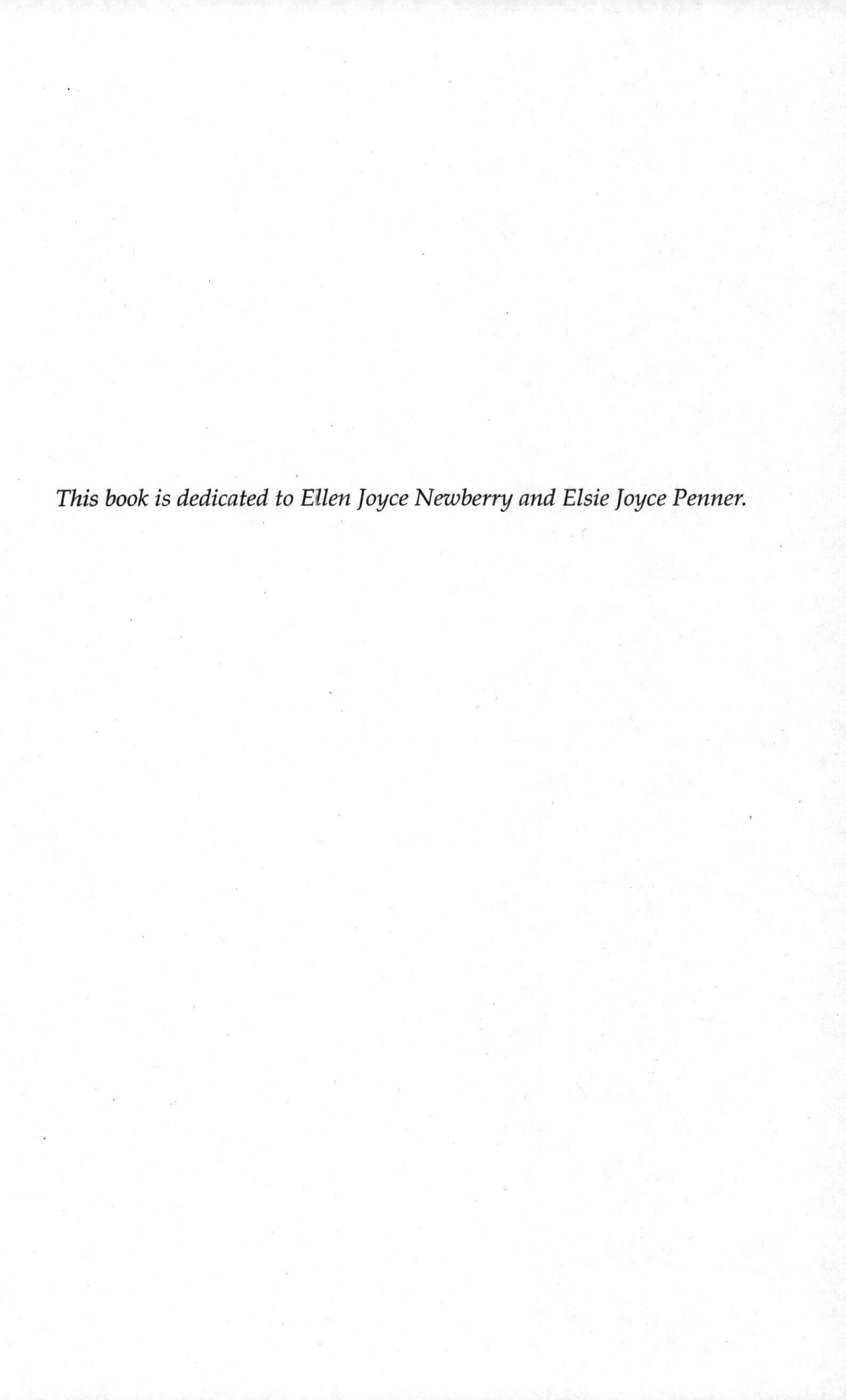

This book is dedicated to Ellen Joyce Newberry and Elsie Joyce Penner.

Contents

Figures

Foreword

Oki niksokowaiksi. It is a profound honour to write the foreword for this book, a work that thoughtfully and ethically addresses the challenges of engaging within Indigenous knowledge systems, while navigating the complex positionalities and representational authority in Indigenous research contexts. As Niitsitapi (Blackfoot) from Kainaiwa (Blood Tribe), I am especially pleased to see a text that amplifies Blackfoot perspectives and enhances the visibility of our ways of knowing and being, particularly within a growing Indigenization landscape where contextuality is often overlooked.

Mainstream discourses often reduce Indigeneity to simplistic monoliths and binaries, failing to capture the rich diversity and contextuality inherent in Indigenous ways of being and knowing. This book disrupts and refines such limited perspectives, honouring the complexity of Indigenous intersectional identities and experiences. In this era of truth and reconciliation, boundaries around Indigenous identity, collectivity, and authority are constantly being contested, exploited, and extracted. While long-standing issues such as cultural appropriation remain critical, newer challenges – such as Indigenous identity theft, often referred to as "pretendianism" – underscore the need for a nuanced approach to safeguarding Indigenous representational authority. Amid these persistent assaults on Indigeneity, the hardening of community boundaries introduces complex ethical considerations for both Indigenous researchers and non-Indigenous scholars engaging in Indigenous research, requiring a critical orientation to Indigenous relationality.

This book is both timely and urgent, illustrating how boundaries are imagined, negotiated, and sometimes refused within Indigenous resurgent knowledge mobilizations. Authored by Dr. Jan Newberry, a non-Indigenous scholar, the book illuminates the relational politics and internal conflicts that arise as both Indigenous and non-Indigenous researchers navigate the complexities of mediating positionalities of power and privilege across cultural perspectives, societal expectations of cultural authenticity, and their own evolving roles as learners of Indigenous knowledge systems. The act of claiming "expert" knowledge as a marker of "authentic" Indigeneity is entangled with various power dynamics and layers of privilege, which this book deftly explores through the Indigenous youth researchers' experiences in the Raising Spirit Project. The thoughtful refusals by Indigenous youth researchers, particularly around the label of "cultural experts," reveal a deep awareness of the complexities and responsibilities associated with such designations.

Newberry employs the concept of the "double bind" in ethnographic research to reveal the tensions in establishing authoritative Indigenous knowledge claims within the intricate web of relationships Indigenous people inhabit – impacted by settler-colonialism, dispossession, and other forms of relational ruptures. This strongly resonates with ongoing critical Indigenous studies debates concerning competing claims to knowledge, authority, and belonging within and across Indigenous communities. This perspective aligns with Daniel Heath Justice's depiction of Indigenous relationality as "a messy thing. It's about what happens when bodies and imaginations come together in a relationship, when boundaries are breached and something else comes into being, for good or ill – sometimes, for both" (Justice 2018, 104).

Newberry's work illuminates what Blackfoot scholar Leroy Little Bear (2000) refers to as "jagged worldviews colliding," particularly within the layered contexts of building Indigenous "expert" knowledge against the backdrop of colonialism and community gatekeeping dynamics. The book thoughtfully navigates these intricacies, identifying dilemmas embedded in the process of making Indigenous knowledge claims – shaped by colonial assumptions of what constitutes valid knowledge, the ongoing impacts of dispossession, and the specific challenges of articulating Blackfoot knowledge within the backdrop of "canonical knowledge of Elders."

Importantly, Newberry's analysis of the "in-between-ness" of Indigenous youth researchers reveals the complexities and challenges inherent in Indigenous knowledge generation and transfer, capturing the unique struggles Indigenous youth face as an "in-between" generation engaging in Indigenous cultural reclamation work. Power dynamics emerge as Indigenous youth – and others who may have been distanced from cultural or traditional knowledge sources – interact with formal Blackfoot systems of law and governance, particularly when Elders and other community gatekeepers view the recognition of these voices as potentially bypassing traditional protocols. In Blackfoot thought, this concept is embodied in poomaksin (transfer rites), a highly regulated socio-legal process affirming the authenticity, relationality, and authority of rights-holders and enforcers of Niitsitapi law (Crowshoe and Manneschmidt 2002). This exemplifies the structured nature of Blackfoot meaning-making practices and institutions, providing context for the anxieties felt by young Blackfoot researchers as they engage with an Indigenous knowledge system that is more formalized and institutionalized compared to other Indigenous cultural traditions.

While upholding Indigenous systems of law and governance is crucial, it is equally important to acknowledge the power dynamics embedded within community gatekeeping practices. The Raising Spirit Project underscores an urgent need for greater accountability to Indigenous youth, revealing that while youth are often envisioned as the future, Blackfoot Elders and Knowledge Keepers hold a profound responsibility to make accessing these ways of knowing less burdensome. Importantly, not all transfers within Blackfoot tradition and culture are "sacred" in the ceremonial sense, though they frequently carry spiritual significance. Blackfoot ways of knowing encompass more than ceremonial rites; they are also deeply social, political, and foundational to community-centred governance.

The Raising Spirit Project further emphasizes the importance of naming and honouring the voices of Indigenous youth, recognizing them as active teachers and leaders in the present. The reflections shared by the young Indigenous researchers underscore the need for more relational approaches to fortify Indigenous knowledge systems. Through Opokaa'sin and the Raising Spirit Project, we find a model and source of inspiration for envisioning the transformative potential of decolonial and resurgent work.

When I was first introduced to the Raising Spirit Project during my last year of high school, I knew little about Indigenous scholarship or Blackfoot ways of knowing, although I had close kinship connections with the communities served by Opokaa'sin, the Indigenous child and family non-profit organization in Lethbridge that partnered with the project. As a youth involved with Opokaa'sin, I was given the opportunity to assist by handling transcriptions and organizing written materials. This experience opened my eyes to the depth of Blackfoot cultural, social, and political thought, revealing how much I still had to learn about Niitsitapiisini (our way of life). Through this project, I came to appreciate the profound role of Indigenous storytelling – a lesson that has since guided my doctoral research on the territorial politics of Indigenous relationality.

Now, more than a decade later, I have acquired various cultural transfer rights in accordance with traditional Blackfoot law, actively participated in the governance structures of traditional Blackfoot societies and am nearing the completion of my PhD in Indigenous politics at the University of Calgary. Reflecting on the Raising Spirit Project, I recognize it as a pivotal experience that not only expanded my understanding of Blackfoot ways of knowing, being, and relating, but also ignited a lifelong commitment to exploring and advocating for critical approaches to Indigenous resurgence, reconciliation, relationality, and decolonization. This involves stronger accountability to Indigenous youth and strengthening Indigenous knowledge systems to support intergenerational knowledge exchange.

In closing, I am deeply privileged to introduce this book, as it represents not only a significant scholarly contribution, but also the genuine allyship that Dr. Jan Newberry embodies. As a non-Indigenous scholar, she has been a steadfast friend to Opokaa'sin and a trusted supporter of Niitsitapi resurgence efforts. Dr. Newberry has generously offered her time and wisdom whenever called upon to support the needs of local Indigenous communities, demonstrating a respectful commitment to Blackfoot knowledge systems and to nurturing the next generation of Indigenous scholars. Her work in this book exemplifies what true solidarity looks like: a careful, ethical engagement that uplifts Indigenous voices and honours the complexities of our communities. For this, I am profoundly grateful to Jan, and I am honoured to introduce her work to a wider audience.

By Ryan Crosschild

Acknowledgments

One thing I learnt from my first fieldwork experience in Java, Indonesia, was that my frequent "thank you" was not being received the way I hoped. Like most folks in North America, I was quick to offer a thank you for any service done on my behalf. It wasn't until late in that first fieldwork trip that I understood that I was offending people who were seeking to establish and maintain a relationship with me by suggesting that it was over with my "thank you." In other words, "thank you," or *terima kasih,* meant that our exchange was finished and done. Instead of offering such platitudes, it was much more important to keep the relationship strong by being ready to give back at some point. I learnt that lesson again during the Raising Spirit Project. The essence of relationality is the building and keeping of relationships with others. Here, most of all, I want to acknowledge this hard-earned lesson and to identify some of those who helped me learn it by supporting the project that has led to this book.

Let me begin at the beginning. The genesis of Raising Spirit was a photo-elicitation project. Dr. Michelle Hogue, Don Gill, and Dr. Steve Ferzacca joined Tanya Pace Crosschild and I to organize giving cameras to caregivers identified through Opokaa'sin Early Intervention Society. As students, Diandra Bruised Head and Joanna Crop Eared Wolf worked with the caregivers and folks they met at powwows. Chloe Crosschild and Maria Livingston did coursework to expand and reinforce what was being learnt during the project. Throughout this long project, Opokaa'sin staff have been supportive and welcoming, helping students and researchers alike. My thanks particularly to Edna Bad Eagle, Deanna Shade, and Jocelyn Davis. Staff who helped with the summer camps included Tico Iron Shirt, Miles Bruised Head, Joey Blood, and Charity Black Rider.

Many Blackfoot Elders contributed wisdom and support during the project, more than I can truly account for here. Even so, I want to particularly acknowledge the contributions of Peter Weasel Moccasin, Deb Pace, Charlene Plume, Rose Fox, Roger Prairie Chicken, Roger Hunt, Francis First Charger, Blanche Bruised Head, and Crystal Shade.

The University of Lethbridge has provided support across the project in a variety of ways. Many students beyond those named here contributed to the project. I want to specifically recognize Cecilia Reid and Zainab Al-Rikabi. And of course, Mikey Lewis made many crucial contributions here both in and outside the classroom. I want to acknowledge too my patient and understanding Anthropology Department colleagues. The structure of the Institute for Child and Youth Studies at the University of Lethbridge was instrumental in providing space and student support. My thanks to Dr. Kristine Alexander who served as its director for much of that time. Her own students Ashley Henrickson and Kaitlynn Weaver provided not only research support but inspiration and moral support to the team. They, along with Kristine, were also responsible for the Elders of the Future Project portion of the project. My thanks as well to JP Marchant for helping train the research team in videography.

In the city of Lethbridge, CASA, the Galt Museum, and the Park Place Mall all offered space to exhibit photographs and other materials from the project. Dr. Anne Dymond and her students contributed support to the exhibit at the Park Place Mall. Darcy Logan helped tremendously with the final exhibition at CASA. Funding was provided by the University of Lethbridge, the Community Foundation of Lethbridge and Southern Alberta, the Urban Aboriginal Knowledge Network funded by a SSHRC Partnership Grant, and PolicyWise for Children.

Bronwyn Davis and Mikey Lewis both helped immensely with manuscript preparation. My thanks to them and to Jodi Lewchuk at the University of Toronto Press, who was everything one could hope for in an editor. I am grateful to the anonymous reviewers who improved this book tremendously. My gratitude as well to Marcia Rich for her wise guidance and generous support.

At the centre of the project are young people, most of whom are not named here. It was their courageous refusals as much as their willingness to share their knowledge that made this project what it was. At the heart of this book are the work, words, and wisdom of Hudson Eagle Bear, Tesla Heavy Runner, and Taylor Little Mustache. I will be forever grateful for their bravery and their willingness to share their personal journeys here. I also want to acknowledge two who did not contribute to this volume directly but were nonetheless very important: Jimmy Vielle and Deanne Provost were important parts of the second summer's research team. And beyond the contributors named here themselves, Taylor Little Mustache's family as well as Hudson Eagle Bear's grandmother were very helpful and supportive of the project and the team.

The many relationships made and remade in this project have changed me and my life. I want to end by acknowledging the people who made it possible for *me* to complete this book and who urged me to honour the work done for the Raising Spirit Project. Dr. Amy Mack and Dr. Erin Spring have been co-conspirators, allies, and friends throughout. I thank them for their support, their understanding, their patience, and their insight. Both have become distinguished scholars and trusted collaborators.

Without Tanya Pace Crosschild, this project would not have been possible. It has been her humour, her knowledge and vision, and her unwavering commitment to young people, including especially Blackfoot young people, that have carried this project forward. In fact, her whole family has been instrumental, including her husband, Patrick, and at least two of her children, Chloe and Ryan. I can't thank her enough. I can only try to live by some of the values she has taught me, including not taking myself too seriously. Blackfoot people often identify their humour as a cultural value. That's true, but it also always comes with the grace and strength of a people who have endured and thrived despite so much.

Closer to home, there is my own little family. Thank you to Ana, Nick, and Elsie. You too remind me what's important in this world.

But mostly, for Steve, my love and thanks for being not only my anthro buddy and fellow traveller, but my first and most trusted confidant. You believed in this book before I did, and it exists because of you. My love and thanks always.

RAISING SPIRIT IN BLACKFOOT TERRITORY

Chapter One

What Ethnography Can and Cannot Do

Prologue

This is not an ethnography. But I did take some ethnographic field notes. Here is an excerpt written towards the end of the Raising Spirit Project, a more than seven-year-long collaborative project between university scholars and a local non-profit dedicated to Indigenous children and their families in southern Alberta. This project began as a pilot attempt to use participatory photo-elicitation to articulate child-raising values among primarily Blackfoot folks. It ended as a collaborative experiment with young researchers, Indigenous and settler, in design-driven ethnographic innovation to deal with the patchy and distributed knowledge encountered and made in the process. The move to co-creation and collaboration followed from refusals by young and Indigenous people to take on the role of culture expert, and the double-binds that come with it. The blogged field notes below describe one of the many ruptures prompted by troubles with the making of ethnographic knowledge across the run of the project.

BROKEN HEARTED (JAN'S FIELD JOURNAL, 11 AUGUST 2017)[1]

"But if you can't stop the horror, shouldn't you at least document it?"

This is one of a series of questions that Ruth Behar asks in her book *The Vulnerable Observer: Anthropology that Breaks Your Heart* (1996). She describes the anxiety of the field researcher who seeks to understand.

"Loss, mourning, the longing for memory, the desire to enter into the world around you and having no idea how to do it, the fear of observing too coldly or too distractedly or too raggedly, the rage of cowardice, the insight that this always arriving late, as defiant hindsight, a sense of the utter uselessness of writing anything and yet the burning desire to write something, are the stopping places along the way" (3).

She tries to give her Aunt Rebecca an answer to what anthropology is by saying: "it is the most fascinating, bizarre, disturbing, and necessary form of witnessing left to us at the end of the twentieth century" (5). And she mentions George Devereux's belief that "observers in the social sciences had not yet learned how to make the most of their own emotional involvement with their material" (6).

I picked up Behar's book after our failed (?) design studio with my anthropology colleagues. It was one of the toughest fieldwork moments of this, or any, project I've undertaken. Yet, I think the painful part suggests the need for more of this kind of work. As we have said all along, this is about risk and vulnerability. And yet we are still taken by surprise when it hurts quite this much. As Behar says, "anthropology has always been vexed about the question of vulnerability" (5).

I want to run away from what happened and from the pain I witnessed (caused?) but I take seriously the importance of witnessing and working alongside. There is a long history of the idea of being a witness or witnessing. There are Christian connotations of witnessing for others. And there is the idea of witnessing at the heart of the truth and reconciliation process that was modeled first in in South Africa. Here is some of what it says about witnessing in the TRC report:

> "Pursuant to the Settlement Agreement, one of the objectives of the Commission is to 'witness, support, promote and facilitate truth and reconciliation events at both the national and community levels.' See the current list of Honorary Witnesses.
>
> The term witness is in reference to the Aboriginal principle of witnessing, which varies among First Nations, Métis and Inuit peoples. Generally speaking, witnesses are called to be the keepers of history when an event of historic significance occurs. Partly because of the oral traditions of Aboriginal peoples, but also to recognize the importance of conducting business, building and maintaining relationships in person and face to face.
>
> Through witnessing the event or work that is undertaken is validated and provided legitimacy. The work could not take place without honoured and respected guests to witness it.
>
> Witnesses are asked to store and care for the history they witness and most importantly, to share it with their own people when they return home."[2]

> Are we, the settlers in this project, witnessing? Is this Geertz's idea that fieldwork is "putting yourself in the way"? Perhaps. But is witnessing too passive? Or can witnessing be the equivalent to passing the mic or boosting the signal? All of these are vexed questions too, and by that I mean: there are no easy answers. And it seems to me the work is sitting with the complications, paradoxes, and yes, the pain as we work this through.
>
> I do know one thing and that is that I am *implicated* by design, by history, by position, by accident. We are all Treaty people and I can't walk away from the table.[3]
>
> I will be spending the next year or more trying to understand what happened that day.

This blog post is dated a month before the end of the Raising Spirit Project. The post describes the effects of several reckonings – with methodological choices, with collaborative research with Indigenous young people, with reconciliation work in Canada after the Truth and Reconciliation Commission's report in 2015, and with what ethnography can be now.

The event described was a failed attempt at collaborative coding of project materials. In this instance, the collaboration was between young project researchers, Indigenous and settler, and anthropology faculty. This combination signified one of the central questions in the second phase of the project: Could young Indigenous people share their para-ethnographic knowledge to identify Blackfoot cultural values? After a first phase of photo-elicitation with Blackfoot caregivers and others had produced 8,000 photographs to code for child-rearing values, the second phase moved more deeply to recognize local cultural values by framing them as para-ethnographic (see Holmes and Marcus 2008; Rabinow et al. 2008). Seeking ethnographic recognition (cf. Coulthard 2014) for everyday indigenous knowledge, young Indigenous people joined the project and were trained in Indigenous protocol and academic research. Their work together across two summers would lead to questions about what ethnography offers in an era dominated by reconciliation, recognition, and refusal.

The move to collaboration in the second phase was driven by the need to build a digital storytelling library with the project materials. The young research team developed a design-inspired method for collaborative coding that exploded any sense of being culture experts. Instead, this method of comparing values across difference showed that the team's refusals to act as culture experts in effect redistributed expertise to circulate across relationships. The possibility of making new publics for this redistributed knowledge was in marked contrast to the blow of the failed collaboration with the "real" culture experts from the Anthropology Department. The heartbreak described above captures the moment when the limits of the optimism about the collaborative work ran aground on older ideas about what ethnography is meant to do. Yet ultimately, the limits of ethnographic recognition led to other possibilities following from the refusal and redistribution of expertise by young Indigenous people – the making and strengthening of relationships across difference.

The arc of this project's development from one aimed at eliciting the latent child-rearing values of Blackfoot peoples after the genocidal effects of residential schooling to design-inspired collaborative coding in the era of reconciliation is the subject of this book. Although the articulation of Blackfoot values was the prompt for the research, this book is not about sharing those values. Instead, it is a consideration of what ethnography can and cannot do now. Across its chapters, the various dilemmas posed by the ethnographic recognition of Indigenous knowledge, particularly that of the young, are considered. The question of para-ethnography and its relationship to a contrast between everyday indigenous knowledge and canonical Indigenous knowledge resurfaces questions about the role of ethnography in understanding knowledge and its production. Placing young Indigenous people as culture experts in-the-making led to refusals of the double bind of translation. Opening up the making of knowledge about values in collaborative design spaces showed its distribution and circulation to be the essence of relationality. The shifts and changes in ethnographic methods across the project and what they say about expert knowledge, research with young people, collaborative design approaches in anthropology, and the role of translation and refusal in ethnography are the focus of this book.

Here, as a prologue to this consideration, the Raising Spirit Project is introduced along with the dilemmas of its writing at a particular time in Canada and in anthropology. Its making resurfaces old dilemmas around voice but in a different context. What can and cannot be written here is described along with descriptions of that context and the central contributors to this volume.

Raising Spirit

The Raising Spirit Project began long before it got its name. It started as a series of informal conversations between Tanya Pace-Crosschild, the director of a local non-profit agency, and me, an anthropology professor at the local university. We were connected by a mutual friend and our first conversations were about a shared problem that we were seeing from very different perspectives. Tanya is the executive director of Opokaa'sin Early Intervention Society. In existence since 1996, Opokaa'sin runs a series of early childhood programs, as well as those to support youth and families. The organization serves Indigenous children and their families in a small metropolitan centre of about 100,000 people in southern Alberta. Approximately 2,500 people identified as Indigenous in the 2016 census of the city (Statistics Canada 2019), and the Blackfoot reserve outside the city is said to be Canada's largest.[4] While Opokaa'sin serves Indigenous or First Nation, Métis, and Inuit (FNMI) children as well as settler children, in practice, most of the people served are Blackfoot.[5] This group is divided into those living on- or off-reserve, and children living with their families or in foster care. There are further differences in age between very young children, teens, parents, and Elders, all of whom come together at Opokaa'sin in various activities, programs, and events.

When we first met, Tanya was watching the push for Head Start programming in Canada from her position as the executive director of a non-profit devoted to Indigenous children and their families in southern Alberta.[6] I was back from fieldwork in central Java, Indonesia, where an explosion of early childhood programs had followed from World Bank dictates to develop early childhood programming (Newberry 2017a). I had begun my career as an ethnographer in Yogyakarta, central Java, in 1992. My work on early childhood education and care (ECEC) began in 2007 as democratic reform, along with tsunamis and earthquakes, were reorganizing both education and government (Newberry 2010, 2017a, 2017b).

What Tanya and I shared was frustration with these early childhood programs aimed at improving societies through promoting healthy development of the very young. Our discomfort was not with the focus on the young, especially those typically denied equal access to quality education, but instead the universal guidelines designed to be implemented anywhere and everywhere to improve the education of the very young with little or no attention to local practices. Conversations between the two of us led to a plan to do some pilot research on how to identify locally meaningful child-rearing values. We described the problem as one of articulation. We began with the presumption that the people we worked with, whether in Blackfoot Territory or in urban Java, had socially legitimate ideas about how to raise children that differed from the normative presumptions of good child-rearing being advocated through the worldwide push for optimal early childhood development. The pilot was meant to facilitate the articulation of those values in local terms.

We started with the premise that people are experts on their own values. This choice would go on to shape the project as it shifted from caregivers to young researchers whose ethnographic expertise was both the trouble with and the source of multiple methodological changes across the second phases of the project. As our goal shifted to building a digital storytelling library and training young researchers, Raising Spirit became a project in research creation as refusals by young Indigenous researchers to serve as culture experts and the problems of who was to code for values drove the need for innovation and design-inspired experimentation. In the end, the Raising Spirit Project illustrated how the desire for ethnographic recognition of cultural expertise lead to a doubling of Indigenous youth in troubling ways even as it points the way to other possible futures.

Writing in Blackfoot Territory in the Era of R's

This project took place during a period of intense social reflection in North America and beyond. The Truth and Reconciliation Commission of Canada was constituted in response to the largest class action suit in Canada, the Indian Residential Schools Settlement Agreement. The TRC did its work between 2007 and 2015. The final report and related information are housed at the National Centre for Truth and Reconciliation at the University of Manitoba (https://nctr.ca/records/reports/). But this was also the era of the rising social movements that would be named Idle No More and Black Lives Matter.

Even if the project described in this book did not start explicitly as a part of the Truth and Reconciliation process in Canada to address the genocidal violence of the residential school system, its later stages were certainly shaped by the shifting social and political landscape of an era that seems to be dominated by R-words (and see Tuck and Yang 2014a): reconciliation, Indigenous resurgence, recognition, and refusal. Political debates still rage about these words and their relevance. Each resonates with challenges to anthropology and ethnographic practices as not-yet-post-colonial, as not nearly anti-colonial enough, and as a continuing exercise of coloniality. The force of this moment of reckoning was undeniable. This book draws on some of the scholarship around the various R's, but its central goal is another *return* to ethnography and what it can and cannot be. Here, the focus is the refusal of ethnographic recognition (Coulthard 2014; Povinelli 2002). Such refusals can challenge the relationship between culture and territory (A. Simpson

2007, 2017; and see the next chapter) and the idea of research on/for/with Indigenous Peoples at all (Tuck and Yang 2014b). Certainly, they challenged the idea of para-ethnographic knowledge.

Although this research was conducted in Blackfoot Territory and among the settler and Indigenous Peoples of Treaty 7, this is not an ethnography of Blackfoot Peoples.[7] It is not about Blackfoot culture or ways of living and knowing in any comprehensive sense, although these are considered in places. Instead, it is a contemplation of what ethnography offers to those who work alongside one another and from different positions but for very different reasons, and how ethnography might provide a space of possibility for contemplating different ways of knowing without presuming mastery (Singh 2018) or expertise and without attempting to resolve – or reconcile – differences. Instead, this work is about the possibility for diplomacy (Latour 2014) between ontologies, epistemologies, and forms of difference. Attention is paid to moments of attunement, adjacency, and alignment in translational encounters that build and depend upon relations and relationality.

In Canada, it is now expected that a land acknowledgment will be offered at the beginning of any presentation. Here, I resist this increasingly empty performance to look instead to how land practices in both Blackfoot ways of knowing and ethnography can model relationship-building in this territory (chapter 2). Audra Simpson's work (2007, 2017) registers the power of the confluence between recognizing the colonial shaping of territory and refusals of what I call here "ethnographic recognition." She, like others (Tuck and Yang 2014a; McGranahan 2016a, 2016b; Cisneros 2018), considers both the limits and possibilities generated by refusals.

Even so, the fact that the work was done in Blackfoot Territory is consequential. The Blackfoot Confederacy stretches across southern Alberta and Saskatchewan and northern Montana and is sometimes described as stretching from the North Saskatchewan River to the Yellowstone River, and from the Rocky Mountains to past the Great Sand Hills in Saskatchewan (see Blackfoot Crossing Historical Park, https://blackfootcrossing.ca/). The nations of the Blackfoot Confederacy include the Kainai, Piikani, and Siksika in Canada and the Amskapi-Piikani (Blackfeet) in Montana, many of whom use the term Niitsitapi, which can be translated as "the real people," to describe Blackfoot Peoples. Siksikaitsitapi is used to refer to the Blackfoot Confederacy Tribal Council (https://blackfootconfederacy.ca/), while the Blackfoot Confederacy is a general term used to refer to these historically and linguistically related groups. Nation members in Canada live across this territory on reserves and in the city, but also in the mostly rural communities that surround the reserves.

Through this project and my teaching, I have become keenly aware of the role of Indigenous Peoples in North America in shaping the discipline of anthropology. Starn (2011; and see Field 1999) charts the rise and fall of this work, and the changing social, political, and economic conditions in North America that accompanied it and its interruption by the civil rights movements of the 1960s, including the Red Power Movement. Vine Deloria's call in 1988 to rethink what anthropology owed was important in shaping the trajectory of the discipline. Starn describes a turning away from the complications of this kind of work that was reinforced through the crisis in representation and the attention to how ethnographers write culture. As Raising Spirit began, anthropology had not yet seen the florescence in work on Indigenous North America or by Indigenous people from North America that Starn (2011) predicted more than a decade ago, although there are more and more signs of it (cf. Cattelino and Simpson 2022). Some of the most trenchant critiques are from those who have left the discipline (Todd 2016) in an era of transformational social change in the second decade of the twenty-first century.

Whether this work is relevant to Blackfoot people is not something I can predict. My concern here is to avoid using what I learnt alongside Blackfoot people as a backdrop to a project of settler redemption through ethnography. This work was produced *with* Blackfoot researchers, young and old, university- and agency-based, in spaces from the open prairie to the city, from the campus to reserve offices, from sacred sites to local arts spaces, from our lab space to the classrooms and gathering spaces at Opokaa'sin. As taken up in chapter 5, this work happened in a kind of third space that was created through this project in Blackfoot Territory.

Enjambment: Refusing and Redistributing Voice

The many starts of this book have begun in a cloud of words: entanglements, encounters, patches, reconciliation, refusal, ontology, epistemology, and collaboration. Many of these resonate with previous assemblages, rhizomes, plateaus, lines of flight, and on and on. Anthropologists are the poets of the social sciences, or so it seems to me. As one ages, the trending word can strike the ear as forced, and indeed, a former student recounted how they had been advised to coin a term to really make it in the discipline. Yet the power of words to capture moments of emergence (look, there's another one) and the slow unfolding of scholarly understanding in moments of awakening and change still thrills me.

But, so many years in, the swirl of words can also overwhelm. Some words return boomerang-like with new power, their unresolved tension revealed in new and undeniable ways: colonial, post-colonial, decolonizing, anti-colonial. Others are origami blooms of scholarship, real-world politics, and career trajectory with the potential to capture something just beyond our current reach. Enfoldment? Has anyone taken that one?

Given the abundance of words and ideas that jostle in anthropology, it was troubling to feel that I had lost my voice as I sat down to write this book about a transformative ethnographic project in Blackfoot Territory. As I try again to do justice to this project, its many participants, voices, outcomes, influences, and effects, I turn to the poet's word "enjambment." Mary Oliver described it this way: "Always, at the end of each line there exists – inevitably – a brief pause. The pause is part of the motion of the poem, as hesitation is part of the dance" (1994, 54). Ethnographers recognize and in fact endorse the pause between time in the field and the writing of it (Gupta and Ferguson 1997). Yet the pause between the end of work on the Raising Spirit Project and the writing of this book was quite long, for a variety of reasons that are described below. To try once again to write this complex, multifaceted, and beautiful project, I take inspiration from enjambment: "When, on the other hand, the poet enjambs the line – turns the line so that a logical phrase is interrupted – it speeds the line for two reasons: curiosity about the missing part of the phrase impels the reader to hurry on, and the reader will hurry twice as fast over the obstacle of a pause because it is there. We leap with more energy over a ditch than over no ditch" (Oliver 1994, 54). The ditch here was dug by the interruptions and obstacles to the writing of this project which ultimately are part and parcel of its power. Using the energy of enjambment, I try again to write about what this project was.

My hesitations about how to write this book have only multiplied since the project ended. The Calls to Action from the TRC's final report (2015a) have been amplified – and rejected – across Canada. Calls to decolonize anthropology echoed the larger boom of attention to the continuing colonial character of the Canadian state, of academia, and of Indigenous–settler relations across North America and beyond. As Zoe Todd (2016) was calling for a reckoning in anthropology while others said let it burn down (Jobson 2020) and Anand Pandian (2019) was looking for its possibilities, the end of my career beckoned. Here was a third space different from the one to be taken up in chapter 5, although perhaps with the same creative potential. My third space follows the first space as a fieldworker in Indonesia and the second as a teacher-researcher in the United States and Canada. In this third career space, my work has been to facilitate the work of others and consistently give way to younger people as researchers, experts, fieldworkers, collaborators, and co-authors. I imagine this is true for many, including those who turn to writing thin books late in their careers to contemplate what it all meant (Geertz 1996, for example). This, again, is not what this book is. Yet writing it does afford me the opportunity to consider the challenges to voice and to standpoint produced at the confluence of this third career space and the predicaments of collaborative ethnography, even as it underlines the centrality of pedagogy in all this work.

When I first wrote as an ethnographer (Newberry 2006, 2013), I made decisions about how to use my voice that reflected a different confluence of issues. For instance, I worked alongside my partner husband, Steve Ferzacca (2001), and in my writing, I took on directly the question of research as a couple and the long history of the wife as helpmeet that Tedlock described (1995). My own dissertation fieldwork arrangements aligned with my research on the making of the domestic sphere in lower-class Javanese neighbourhoods. It also reflected an interest in the everyday influenced by Wolf's (1982) "people without history" and the effects of feminist anthropology's attention to the gendering of knowledge production (Moore 1989). The "I" was firmly foregrounded in my writing as a response to the calls for reflexivity (Marcus and Fischer 1986). The influence of Behar and Gordon's (1995) *Women Writing Culture* was only beginning to be heeded, and I felt quite brave and bold in using my voice in the way I did. It was a claim on ethnographic authority.

In the decades since, many things have changed but others not so much. Second-wave feminism has been superseded and is not infrequently vilified now. The punctuated equilibrium of decolonization in anthropology is once again in a moment of change and challenge that reflects larger political, economic, and social shifts. Since I first wrote as an ethnographer, attention to intersectionality and positionality have become expected components of qualitative research. Even more, questions of ontology and epistemology within the discipline and beyond have further challenged how we know what we know. Calls for design approaches (Gunn et al. 2013) and collaboration (Lassiter 2005; Rappaport 2008) have served to decentre the expertise of the ethnographer in important ways.

The nature and quality of expertise has been the subject of much consideration in anthropology and other social sciences. The critique of the governmentality and the rationalization of expertise along with the continuing anguish about the discipline's sources of authority have made it awkward and uncomfortable – perhaps impossible? – to write a book as a sole author (cf. Alonso Bejarano et al. 2019). This tension has been intensified by Indigenous scholars in the discipline (Tallbear 2014; Todd 2016; Cattelino and Simpson 2022) whose challenges to ethnographic expertise are landing with more force now. The convergence of so many sources of doubt further complicates how to write about a sprawling project, with its many participants, experts, researchers, and authors, not to mention its many phases, objectives, and still-emerging outcomes.

Does a book even make sense? Who is it to be written by and for whom? Collaboratively authored pieces about the project have appeared, including one multi-authored piece (Alexander et al. 2018) that included youth researchers, graduate students, a postdoctoral fellow, and two faculty members. Tanya and I co-authored a photo-essay in 2019, and she had contributed a chapter to an edited volume (Pace-Crosschild 2018). Erin Spring has published on her own Blackfoot projects in that time period (2016; Spring and Fox 2018). Two co-authored pieces with Amy Mack, who served as a lead researcher and project manager as a graduate student, have appeared (Mack and Newberry 2018, 2020). We also worked together on a piece in 2021 for which Erin Spring, who was a postdoctoral fellow during the project, joined us (Mack et al. 2021; and see Newberry 2021). In fact, the three of us – as settler scholars – continue to reckon with the politics of returning to the project to see how multimodality might breach the silos of academic publishing. Given all of this, why a book? A return to a long-form, conventional text implies more coherence and stability than most of us experienced during the project. I was aware of the dilemmas of how to represent this project even before it ended. Perhaps my enjambment began earlier than I even knew. Here is another snippet from my field notes.

THE IMPOSSIBILITY OF FIELD NOTES (JAN'S FIELD JOURNAL, 24 JULY 2017)

This is my first entry despite the fact that I've been involved with this project since it began over 7 years ago. And despite the fact that I preach to all those young ethnographers involved that they must keep good field notes. Given the long delay and my shame over it, it would seem impossible to start keeping field notes now. But, I just had an interesting conversation with a colleague in Singapore. She had begun her career working and researching with Indigenous communities in Australia. The politics of that work and of the whole process of representing others became too much. She subsequently turned to studying urban Singapore. I find my own path to be the reverse of that. My original fieldwork made me an accidental urbanist in Indonesia, and I've come to this project with Indigenous Peoples in Canada at the end of my career. Still, I don't disagree with her: this is impossible work. I knew I could/would never attempt to write and describe the child rearing values of Blackfoot people, but I was interested in understanding how they approached that problem. How do people whose social reproductive practices and transmission of inter-generational knowledge have been so profoundly interrupted by genocidal practices, including residential schooling and the 60s scoop (and now the foster care system and other forms of violence) [[8]] – how do they solve the problem of child rearing? Of preparing their young for what will come? And by staying in touch with the past. By asking that impossible question, I had to shift my position as an ethnographer. Anna Tsing talks about being adjacent. By that I think she means that we can work alongside others rather than studying them as subjects. In part because the problems that we have set for ourselves may be common ones, and how we answer them will produce the world we share.

So, it is impossible for me to accurately represent Blackfoot child rearing values. But I can be adjacent as people strive to articulate their own values as they continue to raise strong and resilient families. And besides, it is the impossible tasks that challenge us to find our common humanity.

But as Amy [Mack] reminds me (yet again) to do field notes, I am reminded first that she is becoming a terrific anthropologist and second that the Raising Spirit project has changed profoundly my own relationship to the field, fieldwork, and therefore field notes. As I have said repeatedly, this project began as a participatory one and has become more fully collaborative at every step. From the original choice to use photo-elicitation as a means to encourage the articulation of values to the innovation of design studio collaborative work on these values, the old-fashioned ethnographic gaze of the trained observer has been unsettled. And there are some implications from this. Perhaps most importantly (and emotionally) for me is that I have ceded control: as fieldworker, as participant-observer and as analyst. This has led to a considerable amount of discomfort. Shouldn't I be doing all of this? And as my primary role has changed in this team project, I find myself struggling with the experiential aspect of fieldwork. If I'm not there all the time as the participant-observer, what can I even say? Both forms of discomfort are very revealing about the fieldwork process. It was only once control was given over (at least in part) that I became aware that control was so central to the method. But as I have worked through this unsettling, I realize that controlling fieldwork is an illusion – and maybe a dangerous one. Collaboration requires the relinquishment of power at some point. And upsetting the power dynamics of traditional fieldwork seems a good outcome for a project being done in the era of reconciliation.

The limits of ethnography are a central question of this project, and yesterday I was reading a piece by Rita Astuti ("On Keeping up the Tension between Fieldwork and Ethnography"; *HAU*, 2017, 7(1): 9–14) [Astuti 2017]. She says: "Moving from fieldwork to ethnography is hard. It is hard because it requires letting go of the participatory experience and, in a way, turning against it." And then later she notes how leaving the field means leaving the "pushback against our analytical simplifications or straightforward misunderstandings" and how "once we are back home, this productive (collaborative) back and forth fades away and our ethnographic analyses can ever so easily lose their anchoring in what they are supposedly about" (10). In many ways, our move to design studios is meant to keep that productive pushback and engagement at the centre of our collaboration as "we continue to create the conditions in which they [our collaborators] can be coproducers of anthropological knowledge" (11).

Despite my concerns, the need to document what was learnt in this project is one reason to write this book, along with the need to honour all the work done on the project. Strangely, perhaps it is my position in a third career space (a kind of third act) that, in a sense, gives me the room to write this, and surely also my position as chief instigator across its many phases. Yet, across the project, its sources of authority have become more and more distributed. So then, from where to speak? And how to speak such that my voice reads as only one of many? Just as the colonial shaping of the discipline is not a new revelation, the question of voice is an old one in ethnographic writing (Stocking 1983; Clifford 1983; Behar and Gordon 1995). Although my first book was sole-authored, I had written as part of a couple and explicitly problematized the voice of the distaff side in an anthropological couple not only to make the domestic visible in my research, but also because it was the subject of my work on women and labour in urban Java. At the time,

I was criticized and questioned by peers about the level of reflexivity and personal disclosure. Now, at the end of my career, I confront a different set of dilemmas that have grown from my original commitments to feminist anthropology, to understanding the local and the least, to emphasizing collaborative approaches, and to the power of anthropology and ethnography to illuminate experiences unsaid.

Yet, one thing that became clear over time was that many of the original participants in Raising Spirit didn't care much about a book as the goal of this project. Instead, they have been driven by commitments of their own: providing social services to Indigenous young people, finishing high school, finishing university, getting a job, raising a child, helping their community, learning their traditions. One issue that continues to trouble this work is not just whether to acknowledge their authorship and expertise, but whether to name young participants. All the ethical concerns that characterize ethnographic work are heightened further in work with the young as researchers, collaborators, and consultants (Soto and Swadener 2016; Sæther et al. 2024). Even so, the protection of vulnerability has been a powerful form of governmentality based on recognition (Coulthard 2014) and the framing of the autonomous liberal subject that has increased harm to the young (Dhillon 2017). Research that seeks to give voice to the young as a form of empowerment may ultimately exploit them without acknowledging the power imbalance involved (Spyrou 2011, 2016; Hartung 2017; Spencer et al. 2020; Komulainen 2007; James 2007). The requirement to use their voices and their names also feels like a kind of fetishization of Indigenous youth.[9] The desire to prove they were involved, that they "were there" (cf. Clifford 1997), becomes an empty performance and a kind of violence when they are expected to "show up," whatever their own needs might be.

So, how then to identify the young participants and collaborators here? I have chosen to name as contributors those whose roles most directly shaped the project, who did some writing about the project, and who have given me permission to do so. By not using many of the names of the young people involved in the project, I am not minimizing their importance or their impact. I am engaged in a different kind of recognition: that the domain of academic scholarship is not important to them, nor need it be. A principle of non-interference has been described as important among Indigenous Peoples in North America (e.g., Wark et al. 2019). There is a widely held value that emphasizes autonomy and non-interference with the choices of others (a subject taken up further in chapter 5). I put that into practice here for the young researchers. I am grateful and appreciative of their time and the gifts of their knowledge, but I do not presume that identifying them here is the way to honour that debt. Rather, recognizing the limits of the kind of knowledge production with which I am engaged here is meant instead to honour other ways of knowing as beyond its remit.

One other source of hesitation in writing this book derives from my own sense of being at the edges of the project that I initiated and guided. The displacement of my voice and my "expertise" from the centre of this project was partly by design, but partly because of its emergence as collaborative and co-designed work from a participatory project. This shift reflects many current realignments in Blackfoot Territory, in Canada, and in anthropology as a discipline. Any authoritative account of the project no longer feels possible if it ever was.

This project has meant that middle and high school students have worked alongside undergraduate and graduate students. Staff at a local non-profit and other community organizations have worked alongside scholars at the local university. Blackfoot Elders have worked alongside professors. Settlers have worked alongside Indigenous people. More than once, participants refused to engage in the manner offered to them, instead offering silence or answers in other registers (Spyrou 2016; Spencer et al. 2020; Lewis 2010; Komulainen 2007). In such a panoply of overlapping and braided conversations, "voice" becomes an ongoing question and not an answer to this writing dilemma.

In this context, Victoria Cooper (2022) provides a provocative challenge to the idea of "giving voice" to children. The idea of recognizing the voice of the young has produced a large literature on child-centred research devoted to their agency and their role as experts in their own lives (e.g., Cooper 2022, 71; Kellett 2011). Noting that attention to children's voices is paradigmatic for the interdisciplinary field of childhood studies, Cooper identifies the limits of understanding voice as disembodied, primarily verbal, and understood as the authentic voice of autonomous, self-aware individuals unmediated by other voices, particularly those of powerful adults. She cites Mayes' 2019 contention that "the voice of the child becomes aligned with voices of other silenced groups and repositioned as subjects with agency, thus defining their capacity to act autonomously and make their own choices" (Cooper 2022, 73; and see Spyrou 2011, 2016; James 2007; Spencer et al. 2020). Cook-Sather (2007, 29) make the connection between first-wave feminist theories in the Western world that "acknowledge women as agents, critics, and creators of knowledge" (Cooper 2022, 73) and the position of children as active subjects who create their own worlds as well. The conceptual conflation of the voice of women with that of children is only furthered when the voices of Indigenous Peoples are added, extending a set of conceptual and political linkages (Rollo 2018a). It is Cooper's attention to "the voice of the researcher within a research assemblage" (78) that is most useful for my dilemma here. She asks, "So, if we suspend the idea that there is one voice – but many – and no such thing as authenticity but relational exchanges, feelings and beliefs interacting as assemblages within complex social systems – what then is the future of child focused research?" (Cooper 2022, 79). Ultimately, that's what the Raising Spirit Project taught me, taught us, and how I came to be able to put this book together after all. The shifting research assemblage across the run of the project aimed at "giving" voice to values instead demonstrated the distributed and decentred character of knowledge across Blackfoot Territory as in-the-making, emergent, and relational, the product of pain and productive of possibility. In keeping with Cooper's analysis, the materiality of our design work, like the original photographs, were active agents in the making of knowledge and relations, and the affective dimensions of ethnographic encounters, on and off campus, were the very stuff of relationality.

So, I have not "found" my voice again. In fact, the search for my own voice serves as a kind of asking for permission to speak that belies the central teachings of the project itself. It was all of us working adjacent and alongside one another that identified the problems with eliciting knowledge and the generative effects of refusing to participate in knowledge understood this way. All I can do here is try to bring forward an account of working alongside others by highlighting their voices braided with my own, sometimes amplifying, sometimes interrupting, sometimes refusing.

In the pages that follow here, I seek to stay with the reckoning over what ethnography can be now by staying with its troubles (Haraway 1991). To do this, I will toggle between an unsettled "I" and "we" in the writing. Embracing the awkwardness of trying to describe what I came to know alongside my collaborators who were knowing in different ways, for different reasons, and at different tempos – and who don't necessarily want to show up here – feels like the most truthful thing I can do.

Even so, the distributed and decentred character of this project poses obstacles to writing a monograph. To illustrate this adjacency and to stay true to how the work on this project happened, I will be drawing on the blog created as a repository for the field notes of several of the young collaborators. In the chapters that follow, the blog will be used to provide the kind of intimate and detailed sense of engagement and entanglement that we expect from an ethnography while resisting its attribution to a single author. So, while many of the people who contributed in some way to the project will not be specifically unidentified, the blog writers whose voices will appear throughout this book are put in context here.

Dr. Erin Spring joined the Institute for Child and Youth Studies (I-CYS) in 2015 as a postdoctoral fellow. Her own work on sense of place in children's literature was expanded through projects on the role of place in children's literature in Indigenous contexts. In her time with I-CYS, she served as a crucial mediator between students (graduate, undergraduate, and younger) and faculty members. Her work alongside Amy Mack as the managers of the lab space across the project meant that they consistently collaborated on issues around the young researchers and the many delights and dilemmas of working with them.

Dr. Amy Mack began her work on Raising Spirit in the period between completing her master's degree and beginning her PhD. During the project, her role expanded from lab manager to lead researcher as she assumed more and more responsibility for the project. Her work on Raising Spirit developed alongside her central research on digital ethnographies, alt-right hate, and white supremacy. Along with Erin, she managed the complex methodological and emotional terrain of working with young researchers across two years of research.

Taylor Little Mustache (M.Ed.) initially joined the project as an undergraduate student completing her combined degree in preparation for becoming a K-12 classroom teacher. Although younger than Amy and Erin, she became in effect the third leg of a team that worked directly with the younger researchers but also with the principal investigators, that being me and Tanya. Taylor's teaching skills – perhaps especially her coaching skills from a career in basketball – made her an indispensable member of this team. Her deep familial connections to the Piikani Nation were equally important sources of connection and knowledge for the team.

In 2016 and 2017, two high school students joined this core team. Both were identified through Opokaa'sin as young people who were in foster care. Both had a mentor assigned by Opokaa'sin to work alongside them. One of the great pleasures of this project was watching these two young people grow. Hudson Eagle Bear was in his third year of high school when he joined the team. His interest in learning and connecting with Blackfoot ways of knowing shaped his involvement in many ways. He had familial connections to the Kainai Nation, but he was living in the city and not with his mother during the project, a situation that was troubling to him. Hudson's deep interests in Blackfoot culture and his sense of humour were important threads that helped bind the team together.

Tesla Heavy Runner is a year younger than Hudson, and she was a quieter contributor to the project. Her steady work, including her developing skills as a photographer, supported the project in a variety of ways. She lived with a settler foster family in a small town some distance from the city, and the need to drive her back and forth meant the weaving of relationships with her drivers (Amy, Erin, me) through conversations on that drive (see chapter 2).

Mikey Lewis joined the team during the final summer of work. A settler undergraduate anthropology major, they joined the project to help with the lab work of transcription, video editing, and the building of the digital platform. Mikey's work supporting the ethnographic research of the rest of the team ultimately provided them with an interesting perspective on the project and the workings of the team. They joined the team during the most intense field season at the end of the project, and their reflections on what they saw and experienced provided an important interpretation to what the project did and did not do. While there were many other young people involved in this project, Mikey's particular perspective captured in blog posts later in this book was generative, especially for this writing project. Their reflections are an especially apt example of the multiple pedagogical contributions of Raising Spirit.

There is one other voice that shaped this project and its outcomes perhaps more than any other, and yet it appears here *sotto voce*. That is the voice of Tanya, my long-term collaborator and friend. As I wrote this, we worked on a second Blackfoot Women's Empowerment Project conference. Strikingly enough, the theme is reclaiming voice. This project caps a set of interlinked projects aimed at the economic empowerment of Blackfoot women that developed out of relations seeded during the Raising Spirit Project. Tanya's steadfast clarity and forthright assessment of what really matters in these projects – helping Blackfoot people, young, old, woman, man, Two Spirit – profoundly shaped Raising Spirit, its methods, its goals, its principles, and values. This influence is marked repeatedly in the pages that come. In a sense she speaks through all of us, an example of the circulation and redistribution of knowledge that is both recognized and produced in the Raising Spirit Project. But although she is implicated and interested in this project, she is driven by other needs. This reality has always served as the most important corrective to any exaggerated sense I might have about what ethnography can do. It is important – I've built my life around it – but it does not save children, at least so far as I know.

All the Things That This Is and Is Not

Before turning to a description of the chapters to come, it is important to identify the many things the book does not do, all the things that it is not. Of course, that is the way of all books, but what this book does *not* do is notable. First, it is not an ethnography, although taking up the ethnographic method and critically considering it is central to its goals. The Raising Spirit Project was first designed as a participatory project to articulate and amplify local child-rearing values using photo-elicitation. That goal was sharpened as later phases of the project responded to the work of Canada's Truth and Reconciliation Commission (TRC 2015a, 2015b) on the effect of more than 100 years of residential schooling of Indigenous children. Yet, this is not a consideration of the commission or its findings, although the research was done with a local non-profit serving Indigenous children and their families in southern Alberta. The project became a multimodal collaboration to build a digital storytelling library in its second phase. But even explicitly collaborative work with Indigenous Peoples became a political question during the time of this project. Settler colonialism and its continued structuring logic (Wolfe 2006) are not the backdrop but rather the warp and woof of the project. Still, this book is not about Blackfoot Peoples or the Indigenous Peoples in Canada, although they were the primary recipients of care at Opokaa'sin and made up most of the participants, including the collaborating researchers.

This book isn't really about child and youth studies either, although this was the domain I was working in at the time of research. Even so, it was the contradictions that follow from recognizing the expertise of Indigenous young people that provides one of its dominant dynamics and central contributions. Neither is this book about Indigenous epistemologies, ontologies, or onto-epistemologies, although their relevance was demonstrated repeatedly. The many times they broke through the project's design, like the many fails in this project, became one of the key teachings in this messy, multi-year project in research creation.

Also, this book is not about visual anthropology, although photographs, videos, a digital storytelling library, and public exhibits were significant aspects of the project, and part of how it was meant to be shared in the community and beyond. It was the making of a digital storytelling library that moved the project from participatory photo-elicitation to collaborative design to respond to a series of refusals. Yet, this book does not offer analysis of any visual representations of culture, tradition, and value. Rather, it was the materials themselves, produced during the project, that gathered relations and forms of relationality that were unexpected, unsettling, and ultimately hopeful (see Newberry and Pace-Crosschild 2019).

Although not fully taken up here, each of these threads contribute to the whole of this work. At its centre, this book is about what ethnography *might* be able to do, even in a period when calls for decolonizing anthropology are being made *again* (Jobson 2020) and various turnings have brought us back to our original sins. It is the dilemmas, the ditherings, and the fails that are foregrounded here as the only way to make sense of what Raising Spirit was and continues to be. The multimodal research creation in its second phase was as much an accident as a finding, one that highlighted the building and bundling of relations of care entangled with photographs and other transmedia materials. It was an improvised experiment in ethnography in its second phase that led to its most significant finding. When young Indigenous people refuse the double bind of ethnographic recognition, they circulate and redistribute the production of knowledge, opening the possibility of new publics and other futures.

This book is not a conventional ethnography, and neither is this introduction. As a kind of prologue, it identifies a series of literatures that inform but do not drive the book, including child and youth studies, Indigenous studies, and visual anthropology. Although placed in the context of Blackfoot Territory in the era of reconciliation, these issues are not covered exhaustively here. Rather, the following chapters identify the ethnographic dilemmas that arose across the run of the project and their implications for the production of knowledge and expertise.

Chapter 2 describes the project's initial participatory pilot on photo-elicitation to articulate Blackfoot values in child-rearing and the shift away from it. This chapter provides a chronological overview of the project and an introduction to its participants. This description is organized around the idea of patchwork in more than one sense (Günel et al. 2020; Tsing 2015). The idea of ethnography as a method in need of a patch is explored, along with the elisions and limits of ethnographic methods for understanding the worlds of young people (Cooper 2022). Experimentation and design-influenced approaches are introduced here (Gunn et al. 2013; Ballestero and Winthereik 2021) along with multimodal research creation (Collins et al. 2017; Varvantakis and Nolas 2019; Pink 2011; Dicks et al. 2006) as ways to patch up ethnography.

Patchwork as the making of a local patch of dense mutuality through fieldwork is also explored here. The idea of Blackfoot Territory as an anchor for both ethnological and local understandings of culture is juxtaposed with the young researchers' experience of its patchy and distributed character. The roles of both the territory and the university lab in making local patches of meaning and connection are considered.

Chapter 3 begins with the question of expertise. The idea of para-ethnography is introduced and its relationships to vernacular, indigenous knowledge. Para-ethnography is meant to capture the analytical competence of elite experts in labs, stock exchanges, and other spaces of knowledge production. The contradictions in this approach to expertise were evident when young people were asked to act as para-ethnographers who were doubled as both insiders with expertise but also ethnographers in training. The need to align vernacular indigenous knowledge with canonical Indigenous knowledge, especially in the era of reconciliation, made them leery of making claims to cultural expertise. The blogged field notes of the young research team from the second phase of work provide ethnographic details on how they experienced being positioned as culture experts through training and fieldwork. Their doubts were compounded by their age and the sense that such knowledge should best come from Elders. Team members, Indigenous and settler, redirected calls to be authoritative as culture experts in-the-making, lighting up the relationship they encountered and built together. Their encounters in the field and in the lab did surface forms of vernacular knowledge, but they refused to claim authority as experts on Blackfoot culture and the doubling required through such ethnographic recognition. In translational encounters at the university, with the partner organization, and in the field, their expertise was unsettled, refused, and circulated among the relationships developed in the project, both among the team and with the people they encountered.

Chapter 4 continues the exploration of what it means to position young researchers as culture experts and again through their own blogged field notes with particular attention to land-based knowledge. The double bind produced through the demand for the translation of cultural knowledge led to the team's refusals to act as culture experts. They were in fact counter-experts (Fortun and Cherkasky 1998) who were multiply obligated; the double bind of their situation was produced through the need to translate "messages coded by different logics, operating within different fields of reference, which often deny the existence of other conceptual orders" (151). It was their refusals to act as culture experts that illustrated the problem with ethnographic recognition of Indigenous knowledge even as they showed the redistribution of expertise and its circulation through relationships.

Chapter 5 describes the dilemmas of coding in the second phase of the project. An experiment in how to code collaboratively was designed, and the design studio method that was improvised changed the project fundamentally. Rather than seeking only the identification of Blackfoot values, although some of that did happen, the team learnt how knowledge and values can circulate in Blackfoot Territory as a kind of pedagogy for all, as who was the teacher and who was the learner shifted across encounters.

This chapter juxtaposes the goal of producing an ethical space between worlds following Ermine (2007) with the diplomatic recognition of multiples worlds created in a third space (Bhabha 1994; Choy 2005; de la Cadena and Blaser 2018). The spaces created through the design studio method offered the possibility for new publics and the enunciation of other ways to be together in the era of reconciliation that challenge two-world models of relations between Indigenous and settler ways of knowing. This chapter ends with a consideration of what non-interference might mean in a pluriversal world (Escobar 2017).

The effects of ethnographic recognition and refusal haunted the project until its end, revealing the problems and possibilities of ethnography. In the final chapter, considering the photographs that anchored the Raising Spirit Project brings together their two contradictory effects: They not only gathered relations through their circulation, but they also produced refusals of the double bind triggered by requests for their interpretation. These effects shifted the focus to what the photographs did as objects in a larger photography complex (Edwards 2012). The colonizing power of photography for Indigenous Peoples in North America is considered here alongside the recirculation of photographs from archives back to family albums (Lonetree 2019). In the Raising Spirit Project, this circulation shows the photographs to be agential objects (Doucet 2018). To understand this, the Blackfoot practice of bundle transfer is put in tension with the abstraction and generalization of local Indigenous terms through anthropology. This chapter loops back to forms of expertise and the question of voice. Gregory Bateson's (1972) double bind is used to consider the transcontextual tangles that are produced when a message is refuted by its medium. The young Indigenous researchers refused ethnographic recognition and the doubling of consciousness demanded in the Raising Spirit Project, and in so doing, moved beyond questions of representation to "whether a knowledge-making practice leads to just and cohabitable worlds" (Doucet 2018, 749).

The generative power of their refusals showed the possibility for new imaginaries and the continued redistribution of expertise as it circulates to maintain relationships in Blackfoot Territory and to build new ones that exceed ethnographic recognition.

NOTES

1 Like all the field notes included in this volume, these have not been edited beyond corrections for clarity which are marked in brackets. They are shared with their typos, their errors in judgements, and their confusions and mistakes as a kind of vulnerability and as a recognition that they are ethnographic.

2 Between 2008 and 2015, the Truth and Reconciliation Commission of Canada, as part of the Indian Residential Schools Settlement Agreement (IRSSA), conducted work to understand the impact of the residential schooling system and compensate its victims. The Commission's 2015 report outlined ninety-four calls to action (Truth and Reconciliation Commission of Canada, 2015a, 2015b). See also the Yellowhead Institute's yearly accounting of how many of the calls have been answered (https://yellowheadinstitute.org/trc/).

3 "We are all treaty people" is a slogan in use during the period around the release of the TRC's final report and developed in pedagogical settings (see https://www.oise.utoronto.ca/abed101/we-are-all-treaty-people/).

4 The 2016 Canadian census puts the number of Blackfoot people in Canada at 22,490 (Dempsey 2019). The reserve system was established through the 1876 Indian Act that identified the lands recognized by the Canadian state as belonging to First Nations.

5 First Nations, Métis, and Inuit are official categories recognized by the Canadian government (https://www.rcaanc-cirnac.gc.ca/eng/1100100013785/1529102490303). The umbrella term "Indigenous" is used throughout this book.

6 Head Start in the United States was part of the suite of programs associated with Lyndon Johnson's Great Society Campaign and the War on Poverty. Initiated in 1955 in America, Head Start aimed at improving outcomes for poor children through early childhood education, health, and nutrition. The Aboriginal Head Start Initiative in Canada was announced by the Minster of Health in 1995 (https://www.canada.ca/en/public-health/services/health-promotion/childhood-adolescence/publications/aboriginal-head-start-urban-northern-initiative.html#a2).

7 Treaties are constitutionally recognized agreements between the Crown and Indigenous Peoples. These agreements are understood to derive from a nation-to-nation relationship based on Indigenous sovereignty recognized at the time of Canada's colonial founding (Dhillon 2017, 243).

8 The "60s scoop" refers to the Canadian policy of facilitating the adoption of Indigenous children by white settler families as an extension of the assimilatory logic of residential schooling (see McKenzie et al. 2016; Milloy 1999).

9 Inspired by a tweet by Erica Violet Lee.

Chapter Two

Patchwork Project

"What happened over the years of my expeditions as a child was a slow transformation of my landscape over time into what naturalists call a local patch, glowing with memory and meaning."

(Helen MacDonald, *H is for Hawk*, 2014, 241)

Patch It Up, Patch Me Through, a Patch of Ground

This chapter only *begins* to describe the methods used for the Raising Spirit Project and the shifts in them that emerged through practices attuned to the needs of the project, its context in Blackfoot Territory in the era of the TRC, and in relation to the young people at its heart. The implications, ethnographic, emotional, theoretical, and practical, of the changes we made to methods across the project are the subject of the chapters to follow. Here, a description of the project's origins and a chronology of personnel and methods is organized around patches understood in more than one way. There were the patches needed to fix ethnographic methods and ruptured relations. And, as it happens, the need for such patchwork reflected the patchiness of knowledge in Blackfoot Territory that shaped the project and that ultimately led to the making of local patches "glowing with meaning and memory" as relations were knitted together across this sprawling, multi-year, multidimensional project.

What most characterized the methodological choices across Raising Spirit was a spirit of on-the-fly innovation to deal with the complex intersections we were facing as project goals shifted: how to collaborate with young people effectively and appropriately, how to deal respectfully with Indigenous protocol and Elders, how to mediate the community and university divide, and whether and how design and digital methods in ethnographic work might help with all of this. At the time, we did not have the language of research creation (Chapman and Sawchuk 2012; Loveless 2015; Fisher 2015), but this is certainly one way to describe what we came to do. The research approaches we took up ranged from fieldwork and participant-observation to standard interviews, but it also incorporated art projects, museum exhibits, and forms of digital engagement between young researchers.

These adaptations and innovations can be read as patches on the standard ethnographic method that has sprung even more leaks recently. In this sense, a patch is a fix, a kind of repair. Across this project, the question of whether and how to repair relations arose repeatedly – in tandem with the return of the perennial question of whether anthropology's colonial origins can be fixed (Asad 1973; Harrison 1992; Fox 1991) or whether it's time to burn it down (Jobson 2020; Todd 2018). Failures and fault lines in standard ethnographic methods required a variety of patches across the run of Raising Spirit, and the devising of these patches was some of the most impactful work done. The need for the patches was a constant reminder of anthropology's use of Indigenous knowledge and ways of knowing, as will be evident across the following chapters.

But another form of patch-making also characterized work done on the Raising Spirit Project, and this was the making of local patches of mutuality and meaning as suggested by the opening quote. Here, I draw inspiration from patch ecology with its attention to the mutuality of dense and overlapping local relationships that form a distinct community, an understanding informed by the work of Anna Tsing (2015; Tsing et al. 2019) but also Joel Hagen (1992). Tsing's work, like Hagen's before it, demonstrates the power of ecosystems thinking and its entanglement with how we conceptualize the social. As Tsing (2015) says, "landscapes and landscape knowledge develop in patches" (227). She recalls her own inspiration upon hearing Dr. Suzuki "treating species in the way cultural anthropologists treat their units" and implying that "the kinds we know … develop at that fragile junction between knowledge-making and the world" (231). The recognition of this fragile junction and what can happen there shaped the second phase of the project, which is taken up in chapter 4 through the question of its role as a kind of third space.

Patchwork through methodological adaptations and innovations took the research team across Blackfoot Territory, from university to Opokaa'sin, from museum to sacred site, from city to Sundance. In the process, the patchiness of Blackfoot knowledge became a central problematic for the research team as it ran up against their expectation for a Blackfoot culture in general and its uniform existence across Blackfoot Territory. Like the patchiness of capitalism in Tsing's analysis, there is reason for hope here. "Patches are productive," and like mushroom spores they can spread. Our patches on ethnographic methods yielded this kind of patch; the space for crafting methods and working across difference knotted together relations (Ingold 2015). These patches were places of meaning, relation, discomfort, and joy. The local patches of connection created through the research done by young people were powerful reminders of what can be possible in research and in Blackfoot Territory.

The evidence for and implications of both kinds of patch-making are developed more fully in the following chapters. Here, the meanings of patch are illustrated first through a chronological description of our methods and the innovations made to address needs and tensions arising from them. Then, two examples of local patches created through the work of the research team are explored. But first, some attention to the calls to fix ethnography is necessary.

Ethnography as Patchwork

We are patching up ethnography once again. For a discipline that likes to stereotype its approach to methods as poorly explicated and just as poorly taught, it is remarkable how much time we spend discussing it. Influences on the most recent return to ethnography and its shortcomings have come from several directions, and no comprehensive mapping is offered here. Rather, a sketch of some of the patches offered is described to illustrate their influences on choices made across the Raising Spirit Project.

George Marcus and his various collaborators advocated the need to "refunction" ethnography for the contemporary era in the 2000s (Marcus 2007, 2008; Holmes and Marcus 2007, 2008; Rabinow et al. 2008), a move that has overlapped with the repatriation of ethnography he had called for earlier (Marcus and Fischer 1986) to deal with some of the contradictions, colonial and otherwise, in the fieldwork tradition. Using ethnographic methods in the spaces of elite knowledge production such as stock exchanges (Riles 2000b, 2013; Zaloom 2004), clinics (Mol 2002) and laboratories (Latour and Woolgar 1986) reflected these influences along with those of feminist science studies (Haraway 1991) on the reversal of the ethnographic gaze. Some of the resulting questions about what counts as expertise are taken up in the next chapter. More recent moves to consider ethnography in relationship to design, both as a practice (Akama et al. 2018) and as a domain for ethnographic work

(Gunn et al. 2013), extend the earlier influences from science and technology studies (STS) as well as more recent critical feminist approaches to materiality (Barad 1998; Grosz 2004; de la Bellacasa 2012). These emendations to ethnographic methods can be read as patches needed after a rejection of the primitive/other duality of anthropology's early assignment to "savage slot" (Trouillot 2003).

Design approaches in anthropology have been enlarged in work by Escobar (2017) to understand the people that anthropologists work alongside as co-creators (Rappaport 2008). This work has affinities with the attention to worlding (de la Cadena and Blaser 2018), which in turn shares much with the so-called ontological turn (Kohn 2015; Parreñas 2020) and post-humanist and more-than-human approaches (Kohn 2013; Haraway 2010; Tsing 2012). Beyond the recognition of alternative ontologies and epistemologies or onto-epistemologies (de la Cadena 2018) and the limits of conventional ethnographic methods in addressing them, Escobar suggests the potential of ethnography for creating – not discovering – new imaginaries in new kinds of ethnographic spaces (see chapter 5).

The elisions and limits of ethnographic methods for understanding the worlds of young people has been taken up in parallel fashion to other currents in anthropology at least since the emergence of child and youth studies in the 1990s (Scheper-Hughes and Sargent 1999; Stephens 1995). Within child and youth studies more generally, the work of Allison James, Chris Jenks, and Alan Prout (1998) is often used to mark the move to centre children in social science research by recognizing their agency and their accounts of their worlds (and see Bluebond-Langner and Korbin 2007; Christensen 2004; Soto and Swadener 2016; Sæther et al. 2024; Lancy 2015). Since then, the field has grown and been reimagined (Spyrou et al. 2018). Using ethnographic and other qualitative methods to address the subjectivity and agency of young people has sponsored a large literature on methods, including those who explicitly consider children as researchers themselves (Alderson 2001; Cheney 2011, 2018; Pole et al. 1999; Solberg 1996; Lang and Shelley 2021; Kellett 2010; Lundy and McEvoy 2011; Skelton 2008; Thomas 2017). Calls for decolonzing child and youth studies have also been made (Abebe et al. 2022; Cheney 2018).

As taken up in the next chapter, the positioning of young people as subjects of attention, ethnographic and otherwise, shares some significant and troubling contours with the subjectivation of Indigenous Peoples generally (Rollo 2018a; and see Cooper 2022). One patch, offered to deal with the question of how to understand the subjectivity of muted groups such as the young, has been the use of visual alternatives to interview-based approaches. Photo- and video-voice are offered as a recognition of different modes of being, interpreting, and representing in the world (Thompson 2016; Wilson et al. 2007; Shah 2015; Clark 1999; Johnson et al. 2012; Luttrell 2010; Varvantakis et al. 2019; Johnson 2011).

Recognizing young people as co-creators and co-analysts (Pole et al. 1999; Mason and Hood 2011; Kellett 2011; Kim 2017; Liabo and Roberts 2019; Lang and Shelley 2021) arises from not only the child and youth studies literature, but also a widespread move towards collaborative ethnographic work. Lassiter (2005) and others have argued for such a collaborative ethnography (Holmes and Marcus 2008; Marcus 2008; Fleur-Lobhan 2008; Mack and Newberry 2020, 2018) whose dimensions exceed earlier participatory action approaches by moving beyond consultation and issue identification to co-conceptualization and co-analysis (Rappaport 2008).

Attempts to patch over the power dynamics of fieldwork are longstanding. And, as with the attention to other worlds/other ontologies/other epistemologies, collaborative ethnographic projects can appear as colonializing refractions of Indigenous research methods, which have been the subject of much attention in critical Indigenous studies in recent years (Battiste 2005; Smith 1999; Wilson 2008; Kovach 2021; Ahenakew 2016; Slater 2021; Barcham 2021; Moreton-Robinson 2009) and among critical Indigenous feminists (Byrd et al. 2024; Todd 2016, 2018; L. Simpson 2022; Sabzalian 2018). Whether the results of unacknowledged erasure or a kind of political and methodological convergence, changes in methods in the Raising Spirit Project brought us to the question of how our methods seemed to mimic, mirror, and extend Indigenous knowledge practices (see chapter 5).

All the elements and issues described above were in some way present in the work done for Raising Spirit, if often unwittingly. The project began as one organized around photo-elicitation and became one that emphasized design, co-conceptualization, and transmedia approaches to shared understandings of values. The project also came to have significant elements of research creation (Chapman and Sawchuk 2012; Loveless 2015) and multimodality (Collins, Durington, and Gill 2017; Dattatreyan and Marrero-Guillamón 2019; Dicks et al. 2006; Varvantakis and Nolas 2019; Pink 2011), moves that ultimately reflected the larger discipline's move towards experimental methods. As Ballestero and Winthereik (2021) note, this move goes beyond questions about ethnographic fieldwork, theory, and writing to how we conceptualize, an expansion evident across the run of the project. Latterly, and specifically in the context of the work done on Raising Spirit, calls to decolonize anthropology and its methods represent yet another return in anthropology, now accompanied by calls for abolition. While some are considering whether to "burn anthropology down" (Jobson 2020), the literatures on collaboration and design in anthropology flourish as patches on existing methods.

In fact, patchwork ethnography has been proposed as a way to express the many, amplifying challenges not only to anthropology's central method, but also to the conditions of knowledge production in university settings and the work lives of those involved (Günel et al. 2020). Many of these challenges were evident in the methods both assembled and created – and often abandoned – in the Raising Spirit Project. Our answers to these dilemmas produced patches of two kinds: ethnographic innovations and the creation of local places of connection, memory, and meaning.

In the next sections, I provide a general overview of the project's three phases: the pilot, the pause, and the renewed project. The first phase was devoted to exploring photo-elicitation as a method for facilitating the articulation of child-raising values among local, primarily Blackfoot caregivers. An unexpectedly large amount of "data" was produced even as contradictions and tensions emerged over how to understand it and who "owned" it. These concerns would ultimately demonstrate the inadequacy of elicitation as a method and lead to changes in our approach. But not before the project ground to a halt when Opokaa'sin's board raised concerns about the goals of the project. After a painful interregnum, the project began again with new funding, a new focus, new researchers, and new methodological approaches.

The project's chronology is sketched in the sections below with attention to the larger social and political context that shaped it. More detailed descriptions of our changing methods and their implications are then developed over the following chapters.

Beginnings: Conversations in a Clash Zone

The subject of the early conversations between Tanya and me was the mismatch between policy mandates on early childhood education and local practices of raising children. Early childhood educators in Indonesia had expressed this very sentiment to me (Newberry 2010, 2017a). One Indonesian child psychologist described her frustration in applying standards such as the *Diagnostic and Statistical Manual* (DSM) to traumatized children in post-tsunami Aceh because it bore no relationship to local child-rearing values. Decades of continuing intervention in Indonesia by successive governments – colonial, modernizing, democratizing – focused on children and childhood as a point for that intervention. The contemporary wave of brain-science-influenced developmentalism (Adriany and Newberry 2022) is only the most recent of these.

In Canada, Tanya was dealing with multiple policy and funding mandates for early childhood programming, just as were the educators and caregivers in Indonesia. The promotion of Head Start in Canada for Indigenous children in the twenty-first century represents an echo of its genesis in the Johnson-era War on Poverty in the United States and its aim of reaching poor, predominantly African American youngsters. Like those educators and activists I met in Indonesia, Tanya recognized the advantages of financial support for early childhood programs, even as she saw the lack of recognition of Blackfoot values in many of these program principles (cf. LaFrance and Bastien 2007). As a Kainai woman herself, Tanya's understanding of the mismatch was grounded in her own lived experience with another knowledge system.

In both of our experiences, local child-rearing values were muted (Ardener 2005), and in both cases as a result of settler colonialism (Veracini 2015; Mignolo and Escobar 2013; Wolfe 2006). The question of whether the frame of settler colonialism works in Indonesia is an interesting one. More than four hundred years of Dutch colonialism and more than thirty years of Suharto's modernizing authoritarian regime had done much to reorganize local child-rearing values in Indonesia (Dewantara 1967; Stoler 2001). Although the Dutch were forced to leave the newly independent nation of Indonesia after the Second World War, the effects of colonial approaches to schooling continue to shape education in Indonesia, although the era of reform, or *reformasi*, beginning in the late 1990s has meant renewed discussions about the role of education in the democratizing nation, including early childhood programming (Newberry 2017a, 2017b; Adriany and Saefullah 2015; Pangastuti 2023).

The schooling of Indigenous children is perhaps the most powerful example of the means, the effects, and the ongoing logic of settler colonialism in Canada (Marker 2000; Donald 2009a, 2009b; Tuck 2009; A. Simpson 2014; Tuck and Gaztambide-Fernández 2013; Sabzalian 2019). In fact, the effects of the long history of residential schooling aimed at "killing the Indian in the child" (Young 2015) were the context that prompted the goal to identify Blackfoot child-rearing values. The residential school system moved Indigenous children out of their homes and in many cases their home communities to a network of government-sponsored religious schools (TRC 2015a, 2015b). Residential schooling was practised for more than one hundred years, with the last closed in 1996, and it followed a longer history of day schools, all devoted to the undoing and remaking of the Indian child (Dhillon 2017, 94). This pattern of violent and assimilatory apprehension of Indigenous children was continued through the Sixties Scoop of adopting Indigenous children out of their communities to white settler families, and now, through a foster care system that continues to disconnect children from their communities (Johnston 1983; Jacobs 2008; McKenzie et al. 2016).[1] These practices are part of the larger eliminatory logic of settler colonialism. Patrick Wolfe's (2006) famous description of settler colonialism as a structure and not an event has particular significance for young people's futures. Michael Marker (2000) describes the extension of this logic into the "clash zone" of debates about education: "It is a complex landscape of colliding interpretations and fundamental goals and purposes across cultural barricades. In short, Indian education is about Indian-White relations. It has been, and remains, the central arena for negotiating identities and for translating the goals and purposes of the cultural 'Other'" (31). As Jaskiran Dhillon (2017, 89) describes, the "salvation project" of education as a solution to the "Indian problem" is not novel or new or over.

As Tanya and I came together, these historical contexts of colonial education were the backdrop to our conversations. We decided to design a pilot research project on facilitating the articulation of local child-rearing values in the face of domination. The first phase would be focused on southern Alberta with the idea that the project would then be extended to work in Indonesia. What we didn't realize as we planned the project was that the work of The Truth and Reconciliation Commission of Canada (TRC) would be nearly simultaneous with the run of the project (see Dhillon 2017 for a useful overview in relation to young people).[2] Between 2008 and 2014, the Commission gathered around 7,000 testimonies to the devastating, genocidal harm caused by the residential schooling system. The second phase of Raising Spirit would be shaped by this work and the momentum of Indigenous resurgence (Alfred 2015; L. Simpson 2016, 2017) and racial reckoning more generally. Informal conversations between Tanya and me began in 2009, and the final exhibit of the Raising Spirit Project was in September 2017. Although not unaware of the TRC's work, its shaping power for the project increased over time in tandem with rising Indigenous political activism such as Idle No More and the appearance of the "Rise-Up Generation" (Dhillon 2017). Now, as I write this, the Pope is making his apology tour of Canada, prompted by the discovery of multiple unmarked graves on the grounds of former residential schools (TRC 2016, vol. 4).

It was perhaps this changing context that prompted Tanya to name the project Raising Spirit when I asked for a name for the second phase of our work together. For this phase of the project, the role of youth, of creativity, and of resurgence would come to be central. To "raise spirit" seemed an apt description for our collaboration with young researchers in tandem with the rising public awareness about the effects of residential schooling and the growing political consciousness among Indigenous Peoples. In its second phase, the project would become a place "where youth develop a critical consciousness through the creation of new media and the use of technology to mobilize" (Recollet 2015, 142, cited in Dhillon 2017, 247). But we began in a different place.

Phase One: Eliciting a Problem

The pilot project designed in 2009–10 was centred on the use of photo-elicitation, in which photographs of children and childcare would be used as prompts to elicit Blackfoot people's understanding of values. This research method derives in part from older cognitive and ethnoscience approaches to understanding local knowledge systems. Like ethnoscience approaches (Spradley 2000; Frake 1961), photo-elicitation is based on the idea that values are generally not articulated and reproduced as a written corpus of organized ideas (Harper 1986; Schwartz 1989; Johnson, Pfister, and Vindrola-Padros 2012; Clark 1999). Instead, they exist as everyday, enacted – and embodied – knowledge that is shared informally. Elicitation techniques are meant to gain access to such knowledge by eliciting its expression through a variety of prompts. In this case, the prompt is a visual one (Pauwel 2015; Bignante 2010; Buckley 2014; Samuels 2004; Harper 1986). Photo-voice, a more contemporary visual method, seems to derive from a similar logic of articulating the unsaid, although it is more explicitly driven by the desire to locate the voice of the marginalized and the dispossessed (Shah 2015; Thompson 2016; Johnson 2011).

My own initial research work had been shaped by ethnomethodology with its assumption that all humans have not only accounts of their lives, but also working theories and social analyses of them. That all social actors analyse their circumstances and devise and carry out courses of action was central to Harold Garfinkel's conception of ethnomethodology (Heritage 1984). Dorothy Smith's (1992) feminist ethnomethodology added the important role of standpoint in shaping such accounts of the social world. In other words, your social position both enables and constrains the kinds of accounts that can be produced. Kimberlé Crenshaw's (2017) groundbreaking work identifies these standpoints as racialized ones, while others have attended to queer standpoints (King 1999).

The "ethno" in all these terms is a recognition of systems of knowledge other to the one identified with the conventional anthropologist – a white European. The existence of other systems of knowledge was central to the emergence of anthropology and its assignment to the savage slot (Trouillot 2003). Audra Simpson (2007) identifies the centrality of differentiation to the ethnographic categories that were the goal of this assignment in knowledge production. From a different perspective, Helen Tilley (2010) considers the identification of "vernacular" knowledge as part of early anthropology's recognition of so-called primitive science, as not lesser than but as different. This history of attending to difference remains in approaches named as ethnotheory, ethnoscience, and ethnomethodology that do not always register the colonial appropriation of vernacular, indigenous knowledge. Contemporary critical Indigenous scholars identify the perils of such extractivist methods and the extension of settler colonialism through them (Smith 1999; Walter and Suina 2019; Tuck and Yang 2014b). The logic of elicitation shares some striking contours with the logic of elimination that Wolfe (2006) identifies as central to settler colonialism. That is, the presumption is that these worlds of knowledge are there to be discovered and extracted by anthropologists and brought out of "other" heads for examination and analysis.

But as we began the project, these problematics were not yet evident to us. Instead, Tanya and I envisioned these methods as participatory and as based on recognizing the expertise of caregivers. The goal was to facilitate their articulation of their own values, suppressed and dominated through histories of marginalization. Ethnoscientists like Spradley (2000) use frame substitution to elicit focal vocabularies and cognitive domains. In photo-elicitation, images are used to provoke responses from the viewer (Pauwel 2015). For the Raising Spirit Project, we were inspired by Kärtner et al. (2007), who elicited parental "ethnotheories" through photographs. For this work, Kärtner et al. (2007) used photographs to provoke an articulation of latent values among mothers in Germany, the United States, India, and Cameroon.

Our choice to use photo-elicitation stemmed from our conviction that child-rearing values among peoples like the Blackfoot existed but were muted in more than one way (Ardener 2005). First, this knowledge is everyday knowledge passed on orally and through the practice of raising children and observing them being raised. The organization and codification of this knowledge depends on the continuity in oral storytelling traditions and daily practices of family life. Residential schooling, the Sixties Scoop, and foster care were violent, genocidal disruptions to this continuity. Yet it was Tanya's conviction that these values were still in practice, at least in part, based on the resilience she witnessed in working with caregivers and children. Indeed, part of her motivation for the project was to demonstrate that children were being raised successfully, not only to the greater Blackfoot community, but also to the local settler community as well. Our working idea was that using photographs to prompt Indigenous caregivers would allow them to articulate more easily the values that underlay their child-rearing choices.

The project itself was always understood as a collaboration between agency and university, with the design and the methods being driven primarily by the needs of the agency. This form of community-based participatory action research (CBPR; see Coghlan and Brydon-Miller 2014 for an overview) was where we began, but across the project, the nature of participation broadened and deepened (see Rosen 2023 and Cahill 2007 for participatory action research, or PAR, with young people). The first change we made to photo-elicitation was to give cameras to eight parents and caregivers, including several agency staff members, to take the photographs that would serve as prompts for interviews (cf. Becke et al. 2019; Varvantakis et al. 2019). In other words, the production of the photographs to be used in the elicitation interviews was itself participatory. The participant-photographers, who included grandmothers, single parents, mothers, and fathers, among others, were asked to take photographs of everyday forms of child raising in their lives.

We tried to provide very little framing for their choices other than suggesting attention to eating, sleeping, and play, and other aspects of taking care of children. Choosing to work with participant-photographers added a layer of data on local values. Not only did they produce the prompts for the subsequent elicitation interviews, their choices about what to photograph and why were taken to represent values as well. This simple choice began an amplifying movement from participation to fuller collaboration through forms of auto-ethnography and the direct shaping of the research by the caregivers' choices in what to photograph. In all, our eight participant-photographers took more than 8,000 photographs of children, youth, and families, a rich set of images of contemporary Indigenous people engaged in raising children.

The photographs were then used as prompts in semi-structured elicitation interviews on childhood and child-rearing values, not only with the broader community of Blackfoot and Indigenous people in the community, but with the photographers themselves to provide context on the choices they had made in their photography. To conduct these interviews, two Blackfoot undergraduate students were hired in the summer of 2010. They were asked to conduct interviews with the photographers using the photographs they had taken themselves to explore what was depicted and why it was important. Again, very little framing was provided. Instead, the student interviewers were asked to follow the lead of the photographers as they described what was represented in their photographs.

Next, the student researchers were charged with taking a set of photographs to powwows in Blackfoot Territory to conduct shorter interviews in response to the photos. To do this next phase of work, the students first had to make choices about a sample of illustrative photos to use in these interviews. Again, their choices represent a layer of data about values. Which photographs would they choose and why? After producing a set of small photo albums, they took this subset of photographs to powwows at Brocket and Standoff in Alberta and Browning in Montana. At each, they set up a small table with a trifold poster describing the project and then gathered responses from self-selected passersby.

These student researchers were joined by staff at Opokaa'sin to conduct a third set of interviews in relation to the photographs. A set of Blackfoot Elders whose wisdom is recognized as authoritative were interviewed. Indigenous agency staff conducted these interviews because of their knowledge of Blackfoot language and the protocols necessary for speaking to Elders.[3] These interviews were quite unstructured and not always especially focused on a photograph. Instead, the interviewers followed the lead of the Elders in contemplating childhood and Blackfoot child-rearing. The interview process was also instructive for Tanya and me. The centrality of the Blackfoot language in describing values became quite clear, along with the lack of fluency among younger people. The power of these interviews for inspiring and motivating those who did the interviewing was also clear.

The training of young researchers would become central to the second phase of the project, but this early phase also provided the grounds for student projects. First, there were the two undergraduate researchers who did interviews with photographers and then with people at the powwow. They were involved as well with interviews with the Elders, but were joined by Tanya's son, Ryan, then a high school student. Tanya's own family played important roles throughout the project. Her daughter Chloe Crosschild completed an independent study to write a Blackfoot guide to childbirth. The materials produced in this phase were also used in an independent study by undergraduate student

Maria Livingston under the supervision of Dr. Michelle Hogue. Her project was an initial collation and analysis of some of the photographs.

The Pause: The Problem of Publics

The original project included not just Tanya and me, but three other faculty members at the university. One from anthropology, one from the fine arts, and one from our First Nations Transition Program. Two were settlers and one Indigenous. They served as advisors in the original research design, and they offered supervision and support to students involved in the project. As this first phase of the project was drawing to a close, I heard from one of these faculty members that there was unhappiness in the community about the project. Questions were being asked about whose knowledge this was. Who did it belong to? Very quickly, the project was halted by the Opokaa'sin Board of Directors.

Both Tanya and I were blindsided by this, and yet what we learnt through this painful pause in the project was tremendously significant for its resumption. The question about whose knowledge it was and to whom it belonged are not new ones in anthropology, of course. Perhaps Vine Deloria's 1969 book serves as a particularly vivid challenge to the work of anthropology, but the problems with anthropology's work with Indigenous populations in North America (Starn 2011), with modes of ethnographic representation (Clifford 1997, 2011), and as the handmaiden to colonialism (Gough 1993; Harrison 1992; Asad 1973) are long-standing. Participatory action research approaches (Coghlan and Brydon-Miller 2014), like the one we chose initially, were one reaction to such critiques. And since the "crisis of representation" (Clifford and Marcus 1986; Marcus and Fischer 1986) and the attempt to recapture anthropology (Fox 1991), these questions have become a conventional (in fact, a knee-jerk) response within the discipline. The project design reflected this. From the beginning, we had agreed that Opokaa'sin owned the data collected and would be the repository for it. This was after exploring and rejecting putting the material in the university's archive or with the local history museum. Although we did not have the vocabulary at the beginning, we were struggling with questions of data sovereignty, which have become a more pressing issue since the project began, especially in terms of digital projects with Indigenous Peoples (Wemigwans 2016; Hennessy 2010; Walter and Suina 2019). These questions would become more pressing and stubborn in later phases of the project. But, from the outset, we had agreed the project materials would belong to and be housed with Opokaa'sin.

Not only had we considered ownership and tried to work to guarantee equal partnerships and voice in the project, we also had followed all of the university's protocols and gone through the human subjects review dictated by the university's research office. And yet, our work together ground to a halt. These institutional protocols did not satisfy the board at Opokaa'sin, and in fact over the course of the second phase, other ethical protocols would be engaged (see below). As we started to pick up the pieces, we realized that another source of tension was a mismatch in reporting audiences in the tempo of that reporting. In other words, we had different publics (Bhabha 1994; Choy 2005; Warner 2002; Nolas 2015; and see chapter 5). As an academic, my timeline for results from such a project is quite a long one (the publication of this book attests to that). There was the collation of data to be done before any analysis, and then of course the write-up of the results of that analysis, and the peer-review process. I expected two years or more before having something in print. In contrast, Tanya's board of directors wanted more immediate results. Opokaa'sin as a non-profit community organization had publics that expected policy-driven results in a much shorter time frame. Tanya's concern was her board; mine was scholarly peer reviewers. Such mismatches in community–university partnerships are not uncommon, of course (Gaudry and Lorenz 2018; Alexander et al. 2018; Haig-Brown 2008). Even so, the long history of bad faith in work with Indigenous communities was the most potent ingredient.

One question that runs as a thread through the project is to whom was it directed? Who was it for? In early conversations, it was clear that Tanya wanted to convey to the local community that Blackfoot families were successfully raising their children as a challenge to discourses, shaped both locally and nationally, about broken families and chaotic child-rearing. Although the TRC's report released during the later period of the project would identify the effects of violent disruptions to families and child-rearing practices, when we began this project, Tanya was identifying this context herself. Even so, it was not clear who she had to convince that Indigenous families were resilient and effectively raising children: the settler community in the city of Lethbridge, Blackfoot peoples living on reserve, or the mixed population of Indigenous and settler families, mostly urban, who made use of Opokaa'sin's programming.

For this reason and for others described below, there were a series of "public" presentations across the project, from consultations held at Opokaa'sin itself to public exhibits in the Lethbridge community. Even the short survey work done at the powwow was a kind of public presentation as it raised awareness about not only the project, but also the issues at its centre. As should be clear in the descriptions that follow, various publics were addressed by this project, and the questions about their constitution and how they are realized weaves in and out of the following chapters.

Ultimately, Tanya and I re-knit the relationship by drawing up a memorandum of understanding in 2013 between the university and Opokaa'sin, itself a fraught compromise. Protocols for working with Indigenous Peoples in Canada were being rewritten at this time. The Social Science and Humanities Research Council had drafted principles to be followed. The Ownership, Control, Access, and Possession (OCAP) were drawn up as principles associated with the First Nations Information Governance Committee (FNIGC) of the Assembly of First Nations (AFN). While the development of such protocols by the Assembly was a welcome addition to those designed by the Canadian government and settler universities, OCAP itself represents a generalization of principles that may differ significantly by local context (cf. Bastien 2004).

Despite all this – or perhaps *because* of the painful breach – our return to the process of rebuilding our relationship with care was crucial to the long-term success of the project. By staying in and working through the issues presented in both contexts, we did the relationship building that many identify as central to Indigenous world-making and knowledge-keeping (Donald 2009a, 2009b; Tuck et al. 2023; cf. Haraway 1991 and Strathern 2018a, 2018b). In the many presentations Tanya and I have made on the Raising Spirit Project, this interruption and what we learnt from it – painful as it was – figures prominently. During the second phase of Raising Spirit, Tanya organized and offered workshops through Opokaa'sin to expand and develop ethical frameworks for work with Indigenous communities. Under her leadership, this work continues at Opokaa'sin as Niitsitapi values are used for human resource policies and more. And during this second phase, the reconstituted research team would foreground the idea of building an ethical space as put forward by Elder Willie Ermine (2007), who describes this as a space between diverse societies "that contributes to the development of a framework for dialogue between human communities" (194). This concept is explored more fully in chapter 4.

Phase Two: Building a Digital Library

The second phase of the Raising Spirit Project was substantially different than the first pilot project on photo-elicitation. Although it began again as a participatory, community-based project, this second phase was more directly driven by Opokaa'sin's needs. The research personnel for Raising Spirit changed, as did the funding, the goals, and the methods. The second life of the project was also fundamentally shaped by the shifting landscape of Indigenous and settler relations in Canada as the TRC was wrapping up its work. The tensions at the heart of many decolonizing research projects were becoming issues of widespread scholarly concern just as the new activities were being planned for Raising Spirit. This second phase of work also marked a return after the misunderstandings and the breakdown we confronted in the first phase. The failure of standard research protocols and agreements that we experienced were a sign of the tectonic shifts in how research was being reframed in Indigenous North America. Even so, these insights were only seeds as the second phase began.

The second phase of the project was initiated by Tanya's request that we put the materials from the pilot photo-elicitation project into a mobile app, one that could be used by young people to gain access to the photos, the values described, and the examples of Blackfoot language to support language revitalization. Tanya's goal was to create a ready way to reach young people and support Opokaa'sin's emphasis on cultural resilience. Welcoming a chance to do more with all the photographs taken and interviews conducted, this reorganization also offered the chance to work more directly with young people. Although the original project was certainly framed around questions from child and youth studies, particularly the values practised in raising children, it was not research *with* young people themselves. By including young people in the research, the hope was also to train them in building and maintaining the library so that when the project ended and all the materials were given to Opokaa'sin, it would become a sustainable community-run resource. Chapter 3 takes up the contradictions and pressures on positioning young people as cultural experts and the burden of being trained as fetishes of futurity and sustainability.

The request to produce a mobile app came as Amy was finishing her own master's work on online gaming communities, work that had her building her own computer while exploring and innovating methods in digital ethnography. She had done this work in the office space of the Institute for Child and Youth Studies (I-CYS) at the university, which meant that she was often in the same space as Erin, the first postdoctoral fellow at the institute, whose research interest spanned education, children's literature, and place. Their interests and mutually amplifying energies were the basis for grant applications, research planning, and ultimately project management. As a result, this phase of the project was better funded as we received monies from the Urban Aboriginal Knowledge Network, PolicyWise for Children & Families, the Community Foundation of Lethbridge, and the University of Lethbridge.[4] It was the synergy of our combined interests that shaped the next directions of the project, including an embrace of digital methods, a focus on the role of place in young lives, and a budding interest in design approaches in ethnographic work.

Although the idea of a mobile digital library had been discussed for some time, it was not until this second phase of the project that this work really began. It meant adding new researchers, gathering, and producing different forms of knowledge, working in different contexts and across media, and developing new methods. These were the changes that moved the project to becoming more fully multimodal and collaborative.

Ultimately, centring the voice of the young and their experience shaped our decisions in the next stages of the project and the ethnographic innovations we made, as will be described in the following chapters. The remainder of this chapter is devoted to a chronological description of project activities and is offered before turning to some of the places that became local patches for the research team.

Summer 2016

Research work for the second phase began in earnest in 2016. Erin was made project manager and Amy lead researcher (and later project manager). As project activities were being organized in the spring semester, Taylor Little Mustache was brought onto the project by Dr. Kristine Alexander, director of I-CYS at the University of Lethbridge. Taylor was taking a history course with Kristine at the time. Ultimately, these three – Erin, Amy, and Taylor – would become the anchor for research activities until the project ended in 2017.

In the summer of 2016, working with Tanya and Opokaa'sin, we identified two young Blackfoot high school students, Tesla Heavy Runner and Hudson Eagle Bear, to join the team for a summer of fieldwork, research, and analysis.[5] Both young people attended school in the city, and both were living in a care setting with foster parents. Each had a mentor through Opokaa'sin as well. The plan was to train them in the methods of ethnographic research and work alongside them to interview Blackfoot Elders about the values that were represented in the original photographs and to put these values in context. Tanya had also requested that we start videoing the weekly traditional storytelling sessions by Elders for children at Opokaa'sin.

The research team's summer work was aimed at adding additional materials to build the library, including traditional stories and interviews with Elders and other cultural Knowledge Keepers. Prior to beginning this work, the undergraduate and high school students were trained in interviewing techniques and the ethics of consent by the university-based team. This was the first instance of capacity-building in the project, as these young team members learnt the skills of research in a university setting. They simultaneously received instruction and apprenticeship in working with Blackfoot cultural knowledge through their participation in the summer camps organized by Opokaa'sin for Indigenous youth. Learning the ethos and appropriate conduct in both settings would prove to be both a strength and a dilemma.

After this orientation, the team started their research in conjunction with summer camps offered by Opokaa'sin. The team accompanied youth, staff, and Elders on trips to cultural sites, including camping trips. In their roles as participant-researchers they helped with camp activities and they made time to interview Elders and document, through videos, photos and field notes, the stories they were told, and the sites they visited. Amy had the team use blog posts to keep track of field notes. It was not just photographs, audio interviews, and videos that made this a transmedia, multimodal project, but a variety of forms of reflecting and reacting to the work being done. This included thinking through how to work with the very young (Clark 2011; Johnson et al. 2012).

One example of this work with the very young had taken place early in the spring semester of 2016. Taylor had sought to interview children in the preschool program at Opokaa'sin about their reactions to the sample set of photos that we were using. Despite Taylor's experience working with children, and her identity as a Blackfoot woman, the interviews were stilted and not particularly productive. She and Amy consulted Tanya who suggested that they reverse roles. Amy, the settler researcher, would conduct the interviews instead. As Tanya noted, this relieved any tension that the children might feel in sharing knowledge with someone they might consider to be an Elder and who might think that they didn't have the appropriate cultural knowledge. By making Amy the person in need of education, the children would be positioned as the experts (see the next chapter). These interviews were much more successful. This shift in position was just one example of the redistribution and circulation of expertise in the project.

During the summer of 2016, Amy worked intensively with the team to do some ground proofing of values identified in the photo-elicitation phase. That is, she organized trips to sacred sites and visits with Elders for the team to see whether the themes that were emerging from the coding of photographs were consistent with land-based knowledge. This was the first stage in identifying emergent key terms and values in child-rearing, and importantly, it engaged conversations among young Indigenous researchers and others: Elders in their community, the agency staff, and us, the university-based researchers. The young researchers were asked to go through the large set of photographs and begin to code them by the values represented. A crucial question arose at this point: who should do this coding and how? This question would ultimately lead to a methodological breakthrough in later phases of the project as is detailed in chapter 4.

September 2016–May 2017

During the academic year, the focus of work was on cataloguing, transcribing, and translating data, conducting community consultations, and videotaping weekly storytelling sessions by Elders at Opokaa'sin. Recording these traditional stories was a particular focus of Tanya's. The Elders who took part in the storytelling always moved between English and Blackfoot to help young children learn the language. As one of the goals for the digital library was to support language learning and revitalization, these stories were an excellent resource. More poignantly, Tanya understood that these storytellers were a precious and diminishing resource. Indeed, several Elders who took part in the project passed away during its run, making the recording of their voices and storytelling even more significant. Amy oversaw liaising with Opokaa'sin to videotape the weekly storytelling sessions held there, and she was also charged with organizing and cataloguing the accumulating data. A settler undergraduate student joined her to help with videotaping and transcribing work.

Twice during this time, we conducted community consultations. These consultations were understood to be part of achieving ongoing consent. In the fall of 2016, an open invitation was sent to the local community to attend the consultation. Invitees were encouraged to bring their own images and photos to add to the library. An early prototype of the mobile app was shared, and Tanya and I were able to discuss the project and its aims. During the event, videos were made with those interested in contributing to the library. Following the work of Christine Walley (2015) on a transmedia project in Detroit, we offered the opportunity for those attending to add their own photographs and stories to the material in the library. The working idea was that the digital library would be a living resource for Opokaa'sin's programming that could not only support the local Blackfoot community, but also foster understanding between Indigenous and settler community members.

What had begun in the summer's work with our young researchers doing some initial sorting of materials became the seed for ethnographic innovations that changed the project fundamentally when we turned to building the digital storytelling library. As the last summer of fieldwork was beginning, our methods came to emphasize capacity, collaboration, and co-creation.

Summer 2017

In the final summer of research, the work of analysing, organizing, and cataloguing the data continued as the work of building the library began in earnest. This summer represented some of our most intense and productive work, and it culminated in a final public exhibit. The project developed along more than one line to support this final public exhibition at a local arts organization and as the focus shifted specifically to building capacity for managing the library. Our research team expanded to aid in this and to begin the process of transferring the library to Opokaa'sin.

The summer work began by growing our research team. We added an undergraduate settler student, Mikey Lewis, to transcribe interviews, edit videos and audio files, and continue the organization of data in advance of building the library. This work also included producing a manual for maintaining and updating the library that would be given to Opokaa'sin along with the library itself. We added two more Indigenous researchers as well. One of these researchers was an undergraduate student finishing her degree in the Faculty of Education. Another young Indigenous researcher who had graduated from high school not long before he joined us had been identified by Opokaa'sin. Tesla and Hudson, the two Indigenous youth researchers from the year before, assumed new leadership roles. They joined Taylor, who returned to take the lead in the most significant work of the summer: designing and running capacity camps.

One of the key goals for the digital storytelling library was to build capacity both at Opokaa'sin and with youth. Capacity here refers not only to the ability to maintain and add to the library, but also to the capacity to grow programs for youth and the capacity for youth to develop skills and competencies that will be useful in other domains. To build this capacity, we again organized a series of opportunities for young people to learn about research methods and protocols in the university setting and in terms of culturally appropriate encounters with Elders and Knowledge Keepers. Taylor took the lead in developing these capacity camps working with Opokaa'sin. The campers were middle-school- and high-school-aged youth who visited the campus, heard from researchers, made trips to collect sweet grass and visit sacred sites, conducted interviews about values, learnt to upload materials to the digital library, and produced artwork to be included in the mobile app and in a final exhibition.

Just as with the research work in the summer of 2016, these youth were doubly exposed: to research and research creation in a university setting and to Knowledge Keepers in the Blackfoot community, facilitated by Opokaa'sin and the Raising Spirit research team. The multiple pedagogical effects of this were evident. As a young undergraduate teacher-in-training, Taylor gained experience in designing the camps and working directly with youth. The youth themselves gained valuable exposure and experience. The result was the development of a library that would be available to youth for years in the future. Even so, we encountered a variety of obstacles in this work, from institutional racism when these young people were suspected of misbehaviour while on campus to the refusal of some young people to participate in the activities. As Dhillon (2017) described in the case of programs to empower and build capacity with Indigenous youth in Saskatchewan, the governmentality of youth programming in settler colonial contexts presented a series of challenges and contradictions to the project. These issues are taken up further in chapter 4.

One of the last activities by the main Raising Spirit team was to train Opokaa'sin staff in upkeep of the library and how to add materials. This final workshop brought together the research team with the staff at Opokaa'sin who had been instrumental in facilitating the success of the project and would now become the caretakers of the library. The transfer of this valuable resource to the community partner was one of the primary goals of the project, and the work simultaneously strengthened and deepened the relationship between I-CYS at the University of Lethbridge and Opokaa'sin, another form of capacity-building. Yet, as we discovered after the transfer, some of the very structural problems that had led to the breakdown in communications in the first phase persisted. How can a busy agency delivering education and care and other frontline social services manage to keep up the digital library?

Fall 2017

The culmination of the Raising Spirit Project was a public exhibition of project materials and original artwork produced in response to it. This part of the project was funded by the Community Foundation of Lethbridge and Southwestern Alberta through a Canada 150 grant.[6]

This facet of the project was directed by I-CYS Director Kristine Alexander, a historian and child and youth studies scholar, working with two undergraduate history students, Ashley Henrickson and Kaitlynn Weaver, in tandem with the regular research team.

This aspect of the project was again built on the desire to find the voices of the young in this transmedia project. Kaitlynn and Ashley, who took charge of this aspect of the project, decided to use art as a way for the very young to respond to the project images. Young preschool children were shown some of the original photos and then given the chance to paint their response. Anchored in the idea that even the very young have a perspective worth sharing and using media other than an interview to facilitate the sharing of that perspective, this work identified the paradox of adult interpretations of child worlds and presumptions of transparency.

An arts-based approach to building the library also informed the capacity camps. Some of the campers were charged with producing paintings that would serve as the icons in the mobile app. In the last days of the camp, they worked on large canvases in the university's art studio. These large canvases were also to be part of the final public exhibit. In these last phases of the project, including the final exhibit, multimodal research creation became a significant focus of the work.

Building the exhibit was used as another opportunity to extend the skill and capacity building aspects of earlier phases of the project. Young people were solicited through Opokaa'sin and through public calls by the local arts organization, Casa. A small group of teenagers worked with Ashley and Kaitlynn and the director of Casa to learn the components of mounting an exhibit of this kind, from design to framing and matting. These students also contributed their own artwork to the exhibit. The exhibit's opening marked the official end of the project and the transfer of the library. It drew a huge crowd and was considered a success by all. Even so, struggles to engage local Indigenous youth in this project demonstrated again the structural barriers to engagement with local institutions.

Lab and Territory: The Work of Ethnography

The many methods taken up in Raising Spirit ranged from standard interviews to multimodal experimentation, and these innovations and adaptations were emergent practices in response to problems as they arose. The many methodological patches applied to deal with the new goals and young participants in the second phase of the project were also inflected by the charged attention in Canada to the questions of residential schooling and the (continuing) damage done to children, childhood, and child-rearing practices. Although these were shadow influences at the beginning, they became pivotal to later phases as young people were centred as researchers and participants. As with ethnography itself, these patches were meant to fix the problems that follow from a continuing logic of settler colonialism and the muting and erasure of the voices of the young and the Indigenous. But this was not the only kind of patchwork done on this project. As the research team travelled across Blackfoot Territory, they created several local patches "glowing with memory and meaning" (MacDonald 2014, 241).

The work of the young researchers illustrated the making of a local patch as a manifestation of relationality built through their research practices, and this was a consequence of the ethnographic innovations designed as a patch on standard methods. In fact, both forms of patchwork for the Raising Spirit Project were the consequence of the patchy distribution of knowledge across Blackfoot Territory as a lived reality for many. The realizations of these forms of patchwork are the substance of the following chapters.

Here to bring this overview of the project to a close, I turn to two local patches made through the work of the research team, because as ethnographic "places" they identify two key dimensions of the project. On the one hand, the space on the university campus called the Lair served as the project's lab space, the place for the design and staging of methodological innovations in the project, some of them to "fix" ethnography. Critically, it was also the crucible for forging relations among the team and patching up differences. In contrast to this space associated with the university and its forms of knowledge, there was the expanse of Blackfoot Territory itself. As a map and model for the breadth of Blackfoot knowledge in most people's minds, the team's experience of it was mediated through the space of the car. Calling to mind the mobility associated with Blackfoot people traditionally, the many car rides across the territory shaped the team's experience of the distributed and patchy character of Blackfoot cultural knowledge and expertise. Indeed, it was this patchiness that led to the methodological patches they worked to make. These car rides also produced another kind of patch: a local patch of dense mutuality and relationship that drew the team together.

The Lab

As with most community-based research, the work for Raising Spirit was divided between time on the university campus and at our local partner organization, Opokaa'sin. These were the twin poles of the project, producing different modes of engagement as well as identification. For the university-based settler researchers, they had to develop a sense of comfort at Opokaa'sin over time. Indigenous undergraduates like Taylor were new to Opokaa'sin but more readily comfortable there, while perhaps not always comfortable on campus where the numbers of Indigenous students remain low. The Blackfoot high school students were new to the university setting but familiar with Opokaa'sin, where they had deeper relations because they were assigned mentors at the organization and often volunteered with other young people there. The differences within the team allowed them to support one another by scaffolding their various backgrounds to help one another.

Opokaa'sin was the site of much of the project's work, from interviewing and interacting with young people through arts-based activities, filming weekly storytelling by Elders, and during the summer work, helping with youth camps. Yet, it was the team's space on campus that figured most powerfully in pulling the team together. The Lair was the name used for the space given to I-CYS on the fourth floor of the university's original building, partly because it was a sort of hidden space on campus. It could be accessed only from the main floors of the building by a single staircase. You had to know how to find it. Its only other access point was a door to the outside via a hallway through student housing. For that reason, it felt both a part of the university and apart from it.

The space itself was in a low-ceilinged section meant for dorms that produced a kind of intimate space. Yet when you entered, it opened to a large main room with a huge window overlooking a green space on campus shaped as an amphitheatre, itself a kind of enclosure. The large owl's nest visible through the window served as a kind of touchstone for the team. The main room had a large seminar table that could sit twelve or more people, and it opened onto three smaller offices and a kitchen. A sink and cabinets in the main room ensured a steady flow of tea, coffee, and snacks. The set-up produced a kind of cozy domestic space.

Before the project, the space was used for I-CYS meetings, but it was also Erin's office during her time as a post-doc. Because Amy had used one of the offices during her master's work, it was natural that the two came to know one another well, and their relationship was one of the reasons that the second phase of the project was begun. Following successful grant writing together, and beginning in spring 2016, the I-CYS Lair became the centre of project activities that would include training in methods, field trips to the reserve, work with the summer youth camps run by Opokaa'sin, and the collation and coding of materials already produced.

The work in the first summer of phase two began with Hudson and Tesla being brought to campus to join Taylor, Amy, and Erin. As mentioned, they were meant to learn a little something about ethnographic methods and consent in a kind of short course taught by Amy, with my help. Erin and Amy became the in-situ supervisors of the research team, a development that aligned with my own move away from direct supervision of the students and project, a move that proved uncomfortable at times. Distance from the field experience has been described as a necessary part of ethnographic writing (Gupta and Ferguson 1997), even as it denies the immediacy of embodied encounters in the field (Astuti 2017). This distance often also characterizes later phases of an anthropology career, as the training of students becomes more important. I felt especially awkward at this point because this distance was opening even as the project became more fully about Blackfoot Territory and the kind of land-based knowledge endorsed as the basis for reconciliation work (L. Simpson 2014; Corntassel and Hardbarger 2019; Tuck et al. 2014; Bartmes and Shukla 2020; Smith et al. 2019; Burow et al. 2018). Still, as my own relationship with the daily research work became patchy, the work Amy and Erin were doing in the Lair was building a local patch of mutuality and connection.

The Lair became a kind of club house for research work. It was the base for gathering researchers and materials, and it was an important meeting place for the many and various participants, young and older, faculty and student, settler and Indigenous, community and university members, and so on. Perhaps most importantly, it was the site for building the core team for both summers of fieldwork. After their initial introduction to the project, Tesla and Hudson came to the Lair each morning in the first summer to work with Amy, Erin, and Taylor. It was the place where they ate, talked, and worked alongside one another. Erin and Amy made sure that we provided them with lunch money, and if they weren't in the Lair, they were at the food court collecting food. Amy and Erin also gave both rides to and from the campus. All team members moved in and out of offices as they did their work. As a less frequent visitor, I was always impressed with the amount of juice boxes, snacks, candy, and teacups in use. Ringing laughter was a consistent part of the soundscape. Over time, a set of shared jokes, nicknames, and a shared language – mediated through phones and social media – led to a family-like feeling between the group members. Tesla and Hudson looked to Taylor who looked to Amy who looked to Erin who looked to me. And yet, this seeming hierarchy was repeatedly undercut based on age, insider knowledge, and daily interactions as the patch was built. In the second summer, these lines of relationship were gone over again, and further moments of connection and conflict made the space a volatile one, if not also often a refuge.

As a staging area for both summers of fieldwork, the Lair was the site for planning and provisioning of field trips and of the "capacity camps" developed in the second summer to help build capacity among young people to add to and maintain the digital library. In the first summer, the core team spent their days organizing materials collected and planning their trips to sacred sites with Knowledge Keepers. Amy took the lead in organizing tasks, depending on a variety of digital methods for staying on top of field notes and information. Positioning Taylor, Hudson, and Tesla as ethnographic fieldworkers, she asked them to keep field notes and to contribute to a project blog. Perhaps it is not surprising that digital media were a key part of a project aimed at building a digital storytelling library. Given that the "creation of new media and the use of technology to mobilize" (Recollet 2015, 142, cited in Dhillon 2017, 247) can help develop a critical consciousness in youth, the role of the Lair as a central space for training and reflection was significant.

Across the second phase of the project, the Lair was the site for training and collaboration beyond the main research team. For example, two undergraduate students spent hours in the Lair doing video work. This work included helping our high school students learn how to shoot a video of an interview or of an Elder telling a story, and it included putting together tutorials and practice runs. We invited a trained videographer for a training session, but ultimately the videotaping was done by project researchers. Mikey spent hours preparing videos for uploading to the platform, including audio work, and adding subtitles and translations. Another undergraduate student provided photographs and videos of the research process itself. The Lair became the site for training students at all levels, mostly under the supervision of Amy and Erin. One of the goals was to introduce Indigenous high school students to the possibilities of university education, and these cross-age collaborations were a powerful way to do that.

The pedagogical aspects of the Raising Spirit Project were multiple and overlapping, especially in the second phase when so much work was done between students and learners at various stages and ages. The co-inquiry and peer teaching that characterized so much of the work was an extension of my own scholarship of teaching and learning (SoTL) research (Newberry and Mikuliak 2020; Awosoga et al. 2020) that demonstrated the scaffolding of learning in the making of a community of practice. The shifting registers of expertise in these moments were yet another manifestation of this, and evidence of how the Raising Spirit Project produced a community of practice among the participants, perhaps especially the young research team (cf. Cahil 2007). Rabinow et al. (2008) and Marcus (2008) have identified the pedagogical benefits of design work (a subject taken up in chapter 5) for graduate students. In the Lair, the benefits of collaboration and co-inquiry were experienced by much younger people.

Perhaps this aspect was most evident in the second summer when we put on the capacity camps. As suggested above, these were meant to build the capacity for Indigenous youth to add to and maintain the library for Opokaa'sin. This work was understood as a participatory and community-based approach to research. These camps also supported Opokaa'sin's summer programming for young people, in this case those as young as middle school. Taylor took the lead on designing the camps, a task that followed on her involvement with Opokaa'sin's youth camps during the first summer. Then, she was charged with supervising Tesla and Hudson as camp counsellors. Her first summer's work, plus her courses in the Faculty of Education, gave Taylor the scope to organize several weeks of activities for young campers in the second summer. As with the first summer's training work, these even younger people came to campus to learn about research protocols and the campus itself along with day trips to sacred sites to hear stories about the land. As the summer ended, they returned to university studios to produce images for the digital library.

During the second summer's capacity camp, Taylor and the other researchers often returned to recharge in the Lair before going out to lead activities and make sure that campers were fed and having fun. The Lair served as a kind of staging area, with many bottles of water, granola bars, and other snacks gathered and stored to be fed to campers and researchers alike. As common wisdom suggests for Blackfoot sociality, food was crucial. The Lair connected local urban spaces – parks, Opokaa'sin, and the university, from food court to art studio – with sacred sites in Blackfoot Territory.

Still, the experience of young Indigenous campers on campus was also troubling. At one point, a security guard aggressively approached a young camper about something observed on a security camera, mistakenly accusing this young person of mischief. The guard was wrong and admitted it, but the moment was a traumatic one for the young person, who never returned to the camp, and for all the adults associated with the project. It was also traumatic for the team. Amy's relationships with Opokaa'sin staff were challenged as the children had been in our care while on campus. Conversations with security services were only marginally satisfying, and the key takeaway for all was that the university was not an inherently safe space for these young people – an understanding at odds with one of the explicit goals of this camp: to make young Indigenous people comfortable on campus. Yet we also came to know that some of our young researchers were using the campus as refuge from complicated family and foster care settings.

Across the second phase of the project, the Lair developed as a local patch of mutually sustaining relationships among the research team across moments both troubling and affirming. This was reinforced in the last stages of the project as the team raced to build the library and prepare for its transfer to Opokaa'sin. The Lair then clearly became the kind of laboratory space envisaged in the design anthropology and STS literature (Rabinow et al. 2008; Holmes and Marcus 2007; Gunn et al. 2013), only staffed by the young and the Indigenous. Chapter 4 describes the process of developing a design-inspired method to collaboratively code project materials. As detailed there, a failed collaboration with members of the Anthropology Department produced a dramatic tear in the fabric of the patch that the team had developed in the space. This breach was patched, but it left a mark.

The Lair was a patch of entangled relations developed within the team through their work together and with the many collaborators who passed through the Lair. It was a local patch of meaning and memory made through the building of knowledge together, along with the mutuality of mentoring and community-building that took place there. Yet, even as the importance of this space as a local patch developed for the project, it was connected to others across two summers of fieldwork and an intervening year of work with Opokaa'sin, mediated through the space of the car.

The Territory

As suggested in chapter 1, in Canada it is now expected practice to offer a land acknowledgment at any public event. These acknowledgements typically identify the traditional lands of the place by using a treaty number to signify its official recognition by the Canadian state, and often with the description of these lands as unceded. What began as a kind of political assertion by scholars and activists quickly became an official practice. Land acknowledgments have accompanied a growing consolidation of calls for "land back" by Indigenous activists and others (Longman et al. 2020; L. Simpson 2014, 2017; Yellowhead Institute 2019). These acknowledgements register the growing recognition of the ontological and epistemological grounding of Indigenous ways of knowing in land-based practices described above.

Blackfoot Territory figured powerfully in the Raising Spirit Project. Yet the use of Treaty 7 to identify it reinforces the governmentality of colonial seizure and control to define the area. Ecosystem thinking offers a different view of territory, one more in keeping with the natural affordances of the environment and its porous boundaries, but also with Indigenous concepts of the territory. The description of the territory used above, as stretching from the North Saskatchewan River to the Yellowstone River, and from the Rocky Mountains to past the Great Sand Hills in Saskatchewan (see Blackfoot Crossing Historical Park, https://blackfootcrossing.ca), is one that I have heard used by Blackfoot Elders. It registers not only an assertion of sovereignty beyond the limits of Treaty 7, but also the recognition of the expanse of land used by Blackfoot peoples historically. For anthropologists, this range resonates with a long-standing approach to culture area that indicates broad patterns of human adaptation to the environment (Wissler 1927; Steward 1972). Attention to the place-based knowledge of territory (Escobar 2008) persists alongside attention to knots and lines (Ingold 2015) and contingent, relentlessly mobile assemblages (Ong and Collier 2005).

I raise the issue of territory here to notice the entanglement of Indigenous conceptions of sovereignty with an ethnological emphasis on the relationship of an adaptation to the environment exemplified by the horse-mounted cultures organized around the bison. This shared sense of culture runs up against treaties, highways, national borders, and dispossession through privatization. Even so, the territory is how many Blackfoot people conceptualize not only their rights to land, but also their culture. My own university has moved to recognize territory rather than treaty in their official "territorial" acknowledgement: "Oki, and welcome to the University of Lethbridge. Our University's Blackfoot name is Iniskim, meaning Sacred Buffalo Stone. The University is located in traditional Blackfoot Confederacy territory. We honour the Blackfoot people and their traditional ways of knowing in caring for this land, as well as all Aboriginal peoples who have helped shape and continue to strengthen our University community."[7]

For the Raising Spirit Project, the territory served as a frame for understanding the reach of the project, even though the work focused for the most part on the southern reaches of the territory within Alberta. Connections with the Siksika First Nation and with the Amskapi-Piikani (Blackfeet) in Montana were not as well developed. As the following chapters will show, the territory was and could only be known through the patches experienced and made during the project. A local patch challenges the idea of "community-based" research and instead aligns with the relationality and mutuality of an ecological system whose porous boundaries are continually being shaped and reshaped by interactions that have local significance and system-wide consequence. Such patches also serve to highlight the distributed and patchy knowledge in Blackfoot Territory and the limits of the conflation of culture and territory in a colonized Canada. Despite the power of Blackfoot Territory as a lodestone for the conceptualization of Blackfoot culture for the researchers, Indigenous and settler alike, the distributed character of cultural knowledge in Blackfoot Territory was realized in travels across it.

One unexpected space of connection for the team members were the vehicles in which they travelled to campus, across the city, to Opokaa'sin, to sacred sites in southern Alberta, to the reserve, to band offices on the Kainai and Piikani First Nations, and to the Sundance. The car might be the personal vehicle of Amy, Erin, or me. It might be the buses and vans used by Opokaa'sin. It might be a vehicle rented for longer trips to sacred sites on rough roads. What happened in all of them was the kind of patch-making that was the most enduring effect of the project. Here, I describe a few of these moments.

Because Tesla's family lived out of town, she often needed a ride to and from campus. Amy did most of the driving, but Erin and I pitched in too. Tesla is generally quiet, but we were also aware that Hudson's age and gender meant that she might defer more than she wanted when with him. These rides became the space for getting to know her better and for attending to what she was learning and what she needed. Relationships were built across our differences in the space of the car.

In the many car rides taken to sacred sites and to offices on the Kainai and Piikani reserve, the car was also the space to build up the courage for the upcoming interviews and interactions with elders and Elders. It was a training ground for all involved. It offered the space for talking over methods before an interview and for considering appropriate protocol before sitting down with Blackfoot participants. It was also a place for reviewing what happened in each encounter. As Stephen Gudeman and Alberto Riveria (1990) describe in *Conversations in Colombia*, the car served as a space for significant interpretive work, both reflecting and shaping the team's engagements in the field. As an ethnographic space it was somehow between field site and the space of final analysis. The space of the car worked the same way for the Raising Spirit Project. First moves towards analysis were made as the research team worked together to understand what happened. Here the embodiment of fieldwork translated within the immediacy of the car ride also worked to continually undercut hierarchy and expertise, even as it strengthened their relationships.

It was in cars on such trips that the young research team shared their own knowledge about southern Alberta, Blackfoot Territory, and

Figure 1. A day in the field.

Blackfoot ways of knowing. Each team member had a different position in relation to this knowledge, and the car was a significant space for filling in gaps for one another. Their trip to the Sundance was a powerful example of this as the next chapter shows. Their anxious preparations and their concern to behave appropriately were mediated through car trips and in the Lair. They mentored one another and scaffolded the knowledge needed within the team and through trusted Elders and others.

In drives to pick sweetgrass, visits to Chief Mountain and other sites sacred to Blackfoot people, and in the many trips in the city to gather gifts and tobacco for interviews on the reserve, powerful relationships were built across difference: settler/Indigenous, university student/high school student, and postgraduate/undergraduate. Even so, they were all young, and all but Erin and Mikey grew up in southern Alberta. The next chapter includes many excerpts from blog posts written by the young research team. These posts reflect time spent in cars moving across Blackfoot Territory, and the kinds of opportunities, dilemmas, hopes, and challenges they faced during their work together.

Can a car be a patch? Perhaps not, but the car rides worked like the digital media that became the backbone of the project (see figure 1). They stitched the team together as they moved across Blackfoot Territory. It was not just that the team was charged with building a digital storytelling library suitable for a mobile app; it was the young team's facility with digital means of organization and communication. The blog posts that figure so centrally in the next chapter are one example of Amy's use of software to organize the work of the team each summer. Even more, social media connected the team – and continues to connect them. At one point, Amy related to me that it was on such a car trip that Tesla and Hudson gave her some insights on which social media were used by young Blackfoot people to share information. Over time, channels of communication using text, Instagram, Facebook messenger, and

Snapchat developed within the team. My own generational positioning was evident in that I was cut out of most of this. Instead, I depended on Amy and Erin to connect with the team.

The patches created in the Lair, through car trips across Blackfoot Territory, and in social media connectivity remain as durable memories of the project. They were relationships built up through the team's patching up of ethnographic methods by adding approaches that were multimodal and experimental. Yet these relationships were also shaped by the protocols for working with Indigenous Peoples, including Elders. Neither influence was determinative, but rather like the twin poles of Opokaa'sin and the university, and lab and territory, they pulled and pushed the team to consider both.

Chapter 4 takes up the idea of third spaces and what they offer to such situations. Indeed, in all the remaining chapters, the contours of identity, expertise, and Blackfoot values are shown to be not only distributed and patchy, but more significantly, emergent – circulated and redistributed – in the relationship-making that was the centre of this project.

Patchwork

A series of ethnographic dilemmas shaped the Raising Spirit Project as methods shifted across the project to match its changing goals, the effects of previous dilemmas, and the contemporary situation in Canada. The original context for the project was the systematic and systemic disruption posed to raising Indigenous children by residential schooling. Then, the final report of the TRC was made public in 2015, two years before the project's end. At roughly the same time, Indigenous scholars were describing an Indigenous resurgence (Alfred 2015; L. Simpson 2014, 2017), beginning with the rise of Idle No More and the protest against Canada's Bill-45 in 2012 (Coulthard 2014, 140). This resurgence only underlined and reinforced the original intent of the research which became the Raising Spirit Project.

Other forms of resurgence further shaped Raising Spirit. There was the return to interest in studying children and youth in anthropology as well as other disciplines. In the second phase of the project, more attention was given to the young. From hiring high school and undergraduate students as researchers to conducting interviews and research creation with young people, the later phases of the project were focused on including young people. Calls to centre the experiences and voices of the young dovetailed with scholarly critiques of the production of expert knowledge, a topic taken up in the next chapter. Yet, across the project as outlined in the following chapters, there were moments of refusal (A. Simpson 2007, 2016; McGranahan 2016a, 2016b; Tuck and Yang 2014a, 2014b) by young people who did not want to serve as cultural experts. It became clear that the politics of recognition (Coulthard 2014; Dhillon 2017) could be used to describe the burdens placed on young Indigenous people to serve as cultural experts, transparent to adult interpretation, and meant to take part in capacity-building and empowerment. The expectation that they would share cultural expertise was a demand for a kind of ethnographic recognition that produced a doubling, both unwanted and generative, as will be explored in the following chapters.

The Raising Spirit Project was shaped by the confluence of multiple ethnographic dilemmas, and in its final stages it was also rocked by some of the same controversies that have rocked anthropology, as the unfinished project of decolonization in anthropology has been taken up again. The chapters that follow take up the dilemmas in detail and the patches applied and made in the process. These were patches in the sense of fixes to something that isn't working, as the central method of sociocultural anthropology is fixed up again to respond to its contradictions and a movement of sweeping social change. Recent proposals to fix up ethnography remain patches on a method that has epistemological and ontological dispositions that remain colonial, and the work on Raising Spirit circled these and the exhaustion of their possibilities.

NOTES

1 The federal government of Canada has settled a class action suit with survivors of the Sixties Scoop (Class Action, Sixties Scoop Settlement, https://www.sixtiesscoopsettlement.info). In April 2023, a revised settlement agreement on harms to First Nations children and their families, including foster care, was reached (https://www.canada.ca/en/indigenous-services-canada/news/2023/04/revised-settlement-agreement-of-23b-reached-to-compensate-first-nations-children-and-families.html).

2 Between 2008 and 2015, the Commission, as part of the Indian Residential Schools Settlement Agreement (IRSSA), conducted work to understand the impact of the residential schooling system and compensate its victims. The final report on the Truth and Reconciliation Commissions' work (2015) states that, "From the outset, this Commission has emphasized that reconciliation is not a one-time event; it is a multi-generational journey that involves all Canadians" (2015b, 262). In addition to documenting these institutions' history of harm and injustice, the report also includes

ninety-four Calls to Action "to redress the legacy of residential schools and advance the process of Canadian reconciliation" (TRC 2015a, 1).

3 The concept of an Elder is the subject of some tension. Respect for older people is an important Blackfoot value, and so all elders are respected. But to become an Elder means to have received community recognition as a Knowledge Keeper (Battiste 2005) and in some cases to have been transferred rights to knowledge.

4 The UAKN grant was part of a SSHRC (Social Sciences and Humanities Research Council of Canada) network. PolicyWise for Children & Families is an Alberta-based policy organization. The Community Foundation of Lethbridge and Southwestern Alberta is a public, charitable foundation that serves the community of southwestern Alberta.

5 This work was supported by additional funding from the Government of Alberta STEP funds (Summer Temporary Employment Program) and Opokaa'sin Early Intervention Society.

6 These grants were offered in recognition of the 150th anniversary of the founding of Canada, the significance of which was not lost on the young research team.

7 See https://www.ulethbridge.ca/planning-and-reporting/iniskim-governance-process.

Chapter Three

Culture Experts In-the-Making

Unsettling Expertise

The question of expert knowledge is at the centre of the Raising Spirit Project. The project began with the goal of eliciting the child-rearing values of Blackfoot parents and caregivers as a kind of expert knowledge. Yet, across its run, the contradictions and tensions in who counts as an expert repeatedly demonstrated how unsettled the question of expertise remains, despite years of attention within anthropology. The Raising Spirit Project showed that recognizing Indigenous young people as culture experts multiplies the dilemmas of expert knowledge.

Recall that the project started as one based on photo-elicitation and then shifted to the building of a digital storytelling library. This shift represented not just a change in methods, goals, and personnel; it was a change in how the knowledge sought was understood. It was a shift from a focus on knowledge elicited to a focus on knowledge made with the young people positioned as cultural experts. Yet this realization was slow in coming. Instead, the second phase began with a turn to para-ethnography as a way to recognize the existing expertise of the young Blackfoot people who joined the team.

Proposed by Holmes and Marcus to refunction ethnography (2006, 2007, 2008), para-ethnography followed from Marcus's (1998) long-standing interest in innovation in ethnographic methods. In the formulation by Holmes and Marcus, para-ethnography was meant to take account of the work of experts in formal institutions such as "banks, bureaucracies, corporations, and state agencies" (2007, 40) and their own social analysis of the situation. Recognizing that experts were engaged in the work of conceptualizing the social as ethnographers were, they identify a "preexisting ethnographic consciousness or curiosity, which we term para-ethnography" (Holmes and Marcus 2008, 82). The "para" here seems to work as it does in "paralegal" – not quite a lawyer but capable of some of the same work as lawyer without the degree and credentials.

In the work of Holmes and Marcus and others (Rabinow et al. 2008), these para-ethnographers were elite experts, whether in the financial sector, the floor of the stock exchange, the atelier, or the lab. These were experts working within technocratic domains shaped by neoliberal capitalism. In their exemplary case of econometric planning and prediction by Alan Greenspan at the Federal Reserve, it was his use of anecdotal information and the fugitive social that first shapes their idea of the para-ethnographic. "It is the so-called fugitive social facts in the continuously changing contemporary that give rise to the sorts of knowledge-making among experts that can be identified as para-ethnographic by the ethnographer" (Holmes and Marcus 2007, 240).

This interest in an anthropology of the contemporary (Rabinow et al. 2008) is taken to illuminate the limits of traditional ethnographic methods. Part of a larger move towards centring collaboration in ethnography (see the first essays in *Collaborative Anthropologies*), para-ethnography is meant to refunction ethnography through "rethinking data-producing relationships in the field" (Rabinow et al. 2008, 118). The experts understood as para-ethnographers are "reflexive subjects whose intellectual practices assume real or figurative interlocutors" (Holmes and Marcus 2008, 82).

Inspired by this approach to ethnographic understanding, I proposed that we see the young Blackfoot researchers engaged in the second phase of the project as para-ethnographers. This decision was meant to acknowledge and honour the cultural expertise we expected them to have. Yet the contradictions of this positioning required an awkward doubling sometimes refused by these young people. The problematic implications of para-ethnography were made clear when young Indigenous people were positioned as experts. Like so much of the work on this project, these problems have taken me back to my early own concerns with ethnomethodology and feminist standpoint theory. Approaches to the para-ethnographic sit awkwardly with those approaches to the everyday, the local, and the vernacular.

To consider the tensions, elisions, and eruptions in the para-ethnographic framing of young Indigenous researchers, this chapter and the next are structured around blog posts made by the young people most centrally involved in the project. A WordPress blog (https://wordress.com) was begun by Amy as a practical solution to keeping track of what was going on with the young researchers and to encourage field note taking and sharing by team members. Like so many of the adaptations necessitated by this project, it was an unexpected affordance that reveals many of the frictions at the heart of a project aimed at capturing and sharing Blackfoot values by collaborators, young and old, Indigenous and settler. But first, some more context on the question of para-ethnography as a kind of expertise.

A Patchy History of Expertise: The Problem with Para-ethnography

The question of expertise has been central to ethnographic work in the last decades, from the influence of Foucault on the discipline's approach to the governmentality of experts (Li 2007; Mitchell 2002) to more recent attention to ethnographic work with experts associated with science and technology studies, as suggested in the last chapter (e.g., Latour and Woolgar 1986; Riles 2000a, 2013; Choy 2005; Mol 2002; Fortun 2001). All this work builds on decades of examining anthropology's own expert systems and ethnographic authority in writing culture (Marcus and Fischer 1986; Clifford and Marcus 1986). Rather than rehearsing all the aspects of this work again here, I point to the threads that came together in the Raising Spirit Project to illuminate some of what has gone missing or is overlooked in attention to expertise when young Indigenous people are understood to be experts on their own culture. As with much of this book, my attention has been guided by my previous ethnographic work on participatory approaches, feminist methodologies, work in child and youth studies, and now on calls to decolonize anthropology and its approach to Indigenous ways of knowing.

Although the shades of older ethnoscience and ethnomethodological approaches are evident in recent STS work, the significance of this debt is not typically identified. Smith's (1992) feminist standpoint theory and Garfinkel's ethnomethodology (2023; Heritage 1984) seem unacknowledged in the turns towards para-ethnography. Yet, ethnomethodology's interest in the accounts people make of their lives (Heider 1975) shares more than a little with the para-ethnographic emphasis on the fugitive social and vernacular theorizing. Perhaps it is because expertise understood as para-ethnographic is meant to be more than local knowledge (Geertz 1983)? After all, Holmes and Marcus (2006, 2007, 2008) and Rabinow et al. (2008) were specifically interested in the para-expertise privileged in technocratic domains. The interlocutors here are elite experts, not young people.

As Daniel Reichman (2011) describes, in this original formulation para-ethnography was used "to show how people in elite professional contexts use personalistic, context-dependent information to challenge abstract, statistically driven models of human behavior" (549). This appears to reverse the move proposed in ethnomethodology and feminist standpoint theory where personal, context-dependent information is the basis for "vernacular" theorizing. Even so, as Holmes and Marcus describe it, para-ethnography "demands that we treat our subjects as epistemic partners who are not merely informing our research but who participate in shaping its theoretical agendas and its methodological exigencies" (Holmes and Marcus 2008, 595).

Likewise, the so-called ontological turn (see Kohn 2015 for an overview), with its focus on ontological difference and perspectivism, seems to resurface an older ethnoscience and its attention to "native" science and world view (Ellen 2004). Interest in the translations between vernacular science and authoritative Western science extends this logic (Tsing et al. 2019; Choy 2005). As Tilley (2010) describes, this concern has been present since the earliest phases of professionalizing anthropology in Europe.

Here, I want to suggest the usefulness of a distinction between "indigenous" and "Indigenous" knowledge. In this usage, lower-case indigenous marks various forms of knowledge that are "other," including those glossed as local, native, insider, emic, ethno, and vernacular. Vernacular knowledge is indigenous, local knowledge. But, as Arun Agrawal noted in 1995 (and see 2009), any simple contrast of vernacular or indigenous knowledge with science falls prey to older contrasts between the engineer and the bricoleur, hot and cold societies, and does not register the effect of locality and heterogeneity in knowledge systems.

In fact, the blurred boundary zone between systems of expertise has facilitated the exploitation of vernacular indigenous knowledge for colonial administration and anthropology. Helen Tilley, a historian of science, revisits the origins of "primitive knowledge" as the subject of objective scientific inquiry between 1860 to 1940, which led to active debates about "the usefulness, accuracy, and commensurability (with other sciences) of vernacular knowledge" (2010, 114). Early anthropologists recognized the importance of these forms of knowledge as commensurate with "science" but in local terms. Yet, as she notes, there were questions about the exact status of this knowledge, which was "increasingly preceded by a modifier such as 'traditional,' primitive,' 'local,' 'native,' 'aboriginal,' 'folk,' 'ethno,' or, more recently, 'indigenous'" (2010, 155). Tilley draws attention to a shift from using "primitive knowledge" to "vernacular science" as the result of patriotic science emerging among experts in the New World. Here, the translation and appropriation of select forms of vernacular knowledge into scientific knowledge was a point of national pride. Vernacular in this usage "signals issues of linguistic and cultural specificity, while also reminding us of the various tensions between universal and particular truth claims; and [it was] necessary in order to highlight the role scientists, including anthropology, played as intermediaries who defined the parameters of this research" (Tilley 2010, 117).

Here, I want to relate this process to the politics of recognition as described by Glen Coulthard (2014; and see Povinelli 2002; Dhillon 2017) for Indigenous sovereignty struggles in Canada and elsewhere. He means most generally the process of pulling Indigenous ideas of governance and land into a grid of intelligibility (Dorrow and Swiffen 2009) driven by the hegemonic governance practices of the Canadian settler state. The idea of recognition in this sense touches on translation and the bringing of subaltern knowledge into the frame of official, authoritative, and legitimate knowledge. For the Raising Spirit Project, the vernacular ethnographic knowledge of young Blackfoot para-ethnographers would be subject to the same translation into an accepted grid of intelligibility through ethnographic fieldwork, but crucially, this vernacular indigenous knowledge exists now alongside a growing canon of Indigenous knowledge.

Anthropology's tendency to focus on indigenous in the lower-case, without acknowledging the growing canon of Indigenous knowledge, can reproduce an equally troubling politics of citation (Ahmed 2017) and canon-building (Durrani 2019). Todd (2016), for example, identifies the continuing colonizing effects in some of the work on the ontological turn: "In order for the Ontological Turn, post-humanism, cosmopolitics to live up to their potential, they must heed the teachings of North American Indigenous scholars who engage similar issues such as Dwayne Donald, John Borrows, Val Napoleon, Audra Simpson, Kim Tallbear, Chris Andersen, Rob Innes, Tracey Lindberg, Sarah Hunt, Vanessa Watts, Glen Coulthard, Leanne Simpson, Eve Tuck, Cutcha Risling Baldy, Erica Violet Lee and so many other brilliant thinkers (this list is not exhaustive!)" (18). Here, Todd is referencing the growing body of upper-case Indigenous knowledge as a political and epistemic intervention though the building of an Indigenous canon. Referring to this as "vernacular" is a problem. It is subaltern knowledge perhaps, in that it is the suppressed knowledge of a people, or rather many peoples. Like the knowledge of Indigenous Elders, this knowledge is not unofficial nor necessarily everyday or ordinary. What becomes clear is that framing para-ethnographic work as a window onto everyday, local, vernacular, indigenous knowledge lies uneasily with the contemporary politics of Indigenous knowledge. While the contrast of Western knowledge with *indigenous* knowledge was central to the making of anthropology as a discipline (Tilley 2010), advocates of *Indigenous* knowledge often seek its unmaking (Todd 2016).

The contrast between being an expert on culture in general and being an expert on one's own culture needs teasing out, it seems. Dominic Boyer (2008) has asked, "On what basis does the representative of one culture of expertise (the anthropologist) claim legitimate analytical jurisdiction over the members of another culture of expertise and how is this claim enacted? How can I document another expert culture without precisely re-framing their expert knowledge in the analytical categories of my own, thus absorbing them into my jurisdiction?" (41). This absorption is at the core of translation and translational practices that seek to bridge vernacular forms of knowledge with official, authoritative accounts (Carr 2010; Choy 2005). The dilemmas of translation shaped the second phase of Raising Spirit as young Indigenous people were asked to translate vernacular knowledge for settler colleagues to serve the project's goals of articulating Blackfoot knowledge in general. To do this they had to navigate the canonical knowledge of Elders and the confusing and patchy landscape of what constituted a good account of this knowledge. Receiving training both in protocol and in ethnographic methods only further confused the question of para-ethnographic "cultural" expertise.

These tensions are only intensified once the question of the expertise of the young is added. As suggested in the last chapter, an emphasis on the voice and agency of the young has been central to child and youth studies since the 1990s at least. In moves that mirror scholarly attention to other subordinated groups, child and youth studies at large has been motivated not only by identifying the voices and agency of the young erased in scholarly accounts of the world, but also by identifying how standard knowledge practices position them as unfinished, not-yet-adults (Qvortrup 2009). Childism (Wall 2022; and see Young-Bruehl 2012) has been proposed to mark the systemic subordination of the young and to propose that attention to this subordination provides critical insights for social analysis more broadly.

Ethnographic work with the young across disciplines has been driven by a desire to understand their experiences from their perspective (Mayall 2008; Bluebond-Langner and Korbin 2007; Soto and Swadener 2016). Mason and Hood (2011), for example, draw attention to how participatory action research approaches have been used with the young, and some researchers have advocated for the role of the young as co-producers of knowledge (Kim 2017; Kellet 2011; Liabo and Roberts 2019; Lang and Shelley 2021; Thomas 2017). Even so, Chae-Young Kim makes a salient point here about the difference between participation as equal and participation for the sake of pedagogy. Some of these issues were at play in Raising Spirit as will be clear in the blog sections below. Recognizing voice, agency, and participation are not the same as recognizing the knowledge of the young as a form of expertise.

The amount of work devoted to children as experts themselves in contrast to the development of expertise directed at the young is small, even less for Indigenous young people. This gap is compounded through the continued conflation of the savage and the child in Western liberal thought (Nandy 1984; Burman 2007; Malkki 2003; Rollo 2018a). From education to the colonizing mission, the equivalence of the child and the Indigene was the motive force for the development and use of expert knowledge. While the contemporary scholarly recognition of the significance of children's accounts of their own lives resonates with feminist and post-colonial accounts of the subaltern, acknowledging the long-standing conflation of the categories of Indigenous and child goes further in unsettling the idea of expertise. As Rollo (2018a) describes, "Well over 1000 years before New World contact with Indigenous peoples, Western political thought and practice were predicated on the political exclusion and violent education of both children and adults who were categorized as children" (66). Across succeeding centuries, this approach to exclusion and education became inextricably combined with civilizational discourses around the backwardness of Indigenous Peoples. The expertise of Indigenous young people is thus doubly denigrated. This doubleness was evident in some of the methodological and ethical problems that arose in the Raising Spirit Project as young para-ethnographers were positioned as cultural experts.

Training Para-ethnographers: The Pedagogy of Expertise

When I had proposed the idea that Taylor, Tesla, and Hudson be understood as para-ethnographers, my understanding of this idea was influenced not just by the work of Holmes and Marcus (2007, 2008), but also participatory and community-based action research (see Coghlan and Brydon-Miller 2014 for an overview). My ideas had been shaped by the emergence of participatory approaches in international development in the 1980s that were meant to recognize the expertise of local farmers and producers. Attention to local expertise and local knowledge was intended to counterbalance the expert systems of international development regimes, at least in some measure. More recently, the proliferation of participatory approaches has led to a recognition that this bureaucratic acknowledgement of local expertise is itself a form of governmentality (Cook and Kothari 2001; Li 2007; Dhillon 2017). For

Raising Spirit, the move to para-ethnography seemed a way to recognize the cultural expertise of the young team.

The team at the centre of the second phase of Raising Spirit was made up of Amy, the newly minted MA in anthropology; Erin, the post-doc with a background in educational studies; Taylor, the undergraduate student training to become a teacher; and Tesla and Hudson, the two high school students. Taylor, Hudson, and Tesla are all Blackfoot. Amy and Erin are settler scholars. Working alongside this team, and occasionally joining in, was Mikey Lewis, a settler undergraduate majoring in anthropology. Who was meant to be the culture expert here anyway?

Blog posts make up a substantial part of this chapter to show how the idea of a *culture expert* cuts in two important ways here. The inclusion of young Indigenous researchers in the project was premised on the idea of their access to and expertise on Blackfoot "culture." That is, there was some expectation that they would be able to interpret and translate cultural values and practices for the settlers in the project. This positioning was undercut somewhat by who was chosen for the project. The young Indigenous researchers were identified through Opokaa'sin and because they were in foster care. That is, they were living in foster care, not on the reserve, and not necessarily in good contact with their families of origin. Indeed, one of the reasons for their inclusion was to bring them in closer contact with Blackfoot cultural practices through project activities.

At the same time, these young researchers were to be trained in ethnographic methods for studying "culture" by experts such as Amy and me. Some of the blog posts below speak to this process and its contradictions, not only for the Blackfoot "para-ethnographers," but also for Amy as a graduate student herself. The blog posts of Mikey, then an undergraduate anthropology major working with the project, provide further insight into being a culture expert in-the-making. In fact, all the young researchers were "in-the-making" during the project. But is it possible to be a (para-)ethnographer in-the-making? Persistent questions about who was training whom, and in what, was one of the clearest signs that para-ethnography doesn't really work conceptually, even as these same issues demonstrated the collaborative learning and teaching that characterized the second phase of the project.

Sections of the blog are shared in this chapter to show some of the dilemmas confronted in the project: how to conduct ethnographic work with young children; how to train Indigenous "para-ethnographers"; how to build capacity for research among young Indigenous people; and how this work can be part of the training alongside of an anthropologist in troubling times. The intertextuality of the blog posts epitomizes what Raising Spirit adds to the question of expertise, its making and remaking, its relationship to the training of ethnographers and to the protocol for dealing with Indigenous knowledge, and the fraught issues of refusal and of cultural reproduction by Indigenous young people. In many ways, Amy and Taylor and their working relationship defined the possibilities of this project.

The context here is important. Taylor was an undergraduate student in the education program at the time. She is now a teacher. She has strong roots in the Piikani First Nation, where her family lives and where they are attentive to traditional knowledge and practices. Amy is a settler whose family has been in Alberta for generations. She had just finished her MA in anthropology based on the digital ethnography of gaming. On the face of it, they were two very different kinds of people, but in fact they shared deep connections with southern Alberta and would spend nearly two years laughing and growing together. Their relationship and how it bridged university and territory was a critical anchor in this project.

Amy and Taylor began working together in spring 2016. Their collaboration followed months of Amy's work recording storytelling sessions by Elders at Opokaa'sin. Taylor joined as a student in the spring semester, and her work involved setting up public exhibits of some of the photos from the first phase and gathering responses. During this period, both were influenced by workshop and conference experiences. For Taylor, the first academic conference she attended was the Congress of the Confederation of the Humanities and Social Sciences in Canada. For Amy, it was a workshop on Indigenous approaches to ethics given by Reg Crowshoe, a respected Piikani Elder, through Opokaa'sin. These experiences show the reversed mirror image of what this project produced: an Indigenous student learning academic protocols and a settler student learning Indigenous protocol.

One of their first tasks together was to capture the voices of young Indigenous children. In keeping with contemporary approaches in child and youth studies, we were conceptualizing the young people attending Opokaa'sin's programs as experts in their own lives, but equally importantly as culture experts. The first phases of Raising Spirit had been about the articulation of values by adult caregivers. Now, Taylor and Amy were asked to gain the child's view of Blackfoot values mediated through the photographs. The quandaries involved in research with the young are clear in this first selection taken from the blog as Amy describes their work. Their methodological adaptations and their reflections reveal some of the dilemmas in conceptualizing young people in this way.

In this blog post, Amy reports on the interviews that she and Taylor conducted with very young children at Opokaa'sin. Although both Amy and Taylor had been visiting Opokaa'sin and were not completely unknown, moving to asking individual children to respond to photographs from the first phase of the project changed the dynamic.

CHILD EXPERTS EXPLAIN THINGS TO AMY (AMY'S FIELD JOURNAL, 9 JUNE 2016)[1]

Taylor and I went back to Opokaa'sin today [9 June 2016] to do some interviews with the 3–4 year olds. I was really nervous because I wasn't sure if a) they would talk to me, b) talk at all, c) articulate answers to our questions. Taylor thought they might end up asking US about the pictures. Anyways, my fears were put on the back burner when we realized the group wouldn't be at Opokaa'sin this morning. So, we decided to interview two kindergarteners who had just brought in forms, and then re-interview some of yesterday's kids to dig deeper into "Blackfoot" values.

Session one [two boys]

Our first session of the day was with two rowdy, Ninja Turtles loving boys. They didn't seem super into looking at the pictures, and took a while to find two that they liked.... While we were talking about play, it became clear that this was about free, imaginative play. They liked to play Zombies, and the one boy told us of the time he fought a wolf at the park. Very creative memories! Fun was key for these two gigglers.

What was really interesting to me was that they would ask each other what was happening in the photo, rather than turning to Taylor or me for answers. Also, when I asked questions, the one boy would whisper an answer to the other. I'm not sure if this was because he was to shy to say it directly, or if he felt like he had to help his friend out. But this was clearly an instance where they were child experts among themselves – no need to ask adults!...

Session two [one boy]

We then brought in a single boy who Taylor knew came from a family very involved in traditional practices. So, we wanted to prompt him to tell us about the culture. We took Tanya's advice and tried to position him as the expert who would be telling me all about the culture. Taylor would phrase questions like "Amy's never been to a pow-wow, what should she know?" and "What can you tell Amy about the dances you do?" And I of course played this up with "What should I know if I go to a pow-wow? Are there rules? What food should I eat?" and "How do you bead? Who teaches you to bead? What do you put beads on?" In order to ask these questions, we used these photos as prompts....

I learned SO much from this little boy. He picked out some pictures that reflected his interest in sports, particularly hockey. His stories really showed how important he thought sports were, and this was definitely reflected when he talked about teaching his little brother to skate and play baseball....

So he told me about pow-wows, what you do at them and what you can't do, how they differ from Sundance, and his experience at Sundance. He also talked about how important his Uncle and Grandma were when it came to taking him to these places and teaching him things. He talked about the food they ate, the different dances and where they slept. He was the first to **specifically articulate** his cultural identity. He explicitly said "in our culture."

He did disclose information that his parents may not have liked, and he talked about the bundles at Sundance – but nothing he didn't have the right to. This has already prompted a conversation between Taylor and I about how we navigate the child's voice. If our methods are supposed to allow the child to a) drive the interview, b) unmute their voice, and c) allow them to tell the stories they want, how do we rectify this with cultural notions of protocol? What happens if a child learns of the inner workings of a ceremony, and tells them to the interviewer when it's not something that should be talked about (e.g. bundles)? I think the answer is we leave it up to Opokaa'sin, as it is their data and they are the protectors and stewards, but this does contradict our methodological framework. And, what do we do with these bits of data? Are they removed permanently, or stored in a restricted section of the server?

I was absolutely stunned by the amount of things this boy had to teach me. I learned so much from him about the difference between pow-wows and Sundance, what they do at each, and what his favourite parts were. He also taught me some words in Blackfoot and about the animals that are important. He said Eagle was phonetically "beeta," though I forgot to ask him how to spell it. Taylor was really impressed as well!

SESSION THREE [ONE GIRL]

We re-interviewed a girl from yesterday. She started to talk to us about beading during her interview, and we thought we might be able to get more out of that conversation. She told us about how her Dad (she said Mom the day before) taught her to bead, and how her Mom made her moccassins. She excitedly asked if she could show them to us!

She explained how to put the beads on and where she wears them. She then told us about pow-wows and how she dances. She happily demonstrated her dancing skills for us, and explained the dresses in [photo 23]. She was very displeased, however, when she talked about the "rules" of pow-wows: 1) girls can't drum – only boys; 2) girls can't sing; 3) you can't eat until you're done dancing; and 4) you get money after if you dance. She clearly articulated the gender roles, but also how displeased she was with them. She really enjoys singing and wants to drum, but was told she couldn't because she's a girl.

She told me that I could have snow cones at pow-wows, which she really likes....

Amy's concerns here capture many of the issues in doing ethnographic fieldwork with the young. The question of expertise is troubled by overlapping ideas of legitimate authority. Such hierarchies are, of course, central to most schooling experiences. Here, Taylor and Amy position the children as having knowledge, but at first, they pursue it using standard ethnographic interview methods. When this kind of "extractive" approach doesn't work, Amy and Taylor shift to letting the children become the teachers. Another standard ethnographic trope is that the fieldworker adopts the child's position of needing to be instructed. But as Amy and Taylor realized, in consultation with Tanya, for a young Blackfoot person to assert "cultural" knowledge when an older Blackfoot person is present challenges deference to Elders. So, they explicitly move to the idea of using Amy's position as a settler outsider, something Tanya called "leveraging whiteness." This idea is picked up in their discussion after these interviews, which was recorded as an interview and transcribed by Mikey.

(MIKEY'S FIELD JOURNAL, 30 MAY 2017)

Taylor: And I think that helped the process a lot more, and I think if we were to go back and do these again, I think I would give them that choice, but then I would also try and maybe do two separate interviews, one with you and then one with me, because like we talked about before, maybe they'll tell you more stuff, and then me, 'cause I felt like they were, like, like Tanya mentioned before, like, they were almost, like, trying not to tell a lot of stuff because I was in the room, as in, like – [5:08]

Amy: – you might correct them.

Taylor: Yeah, yeah, that's. I think that's what was going on, and –

Amy: Test them.

Taylor: Yeah, 'cause especially when we talked to one boy, and he was telling us a lot of stuff about our culture, he kept looking at me, and he kept like, looking for me to like nod, or looking for me to like agree with what he was saying, right?

Amy: Validation.

Taylor: Validation, that's what he was looking for. And, I kinda felt like, okay, I just want this boy to just be him, like, you know? Don't, don't worry about me, like, like I know we're from the same culture, but I wanna hear what he has to say, right? And so I kinda felt like I put that a little bit of constraint on him?

Amy: Okay.

Taylor: Yeah, so.

Amy: And … I mean, Tanya thinks that … the kids will feel as though they're not supposed to be the experts and that they're being tested. Do you think that that is, perhaps, because of the emphasis on learning from your elders? Or, do you think that that's more, just, kids in general should learn from adults?

Taylor: That, that's the, that works in both ways. Um … for, for First Nations children, like for me, for example, I was always taught to listen to my elders. And no matter if they're part of my family, or if they're elders in general, it's part of our protocol to go up to them, greet them, and basically treat them with respect. Because, obviously they have more wisdom than us, and it's, like, we look to them as teachers, and so, for me, I always thought of any elders that I saw as like, you know, my teacher, and so I automatically had that respect. And, even for, let's say non-First Nations, they still have to find that, that figure that teaches them, right? And so I think that what Tanya was trying to say is that yeah, there is that ... that idea of that teacher, being taught kinda thing, and I think it both, works both ways, actually, and so, yeah, I, I'm not quite sure how to finish that off. [laughing]

Upon reflection Taylor adds:

Taylor: But, I, I think I had, I think I went into these interviews with the perspective of, kind of, interviewing an adult, and like, I expected a lotta information from them, but I get that.... I was so wrong, because they're just little guys, and I sometimes think of them as adults, but, through their conversations it's almost as if they were speaking as adults, 'cause they, the two little girls we, we interviewed at one point, they just talked, and they were like, 'member when we went there, 'member when we did this, and like, it's like, we have this term, it's called "old spirits," and, so, like if there's a little, like a, a, child that is, has kinda like adults qualities? We call them, they must have an "old spirit," as in, like they're really, they're already mature, right? And so, it just seemed like I just, it was so fascinating to see how our questions differed from their actual conversations, and I feel, felt as though like, their conversations we got more out of what we were asking, 'cause when we asked the questions, they, they were meant for maybe an older age where they can expand on it, and not just get really vague descriptions and when we did it with the child, the children, the children mainly, did, like, okay, there's two people in here, there's one person on the park, this is what's happening, like, really vague things, and we never really got much from it, hey? But when we let them talk, the two girls just went off, and just like, we played hide and seek here, this is how we play, this is what we do, this is how we like, you know, stuff like that. And so, I think that by interviewing children ... it really changed my perspective and ... my ... my own ways of how to actually interview? So like, I, I learned, I learned a lot to either bring myself up to where I need to be or bring myself down to like, level with them and make sure that I understand what they're saying, right? Yeah.

One of the pleasures of this project was the braiding of voices, experiences, and perspectives. Here, Taylor and Amy consider how to deal with the question of children's cultural expertise and the implications for their interviews. The adaptations and innovations in their methods index the shifting registers of expertise between Amy, Taylor, Tanya, and the young person being interviewed.

These adaptations also were evidence of the project's growing commitment to transmedia and multimodal approaches to understanding expressions of cultural values. For example, during the 2016–17 school year, Amy had recorded traditional storytelling sessions offered by Elders at Opokaa'sin. Children in Opokaa'sin's programs were then asked to produce artwork in response to the stories. Here, Taylor and Amy talk to a young person about the painting they had produced in response to the story about Katoyis.

KATOYIS AND THE MONSTER [1] – KIDS TELL STORIES (AMY'S FIELD JOURNAL, 6 JUNE 2017)

This transcript was completed by Amy Mack on June 6th. This is a transcription of a video file recorded by Taylor Little Mustache. The camera is trained on G's painting of a Blackfoot Warrior, named Katoyis [Blood Clot], killing a monster. In this transcript, he recounts the story [Xxx] (Elder from Piikani) told about Katoyis and how he defeated the monster....

TLM: 'Kay G, we're going. So just explain what the name of it is, and tell us the story again, 'kay?

G: Ah, well, did you start? [TLM: Yep, go.] Well, the story is called the Blackfoot warrior. It's about these people, they found a – this is before the houses came – it's like, they found a blood clot and they cooked it and then when they opened the pot it turned into a baby and they brought it to like different houses 'cause it told them to and then it turned into a Blackfoot warrior. And then people kept getting lost at this one cave, so then he went over there 'cause they asked him to go find them. And then he seen the thing and it ate him up. And then he seen a whole bunch of people – or he couldn't see them, he heard them 'cause it was really dark in there – and he, uh, he put his knife – 'cause he had a knife – he put it on his head and he stabbed the thing in the heart....

Note: G .... was the first student to volunteer to tell a story. We also found that it was a great system to ask the students to tell Taylor the story – despite being older than them, and presumably more knowledgeable – because they knew she hadn't heard the story. In contrast, Amy had been to these storytelling sessions, and despite being a settler, might know the story too. As Tanya says, it's about leveraging knowledge – or a lack of knowledge – in these encounters.

These blog posts illustrate some of the many shifts in who is the expert in a project devoted to cultural values. Some of this is captured in the next post too. It is worthwhile to note the emerging collaboration between Amy and Taylor as they seek to do justice to what they have been tasked with while acknowledging the limits of the context and their own expertise-in-the-making.

PAINTING WITH THE AFTER SCHOOL PROGRAM – REFLECTIONS (AMY'S FIELD JOURNAL, 9 JUNE 2017)

Their voices are important, and we wanted to help them feel like experts in the moment, even if only in relation to us and for a brief period of time. I'm still grappling with this issue of child experts. It's difficult within an Indigenous context like this one where the adults – and especially the Elders – are perceived of as being authorities and the kids are to look to them. So, how do we facilitate their expertise without making them feel like imposters or liars? We don't want them to perform expertise, but to live it. So, we must figure out how to leverage our positions to facilitate this.

We did this when we leveraged my whiteness and perceived (assumed) ignorance. Kids WERE experts compared to me most of the time! And if they weren't, Taylor and I pretended they were. In this instance, we couldn't do this and that's because I had listened to each of the stories they had. I had helped them remember parts they'd forgotten. I was plopped into "adult expert" category. Taylor, on the other hand, had been gone for the year and hadn't heard the stories. So, we could leverage her absence! The kids were empowered to tell her the story because we made it VERY clear that she didn't know them. And I think it worked....

Notice here Amy's return to a standard aspect of fieldwork: establishing her own sense of confidence through developing rapport and building relationships. And yet, these blog posts also show Taylor and Amy moving back and forth between their positions as needed to "leverage" them. This idea of leverage suggests a tactical use of subject position as a means to an end in interviewing. While this might be understood as a method of extraction, the reflections on the process by Taylor and Amy show instead how in specific encounters expertise is defined, enacted, and experienced. Sometimes Amy was training Taylor in ethnographic interviewing. Sometimes Taylor was offering her expertise on Blackfoot ways of being. And of course, the young person interviewed was treated as the expert. Rather than ever achieving some stable form, expertise was fungible in their relationships, continuously established and undermined in each encounter. Elements of age and of identity as Indigenous or settler achieved their salience in the encounters themselves (Faier and Rofel 2014). This point would be made again and again in Raising Spirit, as expertise and the production of knowledge was redistributed to circulate between people and across space.

The role of encounter in the making and marking of expertise became even clearer once Hudson and Tesla joined the project as young researchers in the summer of 2016.

Making Para-ethnographers One Encounter at a Time

It was in the second phase of Raising Spirit that we positioned young people specifically as para-ethnographers. I say "we" here, but in fact I handed off to Amy and Erin the working out of what exactly this para-ethnographic work was to be. They then worked together to set up the space and the approach to training young people as researchers. My decision to delegate to them was in part because of their own training as postdoctoral fellow and graduate student, one of the many pedagogical registers engaged in the project. This distancing from the direct research was not always comfortable for me, but it did reflect what happens across a career as multiple projects demand attention and our responsibilities become taken up with the training of others. Across the project, these training relationships were multiple and changing as knowledge was scaffolded and distributed across the team, consistently undermining any hierarchy. Here, the "we" means at a minimum Amy's day-to-day work with Erin and then Taylor under my supervision.

For this first season of fieldwork with our youth researchers, Tesla and Hudson, we talked about how we wanted them to come to campus to learn about the methods of anthropology but also about campus life – a kind of pedagogy through exposure to post-secondary education and its forms of knowledge. The hope was that this would familiarize them with the idea of university education and lower obstacles for them. Tanya supported this too in keeping with the widespread sentiment in Blackfoot Territory that "education is the new buffalo."

But these young people chosen and supported by Opokaa'sin were also meant to remain connected to the organization, and in fact both had a mentor who interacted with the project as well. In a sense, their position as experts in Blackfoot values and ways of knowing was in-the-making. They were understood as having some knowledge and connection but seeking more. They were to be positioned as researchers on the project, doubling their insider/outsider status in Blackfoot Territory. In fact, the implications of their positions revealed the danger of an unacknowledged slide into the racialization of i/Indigenous knowledge, as the expectation was that because they were Blackfoot and associated with Opokaa'sin, they had access to this knowledge, when in fact it was patchy and shaped by their youth and situation. As will be evident in the blog posts below, their sense of expertise was surfaced in encounters, its fragility and fluidity confounding any notion of stable cultural expertise.

This section begins with a long post by Amy describing their arrival and some of the questions around their training and what they were going to be asked to do. This section also connects the preparatory work done by Taylor and Amy with the work they were meant to do. Again, standard ethnographic methods were tried and amended as needed.

METHODS SO FAR (AMY'S FIELD JOURNAL, 5 JULY 2016)

Something something methods.

We're trying to articulate these innovative methods that we're crafting on the fly in this project, and I've found that it's actually really hard to do. We've been so in the moment that I haven't stopped to think about what it is we're actually doing in those moments. So, to begin with, it might help to recap our first week with the high school students.

[Hudson and Tesla] arrived on Monday morning and I was a bit nervous about having enough work for them to do. We went through the technological bits and they caught on right away – of course they did, I mean they are immersed in it as much as I am – so we ran out of morning activities by 10am. Taylor joined us and we ended up heading over to Opokaa'sin to learn about the field camp they'd be doing . . . which turned out to be the following Monday. So, we got the rundown on that and then headed over to the Mall food court to grab some lunch.

On the way, we headed over to the Casa exhibit to show T & H what Taylor had produced and the sorts of things the project was already doing. It was the first time I'd seen the exhibit and was blown away by how amazing it looked (Great job, Taylor!).

We then went back to the University to eat our lunch and then we wrote some field notes and reflections. Journaling is a really big component of the project so far. We've asked T & H to journal (by hand) every day for at least 30 minutes. These blogs are private, and they can choose to share what they want from them. Then, they are doing weekly blog posts for us in their own Field Journal section on this blog. These posts could simply be photographs of what they've written, a word-for-word retyping of what they've written, a summary of their entries, or a combination of sorts. I do think it's important to have a private field journal; it's a safe space to air your issues and concerns, but also be a little vulnerable. And **no one** would ask to look at mine from my MA! The blog is great because the student reflections are so important to the project (your voices are pivotal, if you're reading this, T & H!) and will be a source of incredible data. So, this is *hopefully* a way to access voices, protect vulnerable moments, and contribute to the project.

We then went through a crash course in interviewing. Jan gave a workshop on anthropology as a discipline, participant observation, field note taking and interviewing. We then crafted new interview protocols for the Elder and Youth interviews they'd be doing at the camp. It was great because we had interviewed T & H the day before using the old Protocol, so they would know what it was like to be on the other end. They were also able to give us some insight into how the questions felt, whether or not they liked them or thought they were effective, and what sort of questions might be more useful.

The next day the students went to do their first interviews! They went to Henderson Lake to hangout with the KinderCare group and Taylor demonstrated an interview. They then broke apart to do individual interviews. When they got back to the Lair after lunch, we listened to and reviewed the recordings. We gave T & H some feedback and I prepared them a field kit for the next week. They did really well. I was impressed!

And now we've thrown them into the field with just a basic understanding of interviewing, participant-observation and field notes. I feel a little bad about it, and wish I could help coach them more. However, if we gave them more training in ethnographic work, would they lose part of what makes them para-ethnographers? And I think their position as para-ethnographers, rather than ethnographers, is a beautiful position for them to be in. They are experts in their cultures and experiences, but are now able to use ethnographic methods.

This long post highlights some of the activities planned and undertaken by the young research team in the first summer of fieldwork. The blog posts that Amy encouraged offered the potential for dialogic interaction, as Amy reminded the others to read and respond to her field notes. They also show some of the scaffolding of knowledge that would take across the last two years of the project, and the development of a community of practice in the process (Lave and Wenger 1991; Newberry and Mikuliak 2020; and see Cahill 2007 for work on young people). While the blogging could be spotty, the team's daily engagements built a shared sense of values and commitments along with trust, not to mention shorthand language for their work and a repository of shared memories that provoked a lot of laughter.

The emerging questions about para-ethnography are noted by Amy. The complication in positioning Tesla and Hudson as young and in need of training but also Blackfoot and in need of greater cultural connection surfaces a tension in the idea of para-ethnography. Do experts need training? When Hudson and Tesla were exposed to and oriented towards particular research conventions and Indigenous protocols, can they be said to be para-experts? Or are they students? Trainees? This tension between participation and pedagogy is explored by Kim (2017) in work on children as researchers. As she notes, there are contending conceptualizations evident in the contrast between children's participation in research to effect empowerment and emancipation as the practice of human rights and participation as pedagogy. As she notes, this distinction maps onto the status of the young as becoming rather than being challenged by so much work in child and youth studies. That is, are they experts now or must they be made into them? Children's research is usually mediated by adults, and she notes that some suggest it may inadvertently contribute to children's socialization rather than their emancipation (Coppock 2011, cited in Kim 2017, 86; and see Hartung 2017).

Kim ultimately questions whether much of the child-led research is really research, a question unsettled further when the young researchers are Indigenous. Her attention to various threshold definitions for what counts as research does not attend to the complexities of current anti-colonial scholarship on what counts as research, an issue central to the work of many critical Indigenous scholars (Battiste 2005; Smith 1999; Wilson 2008; Kovach 2021; Ahenakew 2016; Slater 2021; Barcham 2021). Here is some of the trouble with para-ethnography. Holmes and Marcus (2006, 2007, 2008) identify experts as interlocutors who can share their knowledge arising in response to the needs of their work, that is, the need to understand the social. But there remains a sense of knowledge already there that real ethnographers then gain access to. Teaching a para-ethnographer ethnographic methods seems to contradict the whole premise. Vangkilde and Rod (2015) in fact address this in their description of their training of managers and employees as para-ethnographers in a Danish consultancy firm and a large Danish tech company. Their approach follows from a continuing emphasis on knowledge found and translated rather than knowledge made. Despite para-ethnography's embrace of co-inquiry, it seems to make use of "pre-existing ethnographic consciousness or curiosity" (2, citing Holmes and Marcus 2008, 2) rather than through training in ethnographic methods.

In this context, the conflation of the Indigenous with the child (Rollo 2018a) is not just a violent double subordination but also a doubled challenge to what counts as real knowledge production. That is, could Taylor, Tesla, and Hudson be experts as people both young and Indigenous? As suggested above, if para-ethnographic knowledge is vernacular expertise, then the question of whether it is real is a question about the power to decide what counts as real research and legitimate ways of knowing and who is an expert. Does para-ethnography require the translation of other forms of social analysis into an ethnographic frame for recognition as legitimate knowledge? Our position on Raising Spirit was that Blackfoot values are best identified and curated by Blackfoot Peoples who are the experts. Yet our work with Tesla and Hudson began with training. This was just one of many contradictions we stumbled upon in positioning them as para-ethnographers.

In the next set of blog posts, the team's move into fieldwork is described from several perspectives. Again, encounter (Faier and Rofel 2014) is highlighted but now in relation to place and especially to Blackfoot Territory *as a field*. The patchy, compromised relationships to Blackfoot land knowledge among the team members illustrate again the trouble with para-ethnography.

First, Amy describes her own feelings about going to the field as a settler anthropologist.

IN THE FIELD . . . A REAL FIELD! (AMY'S FIELD JOURNAL, 9 JULY 2016)

Today we (Erin, Jan, Kristine and I) were lucky enough to be invited out to the Opokaa'sin cultural immersion camp that Taylor, Tesla and Hudson have been working at this whole week. They've done an excellent job in interviewing the youth, adults and Elders at the camp, despite a few setbacks (e.g. bears!), which I'm sure they'll write about in their field reports on here. I was a little nervous heading out because of the troubled history of anthropology and Indigenous groups, but sometimes you gotta move forward. I was also really curious about this camp.

Opokaa'sin had organized these cultural camps for young people like Hudson and Tesla, that is, those in care perhaps and needing and wanting more connection to Blackfoot life – or maybe their caregivers wanted this for them. Yet Tesla and Hudson were set apart because of their new position as researchers. In a post by Tesla, her position as para-ethnographer-in-training is clear. Complicating this further were the roles played by Amy and Taylor. While Amy had become in-house anthropology expert in my absence, Taylor was understood as in-house Blackfoot expert. Yet, neither were comfortable with these roles as they both felt too young and too inexperienced. Erin was in the same kind of position as their in loco supervisor when I was not there. Even so, they oversaw Hudson and Tesla as their mentors and supervisors.

To give a sense of how these roles were experienced in their first "field" experiences and a sense of who these young people are, the following blog posts are left long. Posts from Tesla, Hudson, and Taylor comment on the same set of experiences from their individual perspectives. Each of them describes how they navigate the expectations of being researchers alongside their experience as young Blackfoot people called upon to experience, enact, and share cultural experiences.

CAMP FIELD REPORT (TESLA'S FIELD JOURNAL, 11 JULY 2016)

Monday 4th

The first day we got dropped off at the camp was exciting because there were a lot of new people that I haven't met before. I was kind of nervous because I was one of the shyer ones but it all worked out and I began to get comfortable with most of the youth and my surroundings pretty fast. The younger girls showed me to the teepee, helped me set up, and informed me of all the rules and what's going to be happening for the next following days. I warmed up to them all pretty quick because the girls weren't shy to talk to me so that made me feel like I shouldn't have to act shy around them which was good. Afterwards I went to join them down at the river while they all willingly started to float down the river, I didn't want to get into the water because I am constantly cold so jumping into glacier water was not going to happen that day.... When everyone was done having their fun in the water, we headed back to where the camp was set up and enjoyed a bowl of steaming stew for dinner. It was good because everyone seemed to be really cold which made sense because that evening got really chilly. When it was time for everyone to settle down, we all got into warm clothes and sat around a fire in the teepee and then we started to play a game of mash, I haven't played it before nor have I heard of it. It's practically a game written on paper that kind of tells you what your future is going to end up as but it was just for fun. Everyone was tired after the game of mash so we all got into our sleeping bags and fell asleep and I think that that was one of the earliest nights that we had during camp.

Tuesday 5th

The second day we actually started to talk about the interviews with Taylor and we went over who to interview and how to alter the questions for the younger youth. We also drove to Waterton to enjoy some traditional games in a big field with the younger day camp kids that came for the day. The traditional games were interesting because they were nothing like I've ever got involved with. Someone mentioned that the trick is hand-eye coordination which I found interesting. We said goodbye to the day- camp children and headed back to our camp location and started searching for sticks that we were going to roast marshmallows on later that night over the warm fire (it didn't happen that night). Around supper time, we were just heading back from the river and people were mentioning that there was a bear roaming around the tents and the dinner shelter. The thought of the bear kind of freaked me out but at the same time it was exciting because I've never been that close to a bear before in my life. While some of the men were trying to scare the bear away, we got news that all the youth were going to be sent home and a lot of people were sad about that. I left the campground around eight or so with [Xxx] and a few of the other youth and I got dropped off around twelve. It was a tiring day and It was a nice feeling to sleep in my own bed even after one night of being away.

Wednesday 6th

I woke up in my own bed and was only awake for about an hour before I got a call from Taylor and was picked up to go out for lunch to discuss our log book and the notes from the first couple of days that was spent at camp. We later went to opokassin and did some interviews on some of the little kids along with some older women that were there. The interviews seemed successful and it definitely makes it easier if the people are more talkative and open about their stories and the Blackfoot culture and traditions. The plan after the interviews was to find where the next camp location is, which wasn't far from Lethbridge at all which was nice. Once all the youth and everybody else got to the new camp location, we all helped set up our teepee and it was really fascinating to see how it all goes up and the certain ways and meanings that the poles connects to the buffalo spine and ribs. I learned a lot about the teepee and the special meanings it has to it when I was putting it up and overall just staying and sleeping in one for three nights. We did one interview that night with Taylor, most of the youth were really shy when put on the spot.

Thursday 7th

Thursday morning I woke up along with everyone else and headed out with a couple of people to help with breakfast. I feel like everyone was tired that morning but the day got better as it went on, I got over my tiredness and then we sat and listened/learned about the Blackfoot language. The rest of the day was pretty chill and we all just hung around and I felt like every day I came to know someone a little bit more which was always good. The guys did a sweat and the girls participated in opening and closing the cover so that we were involved and again that was a completely new experience to me and probably to a lot of other people too. We finished most of the interviews that evening just as It was getting dark so it was sort of difficult to write down notes and observations but it was still manageable. That night we enjoyed delicious s'mores around the fire and everyone said what they were thankful for while passing around a feather. A lot of people thanked the cooks, the elders who shared the stories, and the friendships that they built. It was nice to hear what everybody learned because it made me think back on all the experiences during the past week and reflect on what I learned from my culture by observing.

Friday 9th

On Friday morning I was kind of happy to be going home, since that morning was probably one of the most tired mornings I had the whole week. I wanted to go home and take a long nap which I did later on in the day. We finished one of the last interviews for the week and it was from an elder, [Xxx]. She had a lot of knowledge about the questions we asked and went into very specific details which is always nice in any interview. [Xxx] talked a lot about her family and her traditions when she was younger, she talked about how different traditions including beading is different today than back in the day. The interview was very successful and it was very easy to get a lot of useful information from her. It was coming to the end of camp.... I took some time to think about the week and how it all went down, it was a good experience to take part of that and I feel like I got the hang of taking care of interviews a lot more in regards of feeling comfortable and making other people feel comfortable in interviews.

Anthropologists will recognize what Tesla describes: the new experiences, the knowledge she did not yet have, the obstacles and successes in conducting interviews in the field, and the exhaustion. Here, Tesla's doubled position is marked when she describes learning about her culture by observing it. Her position as both insider/outsider as a Blackfoot person and as researcher shows how expertise was made and experienced across these encounters.

OPOKAA'SIN FIELD CAMP (HUDSON'S FIELD JOURNAL, 11 JULY 2016)

First Week at Camp

My first day and week at camp went very excellent, we had a very late start to the day but by the time we got to Timber Limits, the experience for me had a very great impression on me that did make me wanting to keep camping and living the way the Blackfoot people did for hundreds of years.... The first day went well because I would make conversation with the other supervisors and elders. I got very good information and knowledge from both the elders and supervisors.... Tuesday I started my day off by walking down to the river with the other guys to wash up for the day and then the girls came to join us but they came to the river for a morning cold swim. Besides all that, our view from the river was just magnificent every time we went down there. Chief Mountain, was always just spectacular just looking at it, each time of the day it had a unique look to it from the sun which made it just stand out from all the mountains....

Later on in the day ... the other children from Opokaa'sin drove out to Timber Limits near Waterton, to join us for a couple hours at our campsite. We set-up a name game for the little kids so that we can get to know each other for the first time, but personally I already knew some of the kids from before by either volunteering at Opokaa'sin at their after school program or by giving the interviews to some of them. We were preparing for lunch.... When we were all finished, we all got prepared to head out to make destination at Waterton for a couple hours. [Xxx] was teaching and showing traditional Blackfoot games and when we started the games, all the kids got very competitive with the types of games we played....

We have been at the river for about 45 minutes and then another supervisor, came down to warn us that there was two bears at our campsite, so then we all gathered our things up into the van with [Xxx] and [Xxx]....

20 minutes pass and the bears were back and they were literally 10 feet away from where I was in the kitchen, every single one of us got into [Xxx]'s trailer to let them pass. [Elder Xxx] then got his rifle to fire off two bullets to try and attempt to scare the bears away. It seemed to not have much effect on them because of the food we had.... Then afterwards the coast was clear from the bears and then after that we quickly gathered up our things from our tipi's very quick.... We left the campsite in no time and in the end of the day we all returned home. The very next day I got picked up so that we can help to set up the camp.... it did not take us very long to set up the tipi's and the kitchen area so during that time I gotten a interview done which took a bit of time but it did go really good for being the first one for the trip, afterwards we then ate supper.... I was also very privileged after to get to sit down with one of the elders to listen to his stories and for him to share his knowledge with me was truly an honour for me because he taught me a lot, including life lessons which I'll strongly pass on to others because the knowledge he did pass on can really be useful to any individual who does need the motivation and knowledge for our everyday lives.

It was Thursday, July 7th 2016 and I woke up just before 9 a.m. so I decided to get up and get ready for the day.... [Xxx] started breakfast, during that time I was with the other male youths doing recreational activities like passing around the football for a bit, when she was done everybody ate so afterwards we were waiting for [Elder Xxx] to start a lesson on Blackfoot words and he was teaching us for about a good hour while we were reviewing various types of Blackfoot words and meanings, we almost gone through all 70 words with [Xxx] but he had something that had came up so he had a bit of an emergency. We then had some free time individually so we got three interviews done during that time so afterwards we got things prepared, collected, and done for the sweat we had, it started at 7:30 p.m. but didn't get the whole ceremony finished until 8:45 p.m.... I was able to interview three people after dinner, I got to chat with [Xxx], [Xxx], and [Xxx]'s wife, they were very interesting people to interview and were also great sources on finding and learning more about the Blackfoot culture itself in general. After everything was done, there was a bon fire made so we then were able to enjoy s'mores for a bit then right after [Xxx] came to sit with us and he told us some stories that were connected to each other in a way and in the end their was very important life lessons to learn and get taught from.

> The next day we got camp all set up like our personal belongings. After that I had coffee so then [Xxx] started breakfast, right when she did that, Jan, Kristine, Erin, and Amy joined us at the camp at about 9:30 a.m. to basically do a mini debrief and talk about what we all did and got done. When breakfast was ready, we all ate together.... before we ate we said a prayer in Blackfoot to bless the food. When we were done I was able to interview [Xxx] about how times and culture have changed and then got a lot of information out of her when I asked how it is different from today. She was very opened about everything and was just an overall good person with a lot of knowledge, I was able to talk about beading and making aboriginal regalia with her and how patience is key in this day of age rather then always trying to rush with things that we can take our time with and to try to make it important, the interview was a huge success with her and the other participants who also did our interview.... I was not able to take down the tipis but it would have been a great learning experience doing it I think.... Personally for me though it was a very terrific and great learning experience to learn and to get more involved with my culture hands on, and also practicing to speak and learn Blackfoot words where I am learning great things to be more involved and taking on new experience for my own personal interests and benefits as well. I would prefer this camp strongly to anyone who wants to learn more about the Blackfoot culture itself, because once you get to the end of the whole camping trip and experiencing it just makes you want to stay longer because the whole trip helps you learn a lot and getting a general idea about fashion, activities, culture, religion, and food in the eyes and perspective in the steps of the Blackfoot people themselves.

Hudson's excitement is palpable as is his doubled in-betweenness. Sometimes he is interviewing others and working with younger people, and sometimes he is learning more himself about Blackfoot knowledge and ways of knowing from older people, including Elders. Sometimes he is the knower and sometimes he is not.

One more blog post from this week adds further dimension. This one is from Taylor, who worked most directly with Hudson and Tesla during the camp. In fact, because of her experience working with youth, she became a mentor to many of the young people in the camp. Her own expertise was recognized and made use of by the camp counsellors and Opokaa'sin staff, even if she wasn't ready to claim it for herself.

OPOKAA'SIN EARLY INTERVENTION SUMMER CAMP REFLECTION (TAYLOR'S FIELD JOURNAL, 13 JULY 2016)

Overall camp experience

From July 4–8, 2016, the summer students and I attended the Opokaa'sin Early Intervention Summer Camp. There were roughly 12–15 youth participants, 8–12 adult supervisors and 2–3 onsite elders. From my understanding all the participants were in foster care or were from group homes and were descendants of the Blackfoot confederacy despite 2 or 3. The camp started on Sunday the 3rd out in Timber Limits on the Kainai reserve. I went out to the camp on Monday the 4th; hoping to find the camp early that morning. However with this campsite being off the map (no listed roads), I ended up becoming lost for three hours.

Events throughout the camp

When I eventually found the camp, we loaded the bus and headed off to see the Buffalos. We all gathered before going into the actual grounds and were given a lesson on the importance of who we are as people and our language. [Xxx] was our elder for this event; he shared with us the rich history of the land and expressed the importance of the buffalo. We then took the tour around the grounds to look at the buffalo and then regrouped at a local campsite to break for lunch.

After lunch we went on two hikes, Bears Hump and Red Rock. The youth and I had a lot of fun, you can tell who where the competitive ones because they often raced me to the top. Every time we reached a new waiting area [Xxx] shared a story with us, it felt as though each meeting area had a distinct meaning and at the end of the day we were left with a full day of different lessons on life. This analogy continued on through the rest of the week. Tesla and Hudson arrived in the evening of this day because their only transportation to get out to the camp site … doubled as errand shuttle that day.

On Tuesday, the day camp children and youth from Opokaa'sin joined us. Our group grew larger and we needed more space to do traditional games.… We were taught stories of Napi, the ones that are told time and time again, and enjoyed by many generations of First Nations families. We were able to use our imagination; curiosity and most of all discover the connection we as First Nation's people have with the land, the water, the animals, and the whole universe. Many of our creation stories are of how things came to be, First Nation's families are strongly encouraged to keep these stories alive; they resemble some of Napi's many lessons that he left with our people. The games that we played represented these stories. This also was the day when we got relocated to our second site because of the bears that decided to make an appearance.

Wednesday was a mixed field day between conducting interviews at Opokaa'sin and then returning to the camp. Our campsite was finally set up around 9 pm that evening. It was also the first time I got to set up a Tipi, [which] was an awesome experience! Our elder [Xxx], who liked to be called grandma; taught us ladies how to put up a tipi. She was unlike any elder I have ever met, She not only gave us instructions but she actually lifted the poles and got on the ground and tied them up. With her instruction and encouragement, I now feel confident that I can set up a tipi without having it crash down on us. Lol

Thursday was a huge day for data collection, we not only conducted numerous interviews but Tesla and Hudson were able to take part in one of our ceremonial practices. This practice is for the men; the women are very restricted in what they can do during this practice. We concluded Friday morning with a huge game of kickball and a big breakfast.

My Personal experience

I have learned a lot from this camp, the elders from the camp contributed a lot to this. The hikes we did on Monday, were so much fun. At the top of Bears Hump, [Xxx] showed us a type of leaf that is used in our pipes. I was also really impressed in how he kept up with us to the top of the mountain. [Xxx] was right behind us and the two youth that I was with, they kept saying "we have to hurry we can't let him get to the top before us." This is where I seen their inner leadership skills come out. They encouraged one another and only stopped twice for a minute each time determined to reach the top. This competitiveness was awesome to see, when we finally reached the top I told the two I was with "If anybody asks, we ran up here" LOL.

On Wednesday night Hudson and I stayed up late telling stories with a few of the elders. It brought back memories to when I was little, sitting and listening to the stories that my grandparents would tell. It was such a humbling night, followed by a bit of frustration with the camp leaders. After our visit with the elders I expected to go back to the tipi and sleep; only to find nothing was set up and their main camp supervisor for the girls was no where to be found. I immediately requested information on

> the plans for the girls but found out that I was the one that got put in charge, this all happened without my knowing and I felt a bit uncomfortable being put on the spot. However with my history in working with youth and children it was easy for me to switch roles and become a more authoritative supervisor. The girls too were also going through a lot of drama, which made the night a bit more frustrating. However as a group we pulled together and moved on, it turned out to be a good night.
>
> Tesla and Hudson, did an amazing job building rapport on the first few days. When we did start interviewing, they were very eager to start the process. This process went well, however some of the participants felt a bit uncomfortable speaking to either of them through this more formal setting. I think this had a lot to do with the fact there wasn't a huge age difference. When you listen to the recordings you can almost hear the lack of confidence in the participants voice when some of the questions were asked. The elders and camp leaders however were delighted to be interviewed, however it was hard to get time with them because everyone was so busy. The data that we collected from the camp was a mix between youth interviews on the pictures, and adult and elder interviews, where they told us stories that related to the pictures and finally recordings of some of the sessions that happened through out the camp.
>
> To conclude this camp we had a closing circle, this was the most inspiring part of the camp. The youth expressed their gratitude toward the elders and camp leaders and talked about what they learned. We then concluded with a final word from [Xxx], who left us with a story that taught us about life and how not to give up; "Iikaakiimatt" (try hard) is what we all went away with from this camp.

The multiple perspectives on the same set of events from these three para-ethnographers-in-training is useful, not only because it registers differences by age and gender, but because these three young researchers had different levels of experience with Blackfoot knowledge, although all of them described learning many new things.

"Para" is an interesting prefix. According to the *Merriam-Webster Dictionary* (https://www.merriam-webster.com), it can indicate "beside," "alongside of," "beyond," or "aside from," but it can also suggest "faulty," "abnormal," "associated in a subsidiary or accessory capacity," or "closely resembling." All these glosses seem to say the same thing: "not the real thing."

When used in the context of young researchers, "para" could well mean "not yet" expert, in the sense that this expertise will be achieved with age and exposure. This not-quite-yet-there aspect of "para" lines up nicely with the understanding of young people as becomings who are not yet beings. And indeed, this is how all three of these young researchers saw themselves: not quite there yet.[2] Yet these young people had been incorporated in the project as cultural experts already – in other words, as beings, not becomings. Their expressed sense of the not-quite-there-yet quality of their knowledge was described, produced, and curated in this project repeatedly, rendering unstable not only their expertise, but also the questions about what constitutes it.

Building Capacity

Even so, producing expertise as a kind of pedagogy became an explicit focus of the last phases of the project in the summer of 2017. As the project shifted to building a digital storytelling library, we had many discussions about how to do this: how to build it, where to build it, and then how it would be maintained. Because this digital resource was meant to be for Opokaa'sin's use in its programming, it was always understood to belong to the organization. But, as suggested, a busy non-profit delivering social services to young people and their families had little time or energy to manage this library. For this reason, we began to consider how to build capacity among young Blackfoot people to be the curators and not just the beneficiaries of this library. To accomplish this, Taylor designed a series of what we called "capacity camps" to train even younger people in how to conduct interviews and research as understood in universities and how to understand and use protocol in seeking knowledge from Elders.

In many ways this was a repeat of what had been offered to Taylor, Hudson, and Tesla themselves the year before. But now, the researchers were even younger people. Although the camps would again be organized by Opokaa'sin as summer camps, now for elementary and middle school students, the design of the camp would be driven by the needs of the Raising Spirit Project.

FIRST WEEK: FAKE IT 'TIL YOU MAKE IT (AMY'S FIELD JOURNAL, 18 MAY 2017)

This was the first week of the summer work!...

Thursday. Today Taylor and I designed the capacity camps we're going to run this summer with the youth at Opokaa'sin. The purpose of these is to ensure that when we hand over the reins to the library, there are folks (especially youth) who have the skills to add to it. I think our plan is ambitious, and I'm sure Tanya will have some suggestions, but I'm confident moving forward! My favourite part is that we'll be giving them training in academic work, but also have more freedom to do things how Opokaa'sin wants. This is because this work will be outside of the University's domain. This is by Opokaa'sin, for Opokaa'sin. My only concern here is the possibility of youth refusal. Will they want to be involved in these camps? If they are told by [Opokaa'sin's Blackfoot youth mentors] that they have to go, will they be grumpy? I would have been at their age.

Amy's concern about youth refusal reflected the rise in scholarly attention to ethnographic refusal during this phase of the Raising Spirit Project (Tuck and Yang 2014a, 2014b; A. Simpson 2007, 2014, 2017; McGranahan 2016a, 2016b; Cisneros 2018). As we found out, her concern was not misplaced (Mack and Newberry 2020).

Amy's worry also reflected some anxiety about the amount of work the team had put into preparing an experience for younger people who were going to be brought to campus. She and Taylor wanted very much for it to be a good one. In the next post, you can see again how they worked to introduce young campers to the knowledge practices of university-based research, while at the same time connecting them to Blackfoot ways of knowing. They were joined by a new team member who played a pivotal role here as a traditionalist and expert on Blackfoot forms of knowledge.

BEGINNING THE PROCESS (AMY, POSTED 27 JULY 2017)

Wednesday was our second Capacity Camp. We met the kids at Tim Horton's and found out we had about half as many as we expected. This was actually great because the number was easier to manage. The day began with my lecture on what anthropology is. I wanted to teach them about the four fields, but also keep it simple. After each brief intro to the field, I asked them to name a pop culture or real anthropologist (Bones, Indiana Jones, Jan, [Xxx] and me!). We talked about where anthropologists worked and what they did like participant observation and field notes. We watched two videos Jan had recommended.

Then we had a pop quiz on the big pieces of brown paper. In their groups (there were two this week) I asked them to answer: 1) what do anthropologists do? 2) Where do anthropologists work? 3) Who are anthropologists? 4) Where would you work if you were an anthropologist? I left the questions broad; though I hoped they would remember the four fields and come up with interesting places they could work.

After I was done, [Xxx] gave a presentation on Blackfoot history and worldview. She talked about Blackfoot conceptualizations of time: it's linear, and only two days in the past and two days in the future. This helps keep them in the present, and it is comforting to know that the ancestors and their power are only two days away. She talked about different prophecies, like [how] this cycle will end when people stop painting their tipis. She talked about learning from the animals and heeding their warnings (e.g. a domesticated wolf moved her pups when she sensed an attack from another group of people). She talked about prayer and tobacco and how you pray for all your relations. It was really lovely.

Then, we made tobacco ties. All the kids were given pieces of fabric and bits of tobacco to tie up. They took one home for themselves and the rest were kept for use in the field.

After lunch – which was filled with YouTube videos, dancing and singing – we showed them the videos that Hudson, Tesla, Jan, and Taylor put together on how to do proper interviews.[3] Taylor was so mortified by her performance that she cowered during it. I laughed ... and laughed ... and laughed! Then we asked the kids which interview was better – and they knew right away it was the one with Tesla and Jan. Then we asked them why it was better and what Taylor and Hudson could have done better. The group was great at critiquing the videos and noticing strengths. For example, they noticed Tesla made eye contact, asked for permission, and let Jan talk. They found Hudson disorganized, noticed that he talked over Taylor, and didn't seem to understand what he was doing! The team did great with the videos.

Then, Hudson and Tesla explained to their groups the interview protocol and had them practice. They had mixed feelings about it, and most of the issues stemmed from not being able to give good answers if they were the ones being interviewed. And that's not an issue for us, really, because they'll be interviewing their Elders and other adults.

After they were done their interviews, we got them to write field notes. They got a big brown piece of paper to write a paragraph about what they learned that day. This was a collaborative approach and one that we'll bring back each day so they can add to it.

There is so much that is wonderful in this post about the overlapping layers of expertise, training, and knowledge exchange between older and younger, Indigenous and settler, insider/outsider, and so on. Some of the moments of collaboration, scaffolding, and learning that made the Lair a local patch are described. These moments, fleeting in many ways, were some of the best of what Raising Spirit achieved. Did they build capacity? I hardly know, but they did prompt encounters that had young people experience positions as expert, as mentor, as trainer. The multiple registers through which learning and knowledge exchange occurred were shaped by encounters on campus, in visits to important Blackfoot sites, at the offices of Opokaa'sin, and in the many trips between these places.

As described in chapter 2, the project developed in patches across the southern part of Blackfoot Territory: in the Lair on the university campus, at Opokaa'sin, and on the Kainai and Piikani reserves, but also in the many vehicles that the team used to travel across the territory. In the second field season, visits to sacred sites, to the locations of the traditional stories told by Elders at Opokaa'sin, to family homes, and to reserve offices brought the team closer together, as is taken up in the next chapter.

Redistributed Expertise

The Raising Spirit blog posts show the limits of "para" as a useful description of knowledge practices outside of scientific laboratories, investment firms, and government bureaucracies. Conceptualizing the young researchers as para-ethnographers meant confronting some of the contradictions in this idea of vernacular knowledge and its relationship to ethnographic authority. Holmes and Marcus (2007) advocated recognizing the social theorizing of elite, technocratic knowledge producers and "the so-called fugitive social facts in the continuously changing contemporary that give rise to the sorts of knowledge-making among experts that can be identified as para-ethnographic by the ethnographer" (240). But what can it mean when young, Indigenous people are understood as experts, particularly experts in their own culture?

Trained in ethnographic interviewing and Indigenous protocol, the young researchers were expected to act as culture experts, but after training in ethnographic ways of knowing to elicit knowledge. Across the project, their position shifted repeatedly between being the knower and the learner. Taylor and Amy learnt in their interviews with much younger people that by leveraging their position as people in need of instruction, their interlocutors were more willing to share their expertise. In their experiences at Opokaa'sin's summer camps, Tesla and Hudson toggled between ethnographer and student of Blackfoot culture. This shifting positioning meant an awkward doubling that pointed to some of the dilemmas of being framed as para-ethnographers. It likewise suggests how endorsing the expertise of the young can be deeply intertwined with ideas of education as empowerment. To train someone in ethnographic methods – that is, as a culture expert in the anthropological sense – poses interesting questions about how the vernacular, everyday knowledge that para-ethnographers are presumed to have can be drawn into the frame of ethnographic recognition.

Amy Mack and I have described elsewhere the use of a para-ethnographic frame for the second phase of Raising Spirit and the dilemmas that arise from it (Mack and Newberry 2020, 78). We describe how the idea of para-expertise was challenged repeatedly, perhaps most notably because we were working with Indigenous people during the era of reconciliation following the work of the Truth and Reconciliation Commission in Canada. Calls for decolonizing methodologies were expanding beyond Linda Tuhiwai Smith's path-breaking work in 1999 (and see the last chapter). The idea of Indigenous knowledge as expertise rooted in ontological and epistemological systems other than Western science is central to current political activism around the environment, settler colonialism, and other ontological dispositions (Todd 2016, 2018; Hunt 2014; Burow et al. 2018; Wall Kimmerer 2013; de la Bellacasa 2012).

To be a culture expert as a young Indigenous person is also complicated by the contrast between everyday indigenous cultural knowledge and canonical Indigenous knowledge, a tension that the young research team felt keenly in their work. In fact, their felt sense of not being expert or not-yet-expert supports conventional understandings of the young as in the process of becoming. Yet the aim and target of training and pedagogy were constantly shifting in their work together. Who the experts were was the result of encounters in the Lair, at Opokaa'sin, and in Blackfoot Territory outside the city. Expertise was fungible, quickly redistributed and recirculated through the group depending on the needs of the moment and the particular encounter between the young and the older, the Blackfoot and the other. In their response to this process of redistributing expertise, the young research team produced among themselves a community of practice, one that learnt and taught together in these encounters.

The blog posts were ethnography in the sense of the writing of cultural difference to make sense of it. Even so, forms of ethnographic recognition that framed the young team as para-ethnographers were sometimes refused in the second phase of the Raising Spirit Project, and these refusals illustrated the circulation of i/Indigenous expertise across relationships, as is taken up in the next chapter.

NOTES

1 For the posts presented here, the date provided is when the notes were posted to the WordPress blog, not when the fieldwork or interview took place. These posts have been shortened but otherwise not edited except where needed to preserve clarity.

2 Although not taken up here, the model of development in Maslow's hierarchy is said to be based on Blackfoot practices. Critiques of Maslow's appropriation of Blackfoot knowledge have been offered, as well as arguments about its misrecognition of actual Blackfoot philosophy and practices (Bear Chief et al. 2022).

3 Tesla's training interview was meant to be exemplary while Hudson's video was meant to demonstrate how *not* to do an interview.

Chapter Four

Ethnographic Recognition and Refusal

Land Back

A consistent thread in resurgent and insurgent attention to Indigenous knowledge in Canada has been the role of land – not only as a stolen resource, but also as the anchor for Indigenous knowledge systems (L. Simpson 2014, 2017, 2022; Longman et al. 2020; "Land Back" 2019; Burow et al. 2018). Calls for land back have expressed not only the intensification of calls for true reconciliation – or the rejection of its very premise – but also an argument that Indigenous ontologies and epistemologies are land-based forms of relationality that deserve respect and recognition. These calls were gaining power during the second phase of the project. And so, although phase two was meant primarily to be about using the photos, stories, and interviews already produced to build a digital storytelling library, the team's trips across Blackfoot Territory extended the training of the cultural experts in-the-making by incorporating learning on the land and in relation to land.

In the following, portions of the blog are again presented to describe some of the team's travels across Blackfoot Territory and to show the effects of ethnographic recognition and its refusal in the redistribution and circulation of expertise among and beyond the team, with particular attention to the role of land-based forms of knowledge.

Grounding Knowledge

Amy was as much a culture expert in-the-making as Taylor, Tesla, and Hudson. She has described her work on the Raising Spirit Project as her first dissertation, and this is a fair assessment. Her energy and planning shaped the second phase, as well as her commitment to learning how to do this work effectively and ethically. Her direct mentorship and management of the young research team and the vast amounts of materials that went into building the storytelling library provided her with the kind of training and experience one hopes will be achieved in doctoral work.

Here, a few excerpts from Amy's blogged field notes are offered to illustrate her sense of her own incomplete, not-yet expert role as lead researcher and newly minted Master of Anthropology, and her experience learning about Blackfoot culture and values alongside as a settler researcher. This first post introduces place, land, territory, and sacred site as active agents in this making of expertise. The 2017 capacity camp included a trip to Writing-on-Stone Provincial Park as well as other sites that are meaningful to Blackfoot Peoples. Amy went along and her reflections identify several key issues in her own development as a culture expert.

IT TAKES INTELLIGENCE (AMY'S FIELD JOURNAL, POSTED 24 JULY 2017)

July 14th, 2016

Today we went to Writing On Stone with the Opokaa'sin crew. I was a little nervous joining them on this trip even though I was invited. I know the project is trying to establish an ethical space in which we know how to talk to one another – and that sometimes means being in an uncomfortable space – but that theoretical or abstract ideal doesn't always make reality easy to negotiate.

Anyways, we left at around 10am in one of the Opokaa'sin vans and were on our way. We had a full van.... Erin stayed in the Lair and Taylor was off winning basketball games with her youth team. Hudson was our DJ for the trip and we jammed out to the best of mullet rock....

Later we headed down to the petroglyphs to listen to [an Elder] explain the carvings. This was really incredible for me as I'd only ever seen the site through an archaeological lense in a geoarky class in my undergrad. We'd talked about it in terms of preservation, erosion and geological processes, and I left with the impression that there was a lack of continuity between those who carved the images and those who were around today.

[The Elder] started out by explaining that the stories were told to him by his father (intergenerational knowledge transmission) as his bedtime stories. He also made a point to (jokingly) point out that he didn't have a radio, TV or the Internet at this time. He told us that the drawings were the stories of people's lives, particularly the men who had come to do vision quests in the valley. During these vision quests they'd have to stay out in the elements for 4 days and 4 nights (more on the number four in my next blog post), and they had to be prepared for what they saw. They might live long enough to return and draw their life story, or they might die young. They had to be prepared to live the life they saw....

[The Elder] asked us to give an offering to Creator and the spirits/ancestors that were there. This was my first time giving an offering of tobacco. [One of the mentors] explained that you can say your prayer out loud (so the spirits hear better) or in your head, and in Blackfoot or in English. [The Elder] led us in a Blackfoot prayer. Once I said my prayer (in my head), I was instructed to make a hole and place the tobacco in it. Then [the Elder] began a song for us, which I believe was typically sung when you'd lost a spouse. This prompted an interesting conversation about heartbreak.

He asked the children what broke their hearts. "It breaks my heart when people swear at me." said a little girl. "That's not what Creator wants. Creator wants us all to be kind to one another," an Opokaa'sin staff member responded. "But it's just dumb white people," she said. I laugh awkwardly. What else can you do when you're the only white person and a kid makes a comment like that? Instantly all the adult heads swivel towards me. And I just keep laughing. It was nice, because I think they recognized that I might be uncomfortable and at least some of them were concerned. [The Elder] followed this up by saying "God doesn't see colour. The only colour he sees is the colour of your heart." Later, when asking them to stay in the circle and pay attention, Peter said, "If you keep running off, the Crow or the Cree will catch you. And you'll have to live with them as they raise you as one of your own." (Again, no free play if you're supposed to be learning from an Elder) "Or the white people!" shouts the same little girl. Again, I laugh. Others laugh too. But the heads once again swivel to look at how I'm reacting. Sigh.

This was a great experience, though. That ethical space is going to be uncomfortable at times. It's also going to be a lot of confronting White guilt and privilege. Even though I'd never done anything to the girl, she's obviously had enough bad encounters with white people to have formed that opinion. And that broke my heart....

[The Elder] also talked about the burden of having to remember everything, and in particular people's names (especially Blackfoot names). He said it's a lot to remember. This was when a very interesting thing concerning our methods came into play: he said the key was to "think in Blackfoot." He began, "All those White people who wrote about us were probably brilliant and talented. But they don't *think* in Blackfoot. They can't." He then made direct eye contact with me and said, "She could learn to speak Blackfoot – and speak it better than me – but she'll never think in Blackfoot. You might be able to speak it, but you won't know the names. You won't know what it means." It was uncomfortable to be stared down by an Elder and told about my positionality, but I remembered Taylor telling me that when an Elder tells you something, you just take it. There is no arguing or retorting to an Elder!

And this got me thinking about PAR [participatory action research] and the importance of Tesla, Hudson & Taylor doing the interviews and being a part of the ethnographic data collection. It's so important that they a) learn these stories for their own lives, but b) collect them for the library. These things need to be transmitted within the community and BY the community. So, again, where is the co-construction? Is this the ethical space? How are we all transformed here? And will the transformations be equal? How might they be transformed by my presence? How does my presence change things?

Amy's post touches on many of the methodological and analytical quandaries that we had centred in this second phase of Raising Spirit. She brings up the idea of ethical space, the concept associated with Elder Willie Ermine (2007) to describe the space between world views where we might meet to share across difference. The team had actively taken up the idea and frequently referred to it in their field notes, and here Amy notes both the discomforts of this space along with its possibilities.

Her own education in how one learns from and with a Blackfoot Elder was deeply impactful for her and it carried through the project as she learnt protocols for approaching and learning from Elders. In this, she was not very different from other members of the team, all of whom felt anxious about how to do this appropriately and respectfully. Just as Taylor, Tesla, and Hudson were being put in the uncomfortable position of speaking for culture, Amy too was made uncomfortable in her search for a position from which to speak in this process as a culture expert.

Amy's attention to intergenerational knowledge transmission is a reminder of the central goal of the Raising Spirit Project. Visits to important sites with an Elder were used by Opokaa'sin to address this lack for young people. But the team had other encounters in the field and on the land in Blackfoot Territory that shaped their experience of being culture experts.

One sort of encounter was visits to sites of official knowledge about Indigenous Peoples in the area, such as Head-Smashed-In Buffalo Jump, a UNESCO world heritage site located in Blackfoot Territory, and the Glenbow Museum in Calgary. Here, in a blog post, Tesla captures some of the many competing forms of expertise and their performance and consumption in such spaces.

POWWOW AT BUFFALO JUMP (TESLA'S FIELD JOURNAL, 27 JULY 2016)

The day we were supposed to be making blog posts and doing more transcribing, plans changed and we heard that there was supposed to be a powwow at Buffalo Jump Historical Museum....

When we got to the top of the hill, We saw a gathering of people right outside the museum and it was sort of interesting to see that the majority of the people were non native people, as was expected because Buffalo Jump is a tourist site I'm pretty sure. We sat down and I started listening to the man that was speaking and Amy and Taylor had pulled out their notes and so I pulled out my notes to and make sure to observe and take in everything I can. I took some pretty useful notes and payed attention to my surrounding a lot. When I first saw the crowed, the first thing I noticed was that there was a lot of tourists and non-blackfoot people and that was really cool to see very interesting. It meant to me that they wanted to take part of our culture and learn more about it. They were their for the same reason I was, to learn and observe the blackfoot culture....

[Later, she puts her own knowledge in context:]

we... decided to go into the museum to look around a bit. Although we've all been there multiple times, we decided to go in anyways. It was cool to see the amount of people that were there that day since whenever I've gone, it was never a big crowd. We walked to the very top and walked outside where you walk out on a trail and can see an amazing view.... So we walked all the way down to Taylor's car in the parking lot and on our way home, we debriefed on what we took notes on a just discussed being at the powwow. It was nice to be able to go a powwow that day, even though it was nothing new to me. It's always something different everyday is what makes stuff like this something to look forward to so I'm really careful on what I should be paying attention to so I would have some ideas to write in blogs like this one.

Tesla's observation of others observing her own culture provides an interesting juxtaposition, as does her turn to record field notes as an Indigenous (para-)ethnographer in-the-making. Her shifting position is realized in encounters as a Blackfoot person and as a young researcher, but also as other to both positions in some way.

What was most influential for the team were their own trips through Blackfoot Territory and their encounters with various experts and Blackfoot ways of knowing. In this next set of posts, Taylor and Tesla describe a trip to pick berries on Taylor's family's land on the Piikani Reserve. I had the great good fortune to go on this trip too and to meet Taylor's family.

BERRY PICKING IN PIIKANI (TAYLOR'S FIELD JOURNAL, 17 AUGUST 2016)

This day was beautiful. My grandparents … invited the team down to their place to pick choke cherries. My grandmother was honoured and happy to have such a wonderful group of people to their house. She mentioned that she was proud of the group and encouraged us to continue the great work.

The day started off by visiting with my grandparents, mother, sister, nephews and uncle. Before we went out, we shared opinions on the pictures in the project and heard Rose express her gratitude to see one of the elders from Piikani in the photos. We were also given a brief history of the area by my uncle who was more than excited to be our tour guide for the day.

My nephews … who were interviewed at the beginning of the project joined us along with their mother.… We started by saying a prayer and making an offering. My uncle … then lead us down into the bush near the Old Man river and we began our berry picking. This was a lot of fun and a great bonding experience for all of us as a team. My uncle shared history, stories and cultural views through out our day here. It was beautiful to see the scenery and be able to experience this day with the team. We collected a lot of berries and joked about the endless things we could make with them. [My uncle] was so excited to be our tour guide that you never heard him stop take a break between his stories. lol He even showed us a tipi ring that was located near my grandparents place and told us about the history of what he knew about them. He then invited the team to his house and showed us pictures and books, that gave evidence to some of the stories he told along the way.

Taylor's uncle is an interesting man. He gifted me with a walking stick. He also talked about how his understanding of Blackfoot knowledge kept him from participating directly in the Sundance. Instead, he celebrates alongside, in a space adjacent. This idea of knowledge alongside became a theme in Raising Spirit. His story also identifies the existence of counter-expertise within the Blackfoot community, unsettling any singular claim to expertise as a community (Fortun and Cherkasky 1998), an issue I return to later in this chapter.

Taylor's close family centred on the reserve represents a set of relations in contrast with Tesla's situation. At the time of the project, Tesla and her sister were living in foster care with a settler family miles away from the reserve. Tesla's connection to Blackfoot Territory and ways of knowing was more attenuated in some ways, but her experience also shows how relationships to land extend beyond a single territory or identity. You get some sense of this difference in her post about berry picking and how her foster family has provided her with access to other communities of knowledge.

BERRY PICKING (TESLA'S FIELD JOURNAL, 26 OCTOBER 2016)

I've only ever been Berry Picking once and it was in newfoundland with my Grandpop. He would take us out into the bushes on his quad and we would pick blueberries and spend the afternoon eating handfuls of berries. So going out to pick choke cherries with Taylors family was a good experience. It wasn't hard to grab a bunch of berries because there were lots of them! We had some buckets and bags that we would keep them in and by the time we finished we had about a whole bag of em. They tasted really good but after a while it leaves a bitter taste in on your tongue.

Tesla begins this post with a reference to her foster family relationships. Throughout this project, I have kept in mind the complex positioning of young people in foster care. The young people served by Opokaa'sin represent a range of living situations, but many are in some form of care by non-Indigenous people and mostly in urban areas. As Tanya would describe for me, the young people served by Opokaa'sin trouble any easy identification with reserve and the uninterrupted transmission of knowledge, and she has worked consistently to reconnect young people with culture to promote resilience. The kin-making (and remaking) of Indigenous Peoples in North America has been continuously and violently disrupted as already suggested here. While the making of kin with the more-than-human (Haraway 2016) has been taken up by academics, for Indigenous Peoples this is a matter of law, rights, and sovereignty (A. Simpson 2014), as well as resistance to the erasure of local kinship-making practices (Innes 2013). Comprehensive treatment of this area of Indigenous scholarship and activism is beyond the remit of this book. Here, I point to how Tesla's kin-making practices were surfaced during project trips across Blackfoot Territory. In her blog post, she weaves together her trips to Blackfoot Territory, and its forms of knowledge, with her own web of relationships reaching to Newfoundland and her foster family there.

In another section of Tesla's blog about the trip to Head-Smashed-In, she describes making kin relations there too:

> Once it ended, Taylor mentioned that her uncle was there, she went to go ask him if we could talk to him for a couple minutes and he generously allowed us to come and let us ask him some questions. At first we introduced ourselves and we told him our last names, as surprisingly he recognized my last name because I feel like the last name "Heavyrunner" is kind of rare. I was also surprised because I don't really know any family of my own. He told me that he knew of someone back when he went to school with the last name Heavyrunner and he was the team's quarterback for football. I thought that was fascinating.

Tesla's kin-making, like her role as a culture expert, was emergent in encounters. The research team had other encounters in Blackfoot Territory that both provoked and confounded expertise. One kind of encounter took place in offices on both the Kainai and Piikani reserves as the team worked on coding values in the photographs.

One of the central questions of the second half of Raising Spirit followed from the first half: Who was going to code all the photographs taken to index the Blackfoot values they were understood to represent? How were the latent values going to be made manifest? The para-ethnographers were meant to be crucial translators in this process. And indeed, in the first summer of work with them, Amy charged them with writing coding notes on the pictures. This work did not proceed very far before the contradictions of their position became clear: They were experts in-the making, doubly inside and outside at once. Our methods would change as a consequence, and the dilemmas of coding and our improvisations to solve them are the subject of the next chapter.

But first, as the initial work of coding was being taken up, we decided that our young research team would go to the reserves and seek out experts to provide a preliminary coding of a set of photographs. Their initial forays across Blackfoot Territory were meant to ground the coding process in the words of those living and working on the Kainai and Piikani reserves. These trips were partly planned and partly serendipitous. In every trip, expertise was surfaced – sometimes performed, sometimes denied, sometimes redirected, but always circulating through relationships. Here is Tesla again.

WORKSHOPS IN BROCKET (TESLA'S FIELD JOURNAL, 26 OCTOBER 2016)

….[W]e had gone out to Brocket another day and talked to some more people and the first thing we did was introduce ourselves in front of a room full of elders and everyone seemed a bit nervous for that. I had handed out offerings after Jan and everyone had spoken about the project and the elders looked super nice and I had even gotten a compliment from one! We still had a few more people to visit and luckily some of them were able to squish us into their very busy work day. After that we had some time until the next meeting so Taylor decided to give us a tour around the small town of Brocket and she showed us all the main important buildings and the neighborhoods. The next meeting was with [Xxx] and she worked at Family and Child Services and she looked very familiar to me so I was thinking that my mom might have known her. She couldn't stay and talk for long since she had another meeting to attend but she did have a bit of time to sit with us and look at a [photo] booklet and say what she thought about them while we all took a bit of notes and I eventually switched off with Erin and recorded the information Trina had about the pictures. By the end of the day we were determined to visit one more place and that was at the Peigan Board of Education and we had interviewed [Xxx] and [Xxx]. Both of the women were very knowledgeable with the culture side of things and they had told us some stories about their childhood as well that linked to the topic of child-rearing practices. It's nice to hear about stories from their childhood because maybe that's one thing that makes them who they are as a person today. [Xxx] had talked about kids and elders and how some children respect elders more than other children and it all depends on who they grew up with, If the children are around adults and older people a lot they tend to act more respectful towards elders and how they attend cultural ceremonies, and that's one of the important things that I picked up on while [Xxx] and [Xxx] were talking to us. We handed them sweet grass and tobacco as a respectful offering and as a "thank you for spending your time to come and chat with us." That day had been concluded with an hour drive back to Lethbridge.

Wednesday were going out to meet with Hudson's Family at a building in Standoff to again, talk to them about the project and allow them to give some of their input. They all seemed very quiet at first and maybe they felt uncomfortable or maybe they just didn't know what to say but then all of a sudden there was more than one person who wanted to say something at once. There was a booklet from the pictures that definitely caught some of the adult's attention more than the others and in more than one interview. Something that they may have wanted to talk from or something that reminded them of the topic of child-rearing practices. A couple of the adults had left the room because again they were busy people and probably had other things they had to get done. The workshop ended with Hudson and I talking about what we have learned and experienced from this summer by being part of the project so that the participants had an idea of who we are and what had to say about the project....

Going to the reserves to speak to people, many of them working in tribal governance, represented encounters with official forms of cultural knowledge for the young research team. Their interactions around the project photos prompted conversations about cultural values. Here is Taylor.

PIIKANI FIELD DAY 2 (TAYLOR'S FIELD JOURNAL, 17 AUGUST 2016)

On August 17, we went out to Piikani for the second time, to meet with more elders and community members for the coding work shops. Now this day was my biggest test that I have ever experienced. I brought the group to the Elders centre and introduced the project and team to them, in the hopes of gaining their blessing and permission to be part of the project. I thought one of the elders I knew would introduce me and possibly assist me in welcoming the team, but instead I stood in the front of the semi circle and introduced myself and the team. I am not one to get nervous in front of crowds but I must say this was by far the scariest presentation I have ever done. I have never stood up in front of elders to speak on anything before, and the nervousness I felt was almost discomforting but I knew this was for a good purpose. It definitely was a awesome experience, although I was put on the spot, I definitely feel more confident in myself to be able to stand proud in front of my elders and speak. I want to thank the team and this project for allowing me to experience this awesome milestone in my life and express my gratitude to be able to take the lead on these community visits....

Taylor's role in the visits to Piikani was particularly important. It was not just that this was the reserve where she grew up or that we visited her family as part of these trips; it was that Taylor, perhaps more than anyone else, was put in the position of acting as the culture expert and as the translator of values, practices, and protocols for the rest of the team. In fact, she repeatedly confessed her worry about her own position as a young person, one who didn't in fact know everything expected of her in these situations. In this instance, she unexpectedly became spokesperson for the project to a group of Elders, acting as translator in front of those she considered culture experts. It was their recognition of her right to do so that made her an expert. Her gratitude to her community is an acknowledgement of that recognition.

Amy describes the same encounter as well in her post. She adds some of the complications of land-based knowledge for those raised in care. See her notes on the social worker who identified making relationships as the crucial point, not specific ties to land. She, like Tesla, had been raised in a settler family and not on the reserve.

FROM CODING WORKSHOPS (AMY'S FIELD JOURNAL, 30 AUGUST 2016)

Noon. We arrived [in the middle of their prayer] at the Elder hall. There were about 20 of them eating lunch in a horseshoe shape. There were about as many men as women, and they were all what [Xxx] called "aged Elders," if not "ceremonial Elders." Taylor made some introductions and Jan gave her bit about the project. Hudson & Tesla handed out the tobacco, and the main Elder confirmed that they would support the project and help us. We then all shook their hands (and they remarked on how cold mine were. Meep).

When we got back to the car Taylor more or less crumpled in on herself. The girl had been *nervous!* But, in classic Taylor style, she hadn't given any outward indication or sign that she was anything other than calm, cool and collected.

1:30pm. We then headed over to Child & Family Services to talk to one of their caseworkers.... [Xxx] was a young Blackfoot professional; sharply dressed and clearly very busy. She looked a little overwhelmed as we all filed into their conference room, and politely listened to Taylor & Jan's bits. She declined being recorded, and prefered to have Erin (and later Tesla) transcribe what she was saying. I gave her the choice between the three books, and she chose the first because of the smiling and happy family on page one.

[Xxx] noted that she hadn't been raised on the reserve, but rather with a white family in Lundbreck. However, she considered Brockett "home" despite now living in Lethbridge with her children. She said that for her, home was here because that's where her family was, and in particular, a Grandma. She said that it's necessary to have ties to *people* on the reserve, and that youth, when searching for something, will use those ties – those connections – to bring themselves home. When asked, she expanded these ties to be to Elders or distant family as well. She didn't seem to think it was a strongly about land or culture as other folks have told us, but instead it was about inter-personal connections. She mentioned that she doesn't practice the culture (so the tobacco and sweet grass weren't something she needed, but accepted nonetheless), and she is "finding a different way in." This really spoke to me and I think our methods, specifically with having youth from the community do the research.

Tesla's post above described some of what happened on the Kainai reserve as well. What she doesn't note was that Hudson's grandmother was a woman of some position in the office, and so, Hudson was both proud and extremely nervous. The encounter was much different than the smaller and more numerous encounters at Piikani, but this one ended firmly on the Kainai reserve at an Elder's house where we watched puppies gambol, looked at the distant horizons that frame the reserve landscape, and listened to stories of his family and the land.

Hudson didn't blog about this event, but his experience in these trips to reserve offices adds important dimensions. While Taylor and her family are from the Piikani reserve, Hudson's family is Kainai or Blood. Until this project, I was unaware of how important this distinction was because the reserves are located close to one another in southern Alberta. It was through this project that I came to understand that these two nations of the Blackfoot Confederacy are often competitive with one another, despite many connections between them. The divide is even clearer with the Siksika located farther north and the Amskapi-Piikani, known as the Blackfeet, across the border in Montana. Most settlers in Lethbridge are blind to these differences. They played a role here because in some ways it seemed as though Hudson wanted to represent his reserve after we had spent more time in Piikani spaces. This had been in part because of Taylor's connections there. In fact, Tanya (a relative of Hudson's) was Kainai. She too had marked the difference as a significant one.

These trips to both reserves were meant to help with coding the photographs, grounding the knowledge on values in Blackfoot Territory, a recognition of the significance of land-based knowledge for Indigenous Peoples.

Refusing the Sundance

There is one last source of landed knowledge and its relationship to expertise that needs describing here and that's the Sundance.[1] No other event prompted more concern and anxiety about what to know and who was to know it. A post by Taylor gives some sense of the stakes.

PRE SUNDANCE (TAYLOR'S FIELD JOURNAL, 17 AUGUST 2016)

Before we went out to the Sundance I took the girls shopping for skirts and hankies. I briefly discussed the importance of how we are to dress when we are going to the Sundance. For example the girls are to wear long skirts out of a sign of respect. Because we were only visitors, I wanted to make sure we were very respectful and not show up in short shorts or tank tops. I also gave them a few important things to remember when we do go there, more as guidance to not over step their boundaries. *I myself am not an expert* [emphasis added] but I passed on the knowledge of what I know. I really hope they enjoyed this day as much as I did, it was fun shopping. I thought this day was important for the girls to experience because in the future they now have an idea of what to wear and a little bit of what to expect.

When Taylor says "I myself am not an expert," even as she shares what she knows with her teammates, we have one of the clearest examples of how experts are made in specific encounters, emerging to meet a need and then relinquishing that role to others when need be. Here is Tesla describing preparations for the Sundance.

SUNDANCE PREP (TESLA'S FIELD JOURNAL, 26 OCTOBER 2016)

When I first heard we were going to be joining Sundance I was unsure of what to expect since I have never attended such a huge sacred ceremony that is very rich in the Black Foot community. I knew practically nothing of what was to be expected or what behavior was most appropriate, but I wasn't the only one who felt that way. Amy along with Taylor needed to find out more information on what to wear and what to do. There is definitely a lot more rules for females and what they are expected to wear than there are for men. It is respectful to cover your legs so wearing a long dress would be the most appropriate for women and for men would just have to wear jeans. I went to some stores with Taylor and Amy to find some of the stuff we were missing like head scarfs and things like that. We went into this really cool store … and Amy found a long skirt for Sundance that she needed. We also searched for scarfs at every store that we visited including the Galt Museum but they didn't have anything that we were looking for or had in mind so we just headed back to the university and talked a bit more about what is to be expected so Taylor decided to call [a youth mentor from Opokaa'sin] and she was really helpful in giving us advice about what to do and what to wear so that we could be all set to head off to Sundance….

It felt different to be there and experience something that I have never got a chance to before. When we showed up, it was overwhelming to see so many teepees all in one area. It was also very cool and eye opening. The whole place seemed really quiet like everyone had gone into hiding but it was also very nice. We had a chance to talk to [an Elder and her husband] and he had LOTS to say and it was all very interesting. He talked about his childhood, a residential ghost story that he had experienced and just the overall cultural side of Sundance that I was very keen on about listening to because it was stuff that I didn't know about that was important to my culture. [Xxx] told many stories and went on for a while with each one, going into depth with the stories he told made in so much more interesting. We had a chance to go to two ceremony's at Sundance and visually watch it take place. Everyone seemed like they knew what they were doing and I just went along with everybody else.

Our time at Sundance was enough to kind of know what it was about, how it made us feel and the things that we learned from [Xxx] was all very interesting. The day was super warm and the sun was intense. It was nice to experience something that I've never experienced before so now I can't say I've never been to Sundance.

Here we see again Tesla's doubled insider/outsider status but also the specialness of the Sundance itself. While familiar with powwows and sites like Head-Smashed-In, she had never attended the Sundance. Her worries about doing the right things echo Taylor's, and she is pleased to learn more from Elders about her culture. Contrast this with Amy's post about the Sundance.

SUNDANCE. OKAN. (AMY'S FIELD JOURNAL, 30 AUGUST 2016)

Preparing. Since the beginning of our fieldwork – even back when we were interviewing little gaffers at Opokaa'sin – Sundance has been a recurring topic of discussion. "Can you explain to Amy the difference between a pow-wow and Sundance?" … "What do you do at Sundance that you don't do at a pow-wow? Do you get your face painted at a pow-wow?" [T. Little Mustache, interviewing a child at Opokaa'sin in June]. *Okay. A pow-wow is more social. You eat fry bread there. You get toys. You see your family. Sundance? There isn't as much dancing. There are more rules. Many children don't go to Sundance. This sort of makes sense....*

"Sundance is much more spiritual. It's more ceremonial. A pow-wow is more social and for fun" [T. Little Mustache, just chatting]. *Okay, so it's more serious. It also lasts longer than a pow-wow and people camp out in their trailers or tipis. Lots of ceremonies take place over the course of weeks. It would be neat for Hudson and Tesla to get to go.*

"You guys should come out and sleep in the tipis! It would be a great experience for all of you" [Opokaa'sin mentor at the cultural immersion camp]. *All of us? Me? Jan and Erin? Oh yikes. Okay, so this is a thing now.*

Hudson told me to watch *Circle of the Sun* [a NFB documentary about the Sundance] to get an idea of what it was like in the Sixties, when people were concerned it would die out. [One person] said to wear a long skirt. Taylor recommended a handkerchief for our heads. Hudson said we had to have closed-toe shoes. [Another person] is uncomfortable telling us what to wear and [yet another] thinks I'd be OK just wearing jeans. [One person] said we can't wear short-shorts, and that we should also cover our shoulders ... and go to the washroom before we leave because the port-a-potties appaul her. *Of course they're more lenient on the outsider's clothing. Much more pressure to do things properly when you're a part of the community. And of course it's gendered; Hudson should wear jeans and a clean top...* [Amy goes on to describe the shopping and the many starts and stops on getting to the Sundance.]

Arriving. You can see the Sundance from the road when it's set up. It was visually overwhelming. Dozens of vehicles were parked near the entrance to the field, and members of the Brave Dog society were there to check the vehicles coming in (even though Sundance is *technically* open to everyone). Then, there was a large outer ring of trailers and trucks. Inside that ring were large tipis. Inside that ring were the tipis of the societies and a field where ceremonies would take place. No wonder the true translation of Okan [I've seen it spelled Ookaan as well] is actually "large encampment" [Elder, interview at his home in August]....

It was pretty incredible, and again, I don't have the rights to talk about it. But it was overwhelming to see so many people come out to watch it and be a part of the community.

I also felt a really strong connection to the land develop as I sat there. We were out in the middle of the prairies, with a panoramic view of the world, surrounded by a ring of tipis. As a local, I've always been partial to the area, and this area reminded me a lot of where my family ranches. But, to witness a group who cares for and stewards the land like the Blackfoot do reaffirmed this connection for me. Which was odd as I'm not of their culture.

But, you know, I noticed the storm clouds in the sky, and how intense they were as they rolled over from the west. The enormity of my view was overwhelming. And I noticed a large bird circling on the air currents above throughout most of the ceremony. A person next to me speculated that it was piitaa [eagle, which one of the boys at Opokaa'sin taught me to say]. When it started to rain, I thought about how I should be happy that we probably wouldn't have grass fires this year, and not be upset with the curly/wavy mess my hair was going to become.

A lot of folks dislike Lethbridge and southern Alberta, and particularly the prairies, but this experience just made me prouder to be from here.

It was also really moving to see so many people – and youth – involved in the spiritual side of their culture, as I know across cultures the youth are more and more disengaged. I'm so glad that Taylor, Tesla & Hudson got to experience this, got to learn more about their culture, and that I got to do this with them. I was really proud of them and all they'd accomplished there and in the days leading up to Sundance.

And again, I was just really honoured to be there and to witness this part of the Blackfoot culture. It meant a lot to be invited (as opposed to just showing up), and to have so many people there making sure I was fed, hydrated and educated. To be in the prayers of the societies carrying out their ceremonies and to feel safe within the encampment. To feel welcome, despite the horrors my people (Canadians and anthropologists) had enacted on the Blackfoot. I learned a lot from the Elders and the family members I met about working together, moving forward together, and accepting forgiveness. I think this was a turning point for me in that I became comfortable in my position within the project. I had been vulnerable and uncomfortable, and was moving towards/helping to produce that ethical space.

The Sundance produces highly charged encounters, perhaps especially for the young researchers who keenly felt the limits of their knowledge. Amy's post reveals her own growing anxiety and the many mixed messages about this very marked event. In fact, the patchy knowledge and incomplete understanding of the Sundance, its events, and its significance held by the young team is true for many Blackfoot people themselves. Here, we also see Amy finally claiming a place for herself in this landscape, perhaps not one as an expert but as someone who derives her sense of self from her own family's relationship to the land and her encounters with experts, young and old, in spaces across Blackfoot Territory.

Yet the trip to the Sundance by the young team also produced a marked refusal, one that Amy and I have written about elsewhere (Mack and Newberry 2020). It happened as the young team got ready to drive home and they realized that they would now be expected to write detailed field notes on the blog about what they had experienced and learnt. Amy described a "collective anxiety that seemed to build as the car neared the city limits. They were not Elders, so what right did they have to share this knowledge" (2020, 88). Amy too "was cognizant that she herself was young and the junior scholar on the project in relation to Newberry and others" (88). There was real concern about honouring established protocols for knowledge transfers in the Blackfoot community. They decided as a team – in the space of the car trip home – to refuse this form of ethnographic recognition. Instead, they would write some heavily redacted field notes.

The Capacity for Refusal and Recognition in the Making of Cultural Experts

Tesla and Hudson each made a blog post after their first summer of work describing what it meant to be a researcher.

WHAT IT MEANT TO BE A RESEARCHER (TESLA'S FIELD JOURNAL, 26 OCTOBER 2016)

When I first got notice of this job I guess I can say I was expecting something different. It was so amazing to work with wonderful people and be able to go different places and learn new things and I know that all sounds a bit cliché but its true! Of course I enjoyed waking up every morning and heading to work always looked forward to the different adventures we would take each day even if some of the days were a bit long and tiring.

I personally have learnt so much from Amy, Taylor and everyone else I got the chance to work with this summer. It was fun to be able to build rapport with everyone. Alongside that, I got a taste of the Lethbridge University, the different courses as some options for when I graduate High school, and of course Anthropology. Anthropology is the study of humans and their culture as well as development, It's a very interesting study that I think may cross my mind somewhere down the path. I got the chance to hang out with some anthropologists over the summer and got a look at what they use their knowledge to do including, field work, interviews, community participation, all of what I have been doing over the course of the summer. We started off with learning of what being on the field is like and how to observe everything and how observations are one of the important key things in field work so we got lots of practice with it then we started with interviews. Interviewed small children, youth, adults, and elders, all which were which important to collect info from. Mid-summer we started transcribing which took time and consistency. We then ended off the summer with workshops.

Being a part of this project has made me more aware of the importance of the First Nations and realized that it is so important to be a part of your own cultural practices. I can immediately say that I have grown on my knowledge about my culture than ever before thanks to Opokaasin and the University of Lethbridge. I've been able to visit many cultural places and go on lots of fun adventures that have made me want to go back and learn and experience what I have done

I am so lucky to have got the chance to be a part of this project and use the skills that I have learnt for things I may want to achieve after high school. This summer has inspired me to think about Post-secondary, something of which I had no clue about before and at least now I have some idea. I hope to come back to this project in the future.

Based on Tesla's post alone, the project was successful in producing encounters with expertise: those based in the university and those based in Blackfoot ways of knowing. Hudson's post underlines the sense of what this project accomplished for the young researchers.

WHAT IT MEANS TO BE A RESEARCHER (HUDSON'S FIELD JOURNAL, 30 SEPTEMBER 2016)

It was defiantly[2] a great and awesome experience for myself, because I was able to meet a lot of great people and as well as it being a summer that I'll never forget. I was able to build rapport and made a connection with everyone that I've interviewed. Everything for me was exciting, and

> honorable experience for me because I was able to be more involved in my culture and to be more knowledgeable about it as well....
>
> I went sweet grass picking for the first time this past summer and I was taught which is real sweet grass and what was fake sweet grass, when you [are] sweet picking as well, you have to sit there and be patient and comfortable enough to spend hours there, if not and you rush to pick it then you could get tricked by Napi, by picking the fake sweet grass. I also [had] the honor to help out at the Sundance with a few of the society members and I also had the privilege of attending some sacred ceremonies which was a great honor for me because it opened my eyes to be a part of something that my people have been doing for hundreds of years, the way I interpreted the Sundance is that it is not a religion or a social gathering but a way of life for the Blackfoot people and it is something I want to be involved with for many more years to come. I was able to visit sacred sites too, as well as climbing Chief Mountain and the Heavyshields canyons. Personally for me it was just a great and unbelievable experience for myself because I learned way more about my culture then I thought I would have and if I have the opportunity to be an interviewer/researcher ever, I'd defiantly take it again immediately because you can meet a lot of great and interesting people, I also learned a lot from a bunch of different people in a short amount of time being around them, the only thing about it is you have to pay very close attention to their stories and what they're trying to teach you.

Para-ethnography is based on a kind of recognition, a recognition of expertise that provides a social analysis other than that by trained ethnographers. How then to understand the work of Hudson, Tesla, Taylor, and all the young people who attended capacity camps? They were trained, albeit briefly, in the methods of ethnography, but they were also chosen because they were Blackfoot young people who were understood initially to have latent cultural expertise that could inform the project's understanding of values in child-rearing. Their doubled positions across the summers of their work prompts questions about the idea of *para*-ethnographers.

As the blog posts show, all three deny being an expert at various points, instead asserting the incomplete and patchy character of their knowledge. In other words, at various times, each member of the research team refused the position of culture expert. The blog posts show that the Sundance in particular prompted several refusals: to record as an observer, to share what was learnt, and to claim any expertise or authoritative knowledge about it. This moment of ethnographic refusal was shared by Amy, who felt equally reluctant to report on what she had learnt at the Sundance even as she felt the weight of the need to advise her young team as another kind of culture expert in-the-making. The team ultimately chose to write cursory notes, leaving out any knowledge that they felt was not meant to be shared. This refusal of expertise was a shared one made by the whole team. Not only does it illustrate the fungibility of expertise and how it is experienced and refused in relational encounters, but their decision argued for the preservation of some kind of a line between knowledge for insiders and knowledge for outsiders.

If "para" is meant to capture the not-quite-expert quality of knowledge, then it is an apt description of the felt sense of the team members. The fragility of expertise was something remarked upon repeatedly. Expertise was unstable in this context, never achieving some final form, but instead shaped in a particular encounter and then just as quickly replaced and redirected in another. Across Raising Spirit, expertise was fungible and redistributed across encounter after encounter, circulating between members and other knowledge keepers, including Blackfoot Elders.

Perhaps Kim Fortun and Todd Cherkasky's (1998) idea of counter-expertise is useful here. Their interest is in collaboration that draws together different interests, perspectives, and skills in organizational contexts.

> Collaboration recognizes that counter-experts are indeed experts, which means that they cannot straightforwardly identify with the demoralized, depoliticized and disorganized people with whom they work. Collaboration stresses the *labour* of working across difference, the *un-easiness* of the counterexpert's responsibilities. These responsibilities are uneasy in a double sense. They involve difficult and demanding work, intellectual as well as political. And the counter-expert's responsibilities are uneasy in that they require that sense of apprehension or trepidation necessary for critical re-examination and re-questioning of cherished assumptions, self-evident ideas, or naturalized alliances. (146)

This description is an unexpectedly apt one for the position that Taylor, Hudson, and Taylor were put in, especially as young Indigenous people during the era of reconciliation and this time of intensive building of an Indigenous canon of authoritative knowledge. Each team member was put in the position of being the expert in various encounters, on campus, at Opokaa'sin, and on reserve. Yet, their expertise was *counter*-expertise because they were young and because they were Blackfoot, and they were meant to identify vernacular indigenous knowledge counter to dominant values.

Taylor, Tesla, and Hudson were positioned both as Blackfoot culture interpreters and as (para-)ethnographers-in-training. This doubling was troubling for them, and yes, *un-easy*. The forms of difference they laboured across included their youth, their roles as mentors and mentees, their relationships to reserve and their family, and their experiences as students on campus. All felt responsible to Blackfoot knowledge and practices as *Indigenous* knowledge, although with varying degrees of intensity. As Fortun and Cherkasky (1998) describe, they were "doubly obligated, multiply and impossibly responsible, while dependent on imperfect schemes and unreasonable alliance" (151). The Raising Spirit Project so often felt like an imperfect scheme that required unreasonable alliances.

Fortun and Cherkasky make use of "double bind" to describe situations in which "individuals are confronted with dual or multiple obligations that are related and equally valued but incongruent" (150). Drawing on Bateson's original emphasis on communication, they note that "the demands of double-bind situations are relayed through messages coded by different logics, operating within different fields of reference, which often deny the existence of other conceptual orders.... An additive strategy is not an option" (151). The implications of the double binds produced by the Raising Spirit Project are taken up more fully in chapter 6, while the relationship of this kind of doubling to the Indigenous concept of two-eyed seeing (Reid 2020) is considered in chapter 5. Here, the focus is how the double bind was produced in a series of translational encounters aimed at the ethnographic recognition of indigenous knowledge.

Taylor, Tesla, and Hudson were consistently put in translational encounters that required a doubled voice, both foreign and domestic as Susan Gal (2015) describes. Speakers in such encounters don't simply inhabit their professional role, here as ethnographer; they are also required to take on a different voice and role than they would with co-experts, that is, other Blackfoot Peoples (Gal 2015, 233; and see Varvantakis et al. 2019). It was clear that this doubling wasn't necessarily comfortable for the young researchers and that it could prompt refusals: to engage, to describe, to share, to discuss. In effect, by asking them to be both trained ethnographers and cultural experts on both indigenous and Indigenous knowledge we were putting them in an unresolvable double bind between subject positions as equals with other university researchers like us and as merely para-ethnographers sharing indigenous knowledge (Mack and Newberry 2020, 98), a position that reproduces the sense of an original distance between worlds (Choy 2005, 11).

Doubling is required not only of the Indigenous, but also of the young. Bronwyn Davies (1982) has argued that children, upon entering school, inhabit a double world: one of children and one of adults. In response to the strangeness they encounter, they create their own rules, which are the basis of a separate culture. Much work in child and youth studies focuses on making the voices of the young available for study. Yet rendering the knowledge of children and young people perceptible (Agrawal 1995, 2009) and visible to adults is yet another kind of politics of recognition, one further complicated when that knowledge is about "culture." Child and youth scholars have problematized the idea of getting at the authentic voice of children (Spyrou 2011, 2016; James 2007; Spencer et al. 2020) and pointed to the significance of silence by child research respondents (Lewis 2010; Komulainen 2007).

In my own work (Newberry 2017a, 2017b), I have considered the terrible burden placed on young people when we demand that their agency and their voice be transparent to adults. Requests to be double may mean being positioned as both inside and outside your own world as a *para*-ethnographer while rendered recognizable and intelligible in frames associated with colonial violence. Dhillon (2017; and see Cooke and Kothari 2001; Hartung 2017) sees the recognition of the participation of Indigenous youth in capacity-building by the Canadian settler state as a continuation of liberal narratives of help and salvation. Calls for healing and reconciliation represent a "trickery of choice" that elides the continuing structural dispossession of Indigenous youth in care.

At the time Amy and I first wrote about the refusals in the project (Mack and Newberry 2020), we heeded Audra Simpson's admonition not to pretend that an even playing field for interpretation exists. There is not just a risk of doubleness, but of "a tripleness, a quadrupleness, to consciousness" (A. Simpson 2014, 8). Now, through returning to their blog posts, it is clearer that the young researchers did not just refuse but rather redirected questions about cultural expertise through sets of relationships that they brought to the project as well as those that were developed through it. It's useful to remember here too the many times when very young people greeted questions about culture with silence as a kind of refusal (cf. Spyrou 2016; Sæther et al. 2024; Lewis 2010). These moments, ethnographic and otherwise, were indeed generative (A. Simpson 2014; Tuck and Yang 2014b), especially in moving beyond the tired binary of insider/outsider (Smith 1999) that is reiterated in contrasts between vernacular and official knowledge, between Western science and Indigenous ways of knowing, between expert and para-expert. As described earlier, Tilley (2010) has outlined how the definition of the vernacular was a result of anthropology's assignment to the savage slot. She provides a useful corrective to the conventional understanding of earlier ethnological accounts as classifying non-Western forms of knowledge as lesser, undeveloped, as "becoming," as not-quite-yet. Instead, she argues that a rejection of that very divide was at the heart of early ethnographic work. The young researchers of the Raising Spirit Project also refused this divide.

Returning to the accounts of the young researchers, including Erin, Amy, Taylor, Tesla, Hudson, and Mikey, I understand refusal differently now. In some sense, the capacity that was built through this project was their own not only to refuse, but also to redirect calls on them to act as cultural experts. When confronted with the need to provide expertise or knowledge they did not feel they had, members of the team would redirect this request to others on the team or in the encounter, recirculating and redistributing it. Relationships – already begun and newly built – were called up, practised, and reinforced as expertise was fungibly and flexibly practised and circulated among the team and across other relationships in Blackfoot Territory (cf. Strathern 2018a, 2018b). Expertise was produced and experienced across relational encounters, but also sometimes flipped and redirected in a single encounter. Who was "para" and not-quite-yet and who was the culture expert was consistently destabilized, making the distinction useless.

By calling on the *para*-expertise of the young and Indigenous, we had been engaging in a politics of *ethnographic recognition* all too familiar. Asking for the translation of vernacular Blackfoot knowledge into recognizably ethnographic knowledge mirrors the problems with the politics of recognition by the settler Canadian state described earlier (Coulthard 2014; Dhillon 2017; Povinelli 2002). In this case, the grid of intelligibility for this recognition was ethnography itself, whether "para" or not. Perhaps it is useful here to note that Glen Coulthard's 2014 book *Red Skin, White Mask* is an homage to Frantz Fanon, and part of a wider renaissance of interest in double consciousness, a subject taken up again in chapter 6.

What then to do with the knowledge made by the team in encounters with one another and other knowledge keepers in spaces across Blackfoot Territory? How to avoid the trap of recognition, of reducing the knowledge of the young and the Indigenous to the not-quite-yet status of "para," while still taking seriously what their multiplied position tells us about the circulation and redistribution of cultural expertise?

Perhaps there is no better answer provided than their own. I end this chapter with the transcription of an extended interview with a young person at Opokaa'sin done by Taylor, Hudon, and Tesla.

This transcription has been left long for a few reasons. It is an example of young people collaborating to interview even younger people. The project's central concern with values and cultural knowledge guides the set of questions asked, even when they don't make much sense to those involved. The tension between participation and pedagogy in collaboration is also evident as the cultural expertise of the young person is sought while Taylor demonstrates ethnographic interviewing techniques for Hudson and Tesla. The interplay between all of them captures so much about the unsettling of expertise through the redistribution of voice and the problems with the "para" position that the young Indigenous researchers were placed in for the project, as well as their work building a shared community of practice. What is clear is that their relationships are more important than the answers to these questions about culture. The playfulness of the interview consistently undercuts the strangeness of the process. When Taylor breaks the wall, so to speak, to talk directly to me, the limits of ethnographic recognition are clear and the possibilities for refusal open up.

INTERVIEWERS: Taylor Little Mustache, Hudson Eagle Bear, Tesla Heavy Runner

INTERVIEWEE: [RXxx]

DATE: 7 July 2016, transcribed by Mikey

TAYLOR: Okay, [RXxx]. So what's gonna happen is that you're gonna be recorded. Alright? Um, don't be shy though, don't be shy, kay? It's just, it's gonna be confidential, so, nobody's really, um, going to know your name when they hear your voice, kay? Um, just talk to me as if I'm the only one here. They're taking notes, but that's basically judging me, okay? That's nothing, nothing's to do with you, um, there's no right or wrong answers, but I do want a little bit more than "yes" or "no," okay? Alright. So let's start, um, so he has CSP8, um, Hudson, do you wanna put this close to, or Hud, Tesla, hold that please, too, so you can hear both of us? Um, so first of all, can you tell me why you chose that photo?

[RXXX]: Yeah, um ... [long pause] Kindergarten, I guess?

TAYLOR: Kindergarten?

[RXXX]: People I know.

TAYLOR: People you know? Were you, are you in that photo?

[1:00]

[RXXX]: Uhh, well, I might be on the other side of it.

TAYLOR: But you recognize those…

[RXXX]: A lot of them.

TAYLOR: Really? Okay, cool! Um, so, obviously it's familiar to you. What's going on in there?

[RXXX]: They're in Remembrance Day.

TAYLOR: And they're singing?

[RXXX]: Yeah.

TAYLOR: Do you remember the song? [Tesla starts to laugh.] Can you sing it for me? [All start to laugh] Just kidding, I'm just kidding, I'm just kidding. Alright, um, so ... what kind of a, uh, does it remind you of any stories you want to tell us about your kindergarten days, or anything about those –

[RXXX]: [Chuckling] I was a little brat.

TAYLOR: You were a little brat?

[RXXX]: Yuh.

TAYLOR: Okay. Um ... do you think going to school's important?

[RXXX]: Yeah.

TAYLOR: Why?

[RXXX]: So you could learn, about lots a things that you don't know, n, n, n, the past.

TAYLOR: Mmkay. Right on. Um, do you think this photo is an example of our traditional child raising practices?

[2:05]

[RXXX]: Yeah.

TAYLOR: Yeah? How so?

[RXXX]: The singing.

TAYLOR: The singing? Can you tell me more about that, though?

[RXXX]: The singing, well ... you gotta learn how to sing because, if you don't know how to sing, it's just not part of the culture, and if you like to sing, the, suspression [trying to say "expression"].

TAYLOR: Mmkay. So, can you tell us more about like, maybe, our, like our powwow singings, or our, you know and like, do you know anything about our ceremonies, and our songs there? Can you tell us more about those kinda songs?

[RXXX]: Well ... the drumming is, part of the, the sound of the drum, and when people hear that drum, makes them want to dance, and sing even more.

TAYLOR: Mmkay.

[3:00]

TAYLOR: Uh, do you think it symbolizes anything?

[RXXX]: The Blackfoot nation?

TAYLOR: Mmkay. Do you feel connected when you hear it?

[RXXX]: Yeah.

TAYLOR: How so?
[RXXX]: I just like to hear the drum, hearin' people sing.
TAYLOR: Right on, okay. Um … do you think there's any value to that photo?
[RXXX]: Yeah, when we were little.
TAYLOR: When you were little? Can you expand a little bit more on that?
[RXXX]: Um … it reminds us when, how small we are, and how different we look, when we grow up.
TAYLOR: Mmhm. Mmkay. Uh, let's move onto PT13, Tesla, you wanna hand her that?
[RXXX]: Oh….
TAYLOR: Alright, so, why did you choose that photo?
[4:00]
[RXXX]: Because it reminds me of my little nephew.
TAYLOR: Aw, okay. Can you tell me more about him?
[RXXX]: He's really cute, he likes to play around a lot, he likes to laugh, he's not shy, he goes to anybody and he just wants to laugh constantly.
TAYLOR: Aw! Too cute! Sounds like Hudson. [All laugh] He's not shy! [Laughter] I'm just kidding. Um … so is that photo familiar to you?
[RXXX]: No.
TAYLOR: Not really?
[RXXX]: No, not really.
TAYLOR: But you connected to it, hey?
[RXXX]: Yeah.
TAYLOR: Yeah? Can you kind of explain that connection a little bit more? Or is it kind of to your nephew?
[RXXX]: [Overlapping] Uh … I like babies, I like taking care of babies, if p-people need a babysitter, I'm here. It just makes me happy seeing little kids, and once they grow up, they're all different.
TAYLOR: Mmkay. Right on. Um … do you think this photo is an example of our traditional child raising practices?
[5:00]
[RXXX]: Yeah.
TAYLOR: Yeah? How so?
[RXXX]: Because if kids weren't in school, and kindergarten, they wouldn't be on Earth right now, because … they'll just be doing whatever they want to be, and they won't be getting a job, and they will just be on the streets.
TAYLOR: Mm … okay. Um … does it remind you of any special story, this photo? That you want to share with us? Or, any story, at all? Doesn't have to be special.
[RXXX]: Um … um …
TAYLOR: Any funny stories of your nephew?

[RXXX]: My little nephew and I we were in the, in the water, and he just wanted to get out, and I was saying, somehow he got out of the, the safety thing, and all the sudden he was swimming by himself for some reason, he was just like, only one, [6:01] and he just started swimming by himself for some reason, and, he just got out, I thought he was gonna [stumbles over words], we thought he was gonna drown. And he kinda slipped, and he kinda went down in the water.

TAYLOR: So you basically taught him how to swi–, taught himself how to swim.

[RXXX]: Yeah.

TAYLOR: Oh, that is so cool! Okay, cool! Alright. Uh, let's move onto LW17.

[PAUSE TO 6:28]

TAYLOR: Alright, so why did you choose this photo?

[RXXX]: 'Cause it reminds me of me.

TAYLOR: Reminds you of you? Tell me a little bit more about that.

[RXXX]: Reminds me of me because I'm always sittin' on the couch, constantly. Learning how to read.

TAYLOR: Mmkay. So, is this familiar with you?

[RXXX]: No.

TAYLOR: No? Well, you, you connected to it, hey?

[RXXX]: Yeah.

TAYLOR: Yeah, okay. You sh-, explain that connection?

[RXXX]: That connection is that um, I'm always sittin' on the couch, just tryna read by myself. I always hate when my little kid, my little nephew is in the background, screaming. [7:01] And I can't, no, I can't [unclear] struggle, 'cause uh, I can't read. And sometimes just trying to concentrate on a book and not them. Concentrate on the book, and just learn how to read.

TAYLOR: Mmkay. Um, so, you think it's important to learn how to read? And to be—

[RXXX]: [overlapping] Yeah.

TAYLOR: Yeah. How so?

[RXXX]: 'Cause if you don't know how to read, uh, then, how can you get a job? How can you finish school? [Taylor: Mmhm.] That's why it's important to go to school, 'cause you'll know how to read.

TAYLOR: Yeah. Um, do you think this photo is an example of our traditional child raising practices?

[RXXX]: Yeah.

TAYLOR: Yeah?

[RXXX]: Because … that, um, kids are in school, that they … they will just try to play around you guys just tell 'em "sit down and read a book," and if they don't know how, you'll teach them how.

[8:00]

TAYLOR: Mmkay. Um, so would you say you would teach your children how to read?

[RXXX]: Yeah.

TAYLOR: Yeah, definitely, hey? That would be a strong thing to teach them, hey?

[RXXX]: Yeah.

TAYLOR: Mmkay. Um ... let's move on to ... what one was that? Over here. Let's move on to, yeah, FT17.

[PAUSE TO 8:28]

TAYLOR: Uh, so why did you choose that photo?

[RXXX]: I choosed this one 'cause it reminds me of my whole family getting together.

TAYLOR: Okay. Um, is it familiar to you?

[RXXX]: No.

TAYLOR: No? Uh, can you tell me about the connection you made with that photo?

[RXXX]: My connection is is that all my family come over, and I will have a dinner together, and then it's good to see them, 'cause it's been, um, for a while that we haven't seen them, and they'll come over and, and have a good dinner....

TAYLOR: Mmkay. Umm....

[9:00]

TAYLOR: Can, er do you think this is a, an example of our traditional child raising practices?

[RXXX]: Yeah.

TAYLOR: Yeah? How so?

[RXXX]: I was told is that, you, if you don't know how to get together with your family ... um ... school will teach you, family will teach you how to get together and learn about the culture, and uh, how to learn about it, and how to get together.

TAYLOR: Mmkay. I like that. Um, is this the kind of value you'd teach your children?

[RXXX]: Yeah.

TAYLOR: Yeah? To be strong [RXxx: Yeah.] with your family? Yeah.

[RXXX]: [Overlapping] Yeah. Yeah.

TAYLOR: Um, does it remind you of any story you wanna share with us?

[RXXX]: Reminds me of me and my family and my cousins, we're hanging out and we got together, and of course, I ate most of all the, the ham. [Taylor laughs gently] And ... somehow we dropped the ham on the floor, and it's been like ten minutes and I picked it up and I ate it.

[10:00]

TAYLOR: [Laughs] You gotta have that ham though, hey?

[RXXX]: Yeah! I gotta have it!

TAYLOR: That ham, though! [laughing]

[RXXX]: I gotta have it! I gotta have that ham!

[ALL START LAUGHING]

TAYLOR: Okay, right on! I would do the same. I don't know with ham, though. Just kidding. [laughing]

[RXXX]: [overlapping] I-I'll have, I need ham.

HUDSON: [overlapping] Baloney.

[LAUGHING]

[RXXX]: Need ham.

TAYLOR: Oh, baloney! Yeah, we have baloney. Just kidding.

[RXXX]: [Joking under Taylor's laughter, saying something unclear about "the baloney"]

TAYLOR: [Still laughing] Oh yeah, [unclear] know what you said earlier. Alright, okay, never mind, change the subject! Next picture! [Giggles]

[ALL LAUGH]

TAYLOR: [Laughing] Do you wanna say in the recording, what your baloney … thing is?

[RXXX]: [Laughing] Baloney makes you horny.

[ALL LAUGH]

TAYLOR: [Laughing so hard she can barely talk] How does it make you … how does it.… We were laughing about that earlier. How, I was like, does it make just *you*, or, does it.… Okay, never mind! [11:00] This is way off topic! Uh, sorry Jan, sorry Jan.

HUDSON: You have to transcript this?

TAYLOR: Yeah, sorry guys, I don't mean to put this in the interview, we'll take this out. Kay, next one. [Taylor and RXxx laugh.] Last photo. Uh, that's EBS1. Be serious guys, kay. Um, why did you choose this photo? [Still giggling]

[RXXX]: 'Cause it reminds me of my little nephew sleeping in the vehicle. [Taylor laughs under RXxx the whole time she says this]

TAYLOR: Wait, wait, wait, sorry, kay, say it again, try again, say it again.

[RXXX]: Reminds me of my little nephew, sleeping in the vehicle. [Taylor: Okay.] So cuddly, so … just so cute, when they sleep.

TAYLOR: Okay. [Still trying to choke back laughter] Um, is it familiar to you?

[RXXX]: No.

TAYLOR: No? Can you explain that connection you made, a little bit more?

[RXXX]: It reminds me of when my f–, my cousin came out … of the hospital, we put him in the vehicle, and he just … fell asleep, then, when we got home, he woke up, and he start openin' his eyes and start smilin'.

[12:00]

TAYLOR: Aw, okay! Um, do you think this is an example of our traditional raising practices? Child raising practices?

[RXXX]: Yeah, taking care of kids. Learning how to ... to, like, when you get a kid, and when, what to do when you get a kid, and how to teach it, and ... just how to know how to take care of a baby when you get older.

TAYLOR: Mmkay, right on. Um, does it remind you of any story you wanna share with us?

[RXXX]: Um, well, when my baby ... cousin were, was in the vehicle, we ... put it in the vehicle and ... my baby cousin started crying, they won't let go anywhere, and we brought 'em inside, I just left 'im there, [unclear], and he fell asleep, on the couch.

TAYLOR: Aw, too cute. Um... [13:00] So, I'm gonna end off with three questions, kay?

[RXXX]: Mmhm.

TAYLOR: Try, try answer them as best you can. Um, gimme a little bit of, little bit ... detail, with it? So, were you taught in our traditional ways?

[RXXX]: No.

TAYLOR: No? Um ... let's say, if you were taught, do you think things would be different?

[RXXX]: Yeah.

TAYLOR: Yeah. Mmkay. Uh, how should our children be raised, should they learn our Blackfoot values?

[RXXX]: Yeah.

TAYLOR: Yeah? Why?

[RXXX]: Why? Because, if we don't know how ... and, they struggle, and the kids will, when they grow up they'll be like ... they'll be like, "why's this person s-speaking this language when I don't understand it?"

TAYLOR: Mmhm. So do you think today was really important, what we did, to, this morning?

[RXXX]: Yeh.

TAYLOR: Yeah?

[RXXX]: 'Cause some of us don't know, how to do Blackfoot.

TAYLOR: Mmhm.

[RXXX]: It was pretty good.

TAYLOR: Yeah. Um, what kind of values would you teach your children, your future children?

[14:03]

[RXXX]: My, I'll teach 'em ... uh, goin' to powwows, sweats, um learnin' Blackfoot, bring the owl there to my house, and, do a smudge and pray.... I'll teach them all of my culture.

TAYLOR: And you think our culture's important, hey?

[RXXX]: Yeah.

TAYLOR: Yeah. Okay, well, that's all I have to say, [RXxx]. Thank you so much. This was by far the best interview I did.

[RXXX]: Yeah.

HUDSON: Yeah.

TAYLOR: You can, just press the—

NOTES

1 Although the term "Sundance" is used here and colloquially to describe these ceremonies, the Blackfoot term for circle encampment is *Aakokatssin* (Bastien 2004).

2 I am pretty sure Hudson meant "definitely," but given the focus on refusal here, I've left his use of "defiantly" in place.

Chapter Five

Coding Improvisations

How Are We Going to Shelve the "Books" in the Digital Library?

Amy asked this simple question as the second phase of Raising Spirit began, and it changed the project fundamentally. By "books," she meant all the various materials produced and collected in the project: photographs, interviews, stories, videos, and Blackfoot words. Although the question sprang from the need to organize the material efficiently and effectively on a user-friendly digital app, it began a crucial and far-reaching rethinking of *who* was going to identify the Blackfoot values meant to be at the centre of the project and *how*. Ultimately, the question of how to code for the values represented in the photographs, stories, and images led to the development of an experimental and design-influenced approach to coding. What emerged from this process was a space for collaboration made through relationships of difference (Choy 2005).

The second phase of Raising Spirit was guided explicitly by the idea of producing an ethical space for engagement following the work of Elder Willie Ermine (2007). It made sense to me to think of this space as a kind of third space, following Bhabha (1994; Kalua 2009), that is, as a space for the emergence and experience of difference. As with much of the work described in this book, STS scholarship in anthropology was an influence on my thinking. It was Choy's invocation of Bhabha and his attention to the making of new publics that shaped how I came to understand what was happening on our collaborative coding sessions. The space produced allowed for the enunciation of difference that made it "knowledge-able" (Choy 2005; following Bhabha 1994) for Blackfoot and settler participants alike.

As I sorted through ways of conceptualizing what was going on in this collaborative space, many approaches to negotiating in-between-ness were available. Was this another iteration of the liberal version of a third space (Pateman 1989; Putnam 2000; Habermas 1989; Fraser 2007)? Or was it a contact zone (Pratt 1991), a clash zone (Marker 2000), a middle ground (White 2006), a site for friction (Tsing 2005), or a jagged edge (Little Bear 2000)? What became undeniable was that what we were calling "experimentation" and "innovation" in this space mirrored long-standing Indigenous knowledge practices. Here, I do not conclude that this is just another act of colonization, although that is clearly a possibility. Instead, I take up the limits of a two-world model, one reinforced through acts of translation and with particular effects for relations across difference. Resisting the demands for ethnographic recognition (cf. Coulthard 2014) and establishing instead diplomatic relations across difference, following Bruno Latour (2014), offers a way out of what is effectively a double bind (Bateson 1972; Fortun and Cherkasky 1998). While the double bind is taken up more fully in the following final chapter, its relevance for young Indigenous people was first evident here in the entangled ethnographic relations and the improvisations designed to help with coding.

This chapter traces the emergence of an experimental and design-influenced approach to coding collaboratively in answer to Amy's question of how to organize the library. Recognizing the effects of this collaborative space created through what we fashioned as design studios fundamentally changed what the project was about and how I understood what it could accomplish. That this was happening as calls for reconciliation were gaining public attention is not coincidental. Instead, the method for coding collaboratively developed in the Raising Spirit Project points the way to the possibility for imagining other futures through forms of diplomacy practised between the young and the older, between the Indigenous and the settler folk, and all those in-between.

As in previous chapters, selected blog posts are used to illustrate key moments and the growing recognition of the relationship of our forms of patchwork to Indigenous ways of knowing.

Coding for Values

The first indication that coding was going to become a problem was when Tesla and Hudson were asked to code the photographs from the first phase of the project. In their first days on the project, Amy sat them down with the catalogue of photos and asked them to start coding the values represented. Approximately 8,000 photographs and associated interviews, transcribed and otherwise, had been collated and organized by the first student researchers and Opokaa'sin staff. This huge amount of material had been brought together with the goal of identifying Blackfoot values.

In retrospect, some of our assumptions about values, their location, and the possibility for their articulation and translation by the young researchers were naive in the most generous interpretation, and colonializing in the least. We expected these two Blackfoot young people to be able to spot and label Blackfoot values. I take some comfort in the fact that our approach was endorsed by Tanya and the folks at Opokaa'sin: these young people would help us identify the Blackfoot values represented in the photographs and other materials. But, in fact, they could not. As the previous chapters have shown, our expectations of cultural expertise in Blackfoot ways of knowing put these young people in untenable situations. We slowly learnt that expertise in ways of knowing were patchy and distributed, emergent in travel and encounters with others in Blackfoot Territory. But at this point in the project, we didn't yet understand this. Nor did we understand the doubled burden we had placed on these young people and what would come from it.

Although Amy soon pulled Hudson and Tesla away from this work to other project needs, the question of how to code for the values we were after did not go away. Instead, it became more complicated once the second phase of the project was devoted to building a digital storytelling library, as Amy's question showed us. How would we link the project materials on the digital platform to values? Who was to do it and how? Our answer would ripple throughout the rest of the project.

In fact, significant coding had already taken place during the project but without remark. For example, during the first phases of the project, the original summer students had made choices of a small selection of photos to share with passersby at powwows. This was in essence a kind of coding as these pictures reflected their choices of which photos showed a variety of child-rearing practices. Later, a similar process was used by the young research team in the second phase of the project to produce coding books to share with people in interviews they were conducting (see figure 2). The Raising Spirit Project and its coding dilemmas led my attention to coding as a particular knowledge practice and its social and political dimensions.

It has become standard practice to code ethnographic material generated through fieldwork, typically using software applications such as NVivo. Students now are trained in using such software to identify thematic patterns and keywords in transcribed interviews and notes. This move represents a generational shift in how to manage ethnographic data. My own original practice had been significantly lower tech,

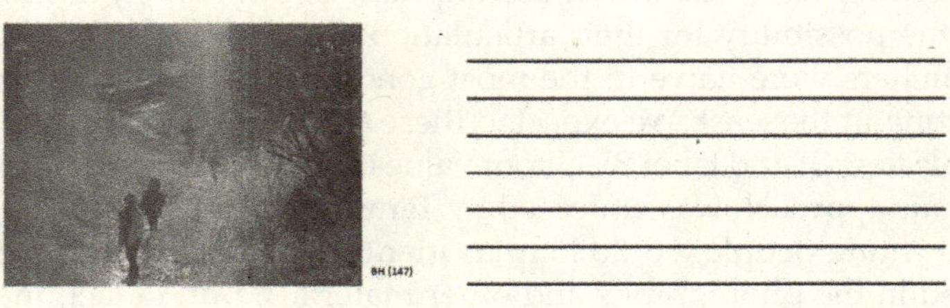

Figure 2. An example of a coding book sheet that would be filled out by participants interviewed in places such as offices on the reserve and in people's homes.

involving lined notebooks, highlighters, and Post-it notes. Yet in both approaches, a crucial part of ethnographic work runs the risk of being hidden (Ballestero and Winthereik 2021). As Eve Tuck and Wayne Yang (2014b) note in their jeremiad against coding in the context of refusal, "code is a word rarely interrogated in qualitative research outside of a few technical definitions" (812). Code is, indeed, a multivalent word beyond its reference to what has become central to qualitative methods.

For example, code glosses forms of language, and of course, this meaning was relevant in the Raising Spirit Project, given that the goal was to identify examples of Blackfoot values that would be used to support language revitalization efforts by Opokaa'sin. In many ways, the project was about moving between different codes, linguistic and cultural. The significant digital component of this project suggests yet another meaning of code, one evident in the team's use of apps for project organization and the many hours of troubleshooting how to move material to the Thing Link platform we had chosen for the library and how to train others to add to the library.

Tuck and Yang (2014b) were also centrally concerned with the codes that govern consent and the treatment of knowledge as property in academic research. They identify a critical interstitial space in analysis that the increased attention to coding has failed to acknowledge, and this is a space for interpretation and translation. But they argue that rather than identifying this as a space for the making of knowledge, codes are represented as found objects. As they say, "after coding, the important decisions have already been made" (812). For Tuck and Yang, this is a significant failing of standard academic research methods and antithetical to other ways of knowing. "Coding, once it begins, has already surrendered to a theory of knowledge" (811). And it is worthwhile here to recall the question of the relationship between para-ethnography and ethnomethodology introduced in chapter 3. Whose theory of knowledge guides the abstraction and coding that takes place (cf. Sharrock and Randall 2004; and see Olszewski et al. 2007)?

The coding dilemmas in the Raising Spirit Project underline these questions about whose codes and whose theory of knowledge, while simultaneously pointing to other possibilities. As Tuck and Yang also note, code "can also refer to a set of ethical commitments" (814). All these connotations of coding were at play in the Raising Spirit Project.

The Design Studio Method

Funnily enough, I had given Amy a design problem to solve by asking her to consider design ethnography as the way to deal with our coding problem. As it happens, she was the perfect candidate to take on all this design work. Her recently finished master's project on online gaming had required her not only to build her own field equipment – a computer capable of allowing her into the worlds she wanted to enter – but also to innovate and invent digital ethnographic methods for this work. She has continued to develop her expertise in digital anthropology as a digital ethnographer of online hate (Mack 2021, 2023).

Perhaps Amy's biggest design problem was how to build the digital storytelling library itself in a space and in a manner that allowed for young people and others to navigate the images, stories, and Blackfoot values and terms that were produced by the project. She and I like to remember the moment when Tanya used her hands to show the need to move between the small space of a cell phone screen out to a sphere that would encompass all that was learnt and meant to be shared and back in again. The library should be able to do this, and the second half of the Raising Spirit Project was devoted to this goal. Yet this design problem was just the newest one for Amy on this project. She had been asked to solve several such problems already. For example, she was the one, along with Erin, who designed a training program for Hudson and Tesla, one that spanned university research protocol and ethnographic methods to Indigenous methods and protocols for working with Elders. Her own knowledge of ethics, sharpened first in her master's work, was expanded through workshops at Opokaa'sin and her engagement with the First Nations Information Governance Centre (https://fnigc.ca/). She also had designed how the team would collaborate effectively on project work, and this had included choosing and using digital interfaces to manage information flow and task assignment.

Even so, it was the question of coding that led to the most significant innovation of the Raising Spirit Project, an innovation that aligned with many of the contemporary challenges to ethnographic methods outlined in chapter 2, including the influence of STS, para-ethnography, collaborative methods, and ethnographic experimentation. Elsewhere (Mack and Newberry 2020), Amy and I have described the period of this design work as the Brown Paper Chronicles, for reasons made clear below. We initially called this work "studio ethnography" but moved to calling the approach "design studios" following Paul Rabinow's usage (Rabinow et al. 2008) to capture the creative, collaborative, open-ended work on how to code project materials. What began from my sketch of an approach and Amy's design solution led over time to powerful collaborative coding sessions that coalesced in the last phases of the project. Ultimately, the collaborative work of the design studios became one of its most significant outcomes.

It is difficult to trace precisely all the decisions in developing the design studios because the method was shaped by so many different elements. For example, I introduced the idea of using the large sheets of brown paper for the collaborative coding sessions that led to our Brown Paper Chronicles description. The use of large pieces of butcher paper to encourage students to collaborate in the production of understanding and knowledge was a practice I had started in my teaching (for example, Newberry and Mikuliak 2020). In fact, much of my teaching practice in recent years has been guided by the same goals at the heart of the design studios: How could students come together to share what they knew, teach one another, and thus collaboratively scaffold fuller understandings of course materials? I hoped to transfer some of what I was learning in my scholarship of teaching and learning (SoTL) practice into our coding practice. Although I was not aware of it at the time, much of the work on collaboration and para-ethnography emphasized its pedagogical opportunities (Rabinow et al. 2008; Marcus 2008).

Our move to collaborative coding was also influenced by my reading and thinking through not only para-ethnography (see chapter 3) but also the growing attention to "design" in anthropology (Gunn et al. 2013; Suchman 2011; Escobar 2017; Smith 2022; Stewart 2011; Murphy 2016; Simeone 2010; Chin 2017; Akama et al. 2018). Initially, I was blind to the overlap of some of this work with Apple-inspired approaches to design thinking in project development. Less comfortable with the corporate tinge of some of these approaches and the uses of ethnography in industrial design, I took more inspiration from STS approaches to the spaces of expertise such as design firms themselves and the potential for using an ethnographic sensibility to problem-solving in those spaces (Gunn et al. 2013). This work was frequently methodological and attention to it was often matched by calls for innovation in ethnographic methods. This refunctioning of ethnography as Holmes and Marcus (2007) would have it was yet another return to sociocultural anthropology's central method, as described in the last chapters. Yet, it was now met with racial reckoning, attention to settler colonialism, Indigenous resurgence, and a move towards experimental forms of ethnographic fieldwork (Ballestero and Winthereik 2021; Alonso Bejarano et al. 2019), not to mention the need to make anthropology "public" (Lassiter 2008; Osterweil 2013; Lamphere 2004) while simultaneously identifying the job skills it produces.

At the centre of much of the design-influenced ethnography, or so it seems to me, is an emphasis on open-ended problem-solving through collaboration that has ethnographers working alongside others. Rather than discovering or extracting data (Smith 1999), ethnographers become co-producers of solutions through collaborative knowledge practices. For the Raising Spirit Project, we were not yet describing this work as research creation (Loveless 2015; Chapman and Sawchuk 2012), but it would come to include significant creative, transmedia, arts-based aspects (Walley 2015). It was in this spirit that I suggested that Amy run something we initially called "studio ethnography" and later "design studios" to code the photographs and other project materials. Relating my nascent understanding of what all this design business was about, I left her to read Marcus and Rabinow and consider how to put it into play.

Amy brought her own research and mentoring experience to this design problem. She had to find a practical solution to designing and building the library by first designing and building a way to code the project materials. She had to do this while continuing to manage the young team who were still actively doing fieldwork, along with all the ancillary work of managing the material amassed in earlier phases of the project.

In the following, I toggle back and forth between blog posts and reflections, some from Amy, to describe what became the design studio process. Here, Amy had brought together the expanded research team from the second summer around a table in the lair over a large piece of brown paper to consider a story recorded for the library.

BEGINNING THE PROCESS (AMY'S FIELD JOURNAL, 24 JULY 2023)

....

Tuesday was our first design studio! Jan had just left for holidays, so we were on our own trying to figure out the process. This was also [Xxx's] first day with us. [Xxx] unfortunately couldn't make it because she had 5 sick kids the night before! And an ER trip! Yikes.

We started with Napi and the magpies, which Mikey had completed the video editing for. [They are] really talented with this, as it requires a lot of trouble shooting to get the blurring right and then the subtitles are very time consuming. Or so [they say]. I haven't had the time to help out on that front just yet. So we were watching for content and for the aesthetics of Mikey's work.

We had the huge piece of brown paper on the table and everyone took notes either on the transcripts or on the paper itself. Then, we came together to discuss the different values that we saw. Of course, everyone saw something different. Often this was along ethnic or gender lines. And the things people shared reflected these categories as well. What Hudson and [Xxx] shared differed from Taylor. Mikey reflected later that [they] felt [they] and I often saw similar things, and I think it's useful to consider how whiteness can often serve as a foil to articulate Indigenous values if only to say "we do things differently. We do XYZ." And I will always think of Tanya telling me that I can leverage my whiteness because I can say, "I don't understand. I don't know the story." But it's expected that Blackfoot folk know these things, and they often pretend they do if they don't. So, one way I can be useful is by asking questions at the table – even if I know the answer – just in case someone else doesn't.

After watching the Elder's story, we broke for lunch. When we got back, we watched the three little kids retell the story. Finally, we worked with Mikey in Quirkos to try and mark-up the transcripts.[1] It was very time consuming and Tesla thought it was way. too. long. Me too Tesla, me too. We did stuff after that, but again, I'm too fried to remember....

One goal for this second phase of the project incorporating young Indigenous researchers along with university-based settler researchers was to produce an "ethical space." This concept is drawn from Elder Willie Ermine (2007): "The 'ethical space' is formed when two societies, with disparate worldviews, are poised to engage each other. It is the thought about diverse societies and the space in between them that contributes to the development of a framework for dialogue between human communities" (194). So, as Amy sought to solve the design problem around coding, she and the rest of the team were guided by the idea that they were working in and honouring a space between world views.

Remembering the early coding failure when Tesla and Hudson were sat down and asked to start identifying values in the materials, we were aware that we needed some kind of a starting point, some initial categorization that would be used to navigate the library. In talking to Tanya, she suggested that we use the Circle of Courage, which is a representation of the Medicine Wheel, a pan-Indigenous concept that is typically broken into four quadrants representing cardinal directions, colours, and values. Tanya used the version in *Reclaiming Youth at Risk: Our Hope for the Future* (Brendtro et al. 1990) to guide programming at Opokaa'sin. This model of development and health is understood to be driven by Indigenous values, and it has been applied widely in health and educational settings as a counter to hegemonic views of health and adjustment. This choice reflects an interesting tension in the development of a pan-Indigenous canon versus the traditional canon of wisdom of a specific people. The Circle of Courage reflects the generalization of knowledge to all of Indigenous North America (Graveline 2000). It is in widespread use and the concept of the Medicine Wheel is deeply meaningful to many Indigenous Peoples. Yet, in this case, this abstraction and generalization was to be re-localized for use in Blackfoot settings. Some of the implications of this kind of disembedding and re-embedding are taken up in the next chapter. In the Circle of Courage model, the four quadrants of the Medicine Wheel are identified as mastery, generosity, independence, and belonging (Brendtro et al. 1990).

We decided that the Circle of Courage would serve as the central image on the landing page for the digital library, and so the design studios were organized around it as well. Each design studio would begin with a drawing of the Circle of Courage Medicine Wheel in the centre of the brown paper (see figure 3).

Back to Amy's blog post, where she describes early attempts to code collaboratively through this emergent method.

On **Thursday** the team met again (Taylor, Tesla, Hudson, [Xxx], and me) to talk about picking wild mint. This time we planned to go through it quicker to avoid burn out. So we nixed the Quirkos coding – who knows when that will get done – and focused on fitting it into two quadrants a handful of the Blackfoot values. We want to have the story telling sessions easily accessible, and so we want them in the quadrants. But we also want them in the values to demonstrate a more nuanced coding. We figure we'll put them in a bunch of places and then pare it down if need be.

I love this story [they had chosen to code a traditional Blackfoot story recorded at Opokaa'sin as an Elder shared it] because I really love being out on the land and foraging. I like it because a) it connects me with the rhythm and spirit of the land, 2) it's very meditative and fun, 3) it upsets the capitalist system that says I have to buy everything at the store! I was really hoping we'd be able to go this year, but we seem to have missed the season.

The design studio approach is going over really well. I think people dig the ability to draw, mind map, use different colours, and work out what we think together. Taylor made a comment that made me think, "Yes! That's the collective sphere! That's the ethical space!" which is exactly what we're going for.

In the afternoon we did a design studio approach to the interview Taylor and I did with [Xxx]. It was almost an hour, so it took quite a while. In the end we decided to break it up into four parts and each part reflected different content (pow wows, Sundance, language, etc.) and therefore different values. So we are going to clean it up in Audacity and add it to ThingLink now. It was also a great process. I was actually pretty pleased with how the interview went in retrospect. Taylor and I did good work last summer.

I think that's it. We tried to find another interview to do, but everything was too long for the amount of time we had left in the day and dang, those design studios are draining. It is really exhausting work to listen, reflect, and share. Articulating how you feel and what you're reminded of is hard to do even to yourself. But then to decide how and what to share to others is even harder. When is it appropriate to use my whiteness to elicit responses? When is it appropriate to share a story from my childhood? Is it ever? In the ethical space or collective sphere I like to think there is some room, but finding its boundaries is tricky. There is a lot of feeling around the edges that sometimes become fuzzy and slip away.... As Rappaport so aptly says, collaboration is hard and it isn't for everyone![2]

Here, Amy and the team consider working through the implications of trying to produce an ethical space as a collective sphere, and in later sections of this chapter, I take up that concept and its

Figure 3. Brown paper used for the design studios.

resonance with third spaces. In this early phase of developing the design studio method, the team was still working out the mechanics of who should be at the table, what materials should be coded, and how to move collaboratively from the material under consideration to a decision about the value(s) represented. In other words, the team worked to move from material such as picture, story, or interview to the Blackfoot value that it would represent in the library. This "coding" made visible the process of abstraction and generalization and its problematics (Riles 2000a; and see Sharrock and Randal 2004).

In her post, Amy notes how long this took and how tiring it was for the team, a result of the process they were developing. They talked through each item and tried to connect it to one of the four quadrants of the Circle of Courage: mastery, generosity, independence, and belonging. The goal was then to start connecting them to specifically Blackfoot values and the words that reflect them. But, given the distributed and emergent nature of the expertise described in the last chapter, these discussions could be long and tentative. Amy encouraged team members to make their own notes on the brown paper as they made connections and noticed patterns. These notes embroidered the edges of the brown paper, and they remain as an archive and index of the entangled character of this collaborative coding (see figure 4). The

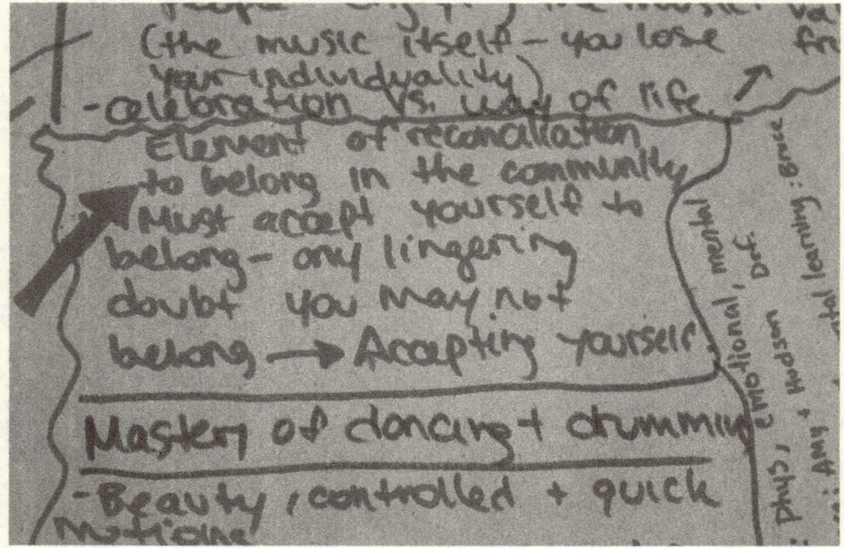

Figure 4. An example of the notes taken during a design studio.

result is reminiscent of the networked UN documents that Riles (2000b) describes with multiple voices and amendments evident in the margins reflecting both the constraints of the form and the opening of space for other interpretations.

These notes remain as a record of the process from the project, one deserving of further attention. In the emerging design studio method, they became the medium through which individual participants moved from image to an articulation of relationship to the four quadrants as values (see figure 5).

The power of this developing process of collaborative coding that we called design studios extended well beyond the Blackfoot members of the research team. Here, in a blog post by Mikey, they reflect on the pedagogical impact of the design studio process.

LOSING SANITY BUT GAINING EXPERIENCE (MIKEY'S FIELD JOURNAL, 24 JULY 2017)

We had a really great design studio this morning. I really appreciated learning more about the line between what's acceptable and what's unacceptable for a non-Blackfoot person to know, and watching [Xxx] and Amy explore that boundary. I was also really interested in seeing the first obvious divide between what the settlers in the group (Amy and I) thought, and what the Blackfoot people heard or saw in the stories we had listened to. We also had a new person, [Xxx], join the meetings, whose energy and perspective I really appreciated.

Design studios are a really great opportunity for learning, in so many ways. I'm developing skills in cultural sensitivity, communicating my ideas, when and when *not* to communicate those ideas, active listening and thought processing, as well as being introduced to traditional Blackfoot stories, and learning more about the values that the elders selected to be a part of the Circle of Courage.

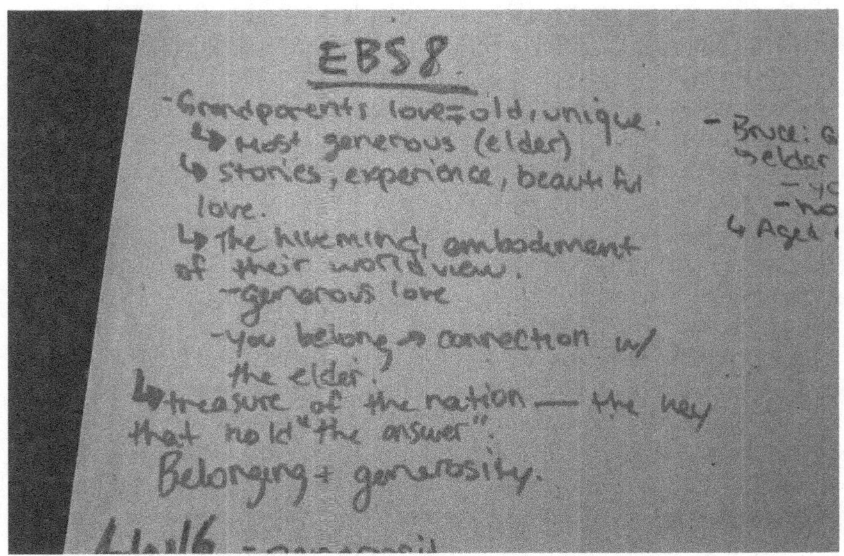

Figure 5. Notes were used to make connections to the values being described and discussed.

The Space That Was Made

While the earlier phases of the project took a conventional approach to methods for eliciting Blackfoot voice and value, the development of the design studio approach in the second phase of the project changed things by emphasizing collaborative problem-solving in an ethnographic mode. This shift meant that the design studio process was opened to "mixed" groups. Indeed, one of the first trials of this approach was organized by Amy to include several undergraduate students recruited through her connections in the Native American Students Association (NASA) on campus. The first design studios included Blackfoot students, but also students who were Métis and those from First Nations other than the Blackfoot. This design studio produced the most oft-repeated epiphany from the project (Mack and Newberry 2020). As the story is told, there was a picture of a caregiver reading a book to a child. In considering what Blackfoot values were represented by it – and in relation to the Circle of Courage – one of the settler participants suggested "mastery." After all, the child was being taught to master the skill of reading. This aligned with a conventional "settler" understanding of education. But, after a pause and further contemplation, one of the Indigenous students suggested quietly that instead "generosity" was what was being illustrated. Teaching and learning, in other words, are about an exchange, one that depends on the generosity of giving. This aha! moment prompted a seismic shift in both the design studio process and in our thinking about what was happening in the space of these collaborations.

We came to see that the design studio process allowed for the expression and exchange of different sets of values in a shared space. Neither set of values was understood to be definitive; rather, team members and visitors realized that two sets of values might coexist – comfortably or not – within that shared space. When Amy invited a mixed group to take part, a space was opened for multiple values to be expressed and considered by the group. What this meant practically, but also conceptually, was that we no longer thought that only Blackfoot Peoples should be talking about values in the design studios. The larger impact of this work was what can be offered by anthropology and ethnography more generally: a contemplation of possibility and access to other imaginations and ways of knowing and being by working collaboratively to solve a problem. These possibilities were being realized by other ethnographers in other places and contexts (Fortun 2005; de la Cadena and Blaser 2018; Escobar 2017; Tsing 2005, 2015), and by child and youth scholars as well (Daelman et al. 2020; Clark 2011; Cahill 2007; Leon and Rosen 2023). For the Raising Spirit Project, the practice of the design studios illustrated the possibilities for creating ethical third spaces where new publics could be produced, new imaginaries could be enunciated, and new forms of diplomacy could be practised, outcomes I will return to below.

Three other iterations of the design process are worth considering here to demonstrate how this method came to do more than sort materials for the digital storytelling library. First, this collaborative method continued to mesh with my own teaching, both shaping and being shaped by it. In the first iteration of an undergraduate course that I developed in response to the TRC's Calls to Action, I asked Amy and Erin to run a design studio with undergraduate students. The course was a second-year anthropology class organized around child and youth studies in anthropology but in the context of Indigenous North America. I was out of town, and so Amy and Erin did this without me. It was early days in the development of the process, and they weren't entirely certain it had been successful. But, to my eyes, what had been successful was the engagement of mostly settler students with the question of conflicting values around something as central as raising children. Not surprisingly, many of these students were reluctant to qualify what they were seeing in the photographs, not wanting to pass judgement even on depictions of very familiar and conventional moments of play in parks, of dinner time, and so forth. Their reluctance registered many things, including their awareness of the possibility of unrecognized differences in values. As an anthropologist, I was very happy with this outcome, whatever their discomfort. The confrontation with the possibility of significant differences in meaning even in everyday practices conducted within the same community was a powerful opening. Amy would go on to conduct abbreviated versions of the design studio in public spaces on the university campus, less with the hope of sorting materials for the library than with continuing what was important reconciliation work. The design studios with university students offered moments of rupture to contemplate, even briefly, the possibility of different value systems alongside the naturalized ones they did not question. The question of how to raise children is a particularly powerful point of entry in this, especially for young people. In the context of the growing recognition of the damage of residential schooling in Canada following the work of the TRC and its 2015 Calls to Action, these moments of prompting to consider what was at stake in the values around raising children were significant.

Even so, the goal of sorting materials in the digital library for Opokaa'sin was still before us. While recognizing what these collaborative coding sessions were doing in mixed groups, we still needed to connect the quadrants of the Circle of Courage to values and terms relevant to *Blackfoot* Peoples. To that end, we organized a design studio session to be held at Opokaa'sin with Elders who worked with the organization.

DESIGN STUDIO – ELDERS (AMY'S FIELD JOURNAL, 30 MAY 2017)

April 10, 2017. Jan, Amy, and [an undergraduate Anthropology student] joined Tanya [and eight Elders] at Opokaa'sin for a design studio.

This design studio was the second round of meetings organized by Dr [Xxx] at the request of Tanya. This was a way to get the Elders more involved in the project and to have them articulate – in Blackfoot – the childrearing values they thought should be included in the Circle of Courage. In fact, one of their goals was to make the Circle of Courage reflect Blackfoot values, rather than the Sioux-inspired pan-Indigenous values it currently has. They were going to help guide the coding of the photo-elicitation books into the circle based on the four quadrants and the values they developed.

The first meeting, which I was invited to for about an hour a couple weeks prior, involved this process of talking about values and placing them into the circle. Tanya asked me to come in and tell the Elders a bit about the project. This. Was. Terrifying. While I had met many of the Elders previously, I was nervous AF. [Amy: Apparently, I looked as nervous as I felt – Tanya would later mention this to Charity, who would relay that to me!] Jan called me before hand to tell me that Tanya was really worried that mentioning "research" would be triggering for the Elders given the horrible history of colonial researchers using Indigenous people for their research gains. And being just generally crappy people. So that added to the general nervousness.

But, it went fine. Tanya introduced me and told the Elders that I'd been working on the project for over a year and that I'd learned a lot (that was probably an exaggeration on her part). I briefly explained the project, my role, and all the amazing things Hudson and Tesla had done over the summer. [Xxx] talked a little bit about the progress they'd made, and that they were going to go back to it in the afternoon. Elders gotta eat! Tanya had also sent someone to pick up cameras for the Elders so they could take photos of the values and contribute their own images and reflections to the library too.

So this is what we started with on April 10th. We had a group of Elders who had been sent off to do some homework and were ready to code the books and their own photos according to the values they articulated in the previous meeting. We all arrived and sat in the main area of Opokaa'sin while we waited for everyone else to arrive. I had a nice chat with [Xxx] and [Xxx], while [Xxx] was hustled over to do storytelling in addition to the Elder design studio – busy lady! Jan showed up and began chatting away with [Xxx] about dogs.

Tanya then snagged Jan and me to talk about the game plan for the day. She had some very specific goals and objectives that she wanted to accomplish. We agreed to give [Xxx] control over how the day would go as she was really in the best position to lead the discussions....

So we headed up to the boardroom on the second level of Opokaa'sin. I think it was the only room big enough to accommodate us all. We sat around the big table and took turns introducing ourselves. Those with Blackfoot names gave them first, and then followed with an English explanation of what they'd said. I always struggle here. How do I introduce myself? What matters to this community? Folks will say where they're from and who their family is. But, does that mean anything to them coming from me? I mean, I am a local, having grown up in Claresholm, but my family name means nothing. Do I talk about where my family emigrated from? Does it matter that I'm German and Scandinavian? Should I lay out my settler status in that way, or is it assumed?

Anyways, so we got going. [Xxx] asked everyone to talk about the terms that they had discussed last time. One of the staff at Opokaa'sin had typed out the Blackfoot words and placed them in the circle, and the Elders were asked to confirm the terms. There was a lot of discussion about the pronunciation and spelling. In fact, some of the terms were unrecognizable on the paper for the oral speakers. It was fascinating to watch people try and decipher what they had meant by the written word, and then debate if it actually fit what they were trying to capture. Then trying to come up with an English equivalent was almost impossible at times! I'm really looking forward to when Hudson and Tesla ask the Elders to pronounce the word and explain it using a story. This took most of the morning.

Then the Elders showed the photos they had brought in. What was interesting was that the photos were all old. By this I mean instead of going out and taking photos they felt captured the words/values they had articulated, they had found cherished photos that they wanted to be included. Then together they decided where the photo fit, but the Elder who submitted the photo had the final say.

It was also interesting because we thought many of them would talk about the specific values, but most ended up simply placing it in one of the four quadrants. We were worried that the circle was too rigid and too structured, but I think people get it. Maybe we need to give them more credit? With the added layers of the values, I think it will work just fine....

After lunch we wrapped up the coding session with the submitted photos, and broke out into smaller groups to talk about the books. Jan was assigned (by [Xxx]) to the [group made up of men]. This was a funny moment because Tanya was really hoping that a male staff member would take up this role, but no one was available. When she made a quip about being stuck with the guys to [Xxx] Jan was simply told "what you don't know won't hurt you!" I remember the Cree Elder from my Allying workshop talking about how older women are allowed in ceremonies that younger (especially menstruating women) aren't. This has to do with the attention the spirits/ancestors give these younger women during that time, and how the older women will have already been through this process and don't distract the spirits in the same way....

It took us a couple hours to get through this process, and my group only managed to finish one – whoops! But Jan's group finished pretty quick; they were apparently straightforward and to the point. They also had *zero* interest in drawing on the big off-white pieces of paper we had supplied. Once they were done, the men went home and Jan joined Tanya's group. This group got really creative with their paper and drew MASTERY, GENEROSITY, INDEPENDENCE, BELONGING in big letters on the sheet. My group took notes all over the paper and wrote down the codes as [Xxx] deliberated. These are really neat traces of evidence for us to consider when writing about the process....

One of the comments that really struck me was when [Xxx] thanked Jan, [Xxx] and me for our work on the project and for giving the Elders an excuse to get together and just talk to one another in Blackfoot. She said that it's not common for folks to just meet up, drink coffee and talk. She noted that it's something she wished they did more of. That was a really nice moment; we saw that they had gotten something valuable out of this too. Fieldwork with Indigenous folks should be reciprocal and mutually beneficial, and I feel like this comment pointed to how our project achieves that (sometimes).

Tanya would later say that if nothing else came of this project, these meetings with the Elders would be enough. She felt really validated and that the Elders recognized and appreciated all the work they do at Opokaa'sin. And, given how much Tanya does to facilitate this project, that also makes me feel good. She should be getting something out of the process too – not just the product for her kids.

Many of the themes from the last chapter are illustrated again in this post. We can see, for instance, the shifting and distributed character of expertise and the expression of identity in encounter – quite literally translational encounters in this example. But Amy's reflections also demonstrate how the design studio method was an adaptable innovation that provided for the articulation of Blackfoot knowledge and ways of knowing among a group of Blackfoot folk. That this work was done alongside the Raising Spirit team opened up possibilities for all. For my own part, the details of my own gendered and generational position complicated by my presence as an anthropology professor were familiar feelings from my other fieldwork positions. Still, as with my other, necessarily limited, direct fieldwork experiences in this project, I relished the chance to take part in this design studio. What was so striking to me was the shared work around finding Blackfoot words for the values that were being identified through other design studios. At the big table in the Opokaa'sin meeting room, the various Elders would suggest a word and the others would quietly listen and take a few moments before responding to support, amend, or extend a suggestion. It became clear that not only were there differences in fluency based on life experiences (including time in residential schools), but there were also different dispositions towards which version of Blackfoot would be used: older forms or more recent modifications reflecting how Blackfoot was currently being spoken. I watched as these esteemed Elders would taste a word, comparing notes on what it contained and might extend to include. The capaciousness of the Blackfoot words to incorporate multiple senses and meanings was evident. We were in no position to make final decisions, and in many ways, these Elders left some of the terms open for further discussion and elaboration in use, an apt metaphor for the values to be represented in the digital library itself.

As Tanya and other participants noted, what was most important here was the chance to sit down and talk like this about values and language. These discussions were facilitated and organized through the design studio process as a kind of problem-solving alongside, which again opened the possibility for multiple meanings and values to be expressed without any final determination. This is not to say that terms were not identified along with associated values, but rather that the process demonstrated how their interpretation remained open to multiple readings.

Our experiments with the design studio process, to solve the problem of who codes and how, produced some of the most powerful moments around values in the project. People sitting together around pieces of brown paper recognized the entangled character of their values and their ways of knowing and being and they became yet more entangled. The process developed and deepened as it was practised with mixed groups, on campus, off campus, and with Elders. Most design studios, however, were conducted by the team itself in the summer of 2017. As Amy related to me, recurring patterns were identified and as some of the more chaotic and creative moments of the earlier moments receded, the process became shorter and less intense.

Even so, design studios still had more lessons to teach us.

When Collaboration Fails

HEAT WAVE (MIKEY'S FIELD JOURNAL, 1 AUGUST 2017)

Tuesday morning was *rough*. I'm not even sure how to verbalize it, or how much of it all I want to verbalize. Maybe just a "simple" summary will do.

Jan invited the Anthropology department down to our office to check out the work that Raising Spirit is doing, have exposure to a new kind of methodology, and get some feedback from them. I think we all had very different ideas of what the morning was going to look like, but from my point of view, I was really excited for some of the dialogue that I hoped would happen during and after the design studio. I love anthropology, and I respect many of the professors at this institution, and I was excited to see what a hive mind of anthropologists would sound like.

The story of what happened that day goes far beyond the design studio method and questions about ethnographic method, even as it demonstrates what can be produced and what can be missed in such an experimental moment. It is also a humbling reminder of the limits of ethnography to capture personal and social complexity.

In their post, Mikey describes their positionality through their own relationships with these faculty members, people with whom they had taken or would take courses. Mikey's understanding of what happened that day, like the understanding of all members of the young research team, reflects the contingency and partiality of their positions, and rightfully so. Their reactions were shaped both by their felt position of being junior to the visiting faculty and in positions of less power, but also by their pride as accomplished practitioners of this method that they had been developing and using for some time. My own position meant that I read what was going on in a much different way, one informed by long-term personal and indeed intimate knowledge of why some of the reactions took the shape they did. Because as Mikey notes, things went wrong. They continued in the blog post:

> Unfortunately, the meeting did not go as planned. As Jan acknowledged this morning (I'm writing this a week later), she didn't set up the meeting with the utmost clarity It sounded more like she wanted her own thought process critiqued, rather than for the anthropologists to participate in a design studio, or even to observe it unfold....

I had failed. I had failed my team, failed my colleagues, and failed to accomplish what I had hoped. I had thought that the break with Opokaa'sin in the early phases of the project was painful; that was nothing compared to this moment of failure and refusal, although ultimately there would be some repair.

I have left out a longer description of Mikey's reaction which captured the confusion, pain, and anger at what the young research team understood as a rejection of the process – in fact, a refusal to even engage with it seriously. They saw in this both evidence of a colonial mindset, but also a dismissal of younger, Indigenous, and female researchers. I was sitting at the table as an ethnographer – but I was also there as partner, colleague, mentor, supervisor, and team member. For this reason, it is particularly important that I claim my own voice and my own experience, not just because it was I who bore the greatest responsibility for what happened, but also because I still believe in this part of the ethnographer's magic: a first-person account of a happening in the world in all its messy complication with due attention to the interpretive frame.

Mikey was right. What happened was the result of how I had set up this instance of the design studio process. As the method was emerging, we were shaping it and it was shaping us. I had grown more excited about its possibilities to move ethnography towards collaborative problem-solving across difference. I wanted my fellow ethnographers to consider this method and let me know if they too saw its promise. Having them participate directly would give them the most direct engagement with the process. At the same time, my hopes about what this design studio process could do more generally had grown.

Perhaps a collaborative values session around a design problem could be a kind of reconciliation work between Indigenous and settler peoples in Canada opening the space for new publics and the enunciation of new imaginaries (Choy 2005; Bhabha 1994; de la Cadena and Blaser 2018; Escobar 2017; Tsing 2015). The Truth and Reconciliation Commission had issued its report and its ninety-four Calls to Action in 2015. We were developing the design studio process while the report was generating greater public awareness. The potential of the design process to bring people together to reconcile their accounts of values seemed significant. And this was how I was describing it to the young team, who were flush with the sense of the kind of conversations that could be held around tables such as this.

So, I arranged a time for my colleagues to come to the Lair, and the team under Amy's supervision, set up the table and chose the material to be coded. It was decided that Taylor should take the lead in running this iteration of the design studio. The faculty trooped in and were shown a video after Taylor shared the instructions for the design studio process. They should take notes on the brown paper about the video and enter a discussion of the values at play. Instead, they offered up critiques of the method, noting its shortcomings and talking to one another about it. One colleague did their best to follow the instructions as a collaborator. Another colleague described the process as a version of a focus group interview. Another was befuddled about the doodling on the paper. Another, returning after a long hiatus away from the department, wanted to use the occasion to re-enter scholarly discourse with colleagues. The problems of using a pan-Indigenous concept like the Medicine Wheel to address local Blackfoot values became a point of scholarly consideration. But what the team heard was a dismissal of Indigenous values. The young team members looked on in dismay, feeling silenced. I tried to intervene, but tensions grew rapidly for the young people particularly. The faculty weren't entirely aware of how the mood had shifted. In a testament to the power of the work they had done together thus far – and perhaps the design studio process itself – the team was extremely attentive to one another's emotions and engagement. Ultimately, I cut the conversation short, and I left the Lair with the other faculty.

Even now, I cannot adequately explain my choice to leave, although I think I had put myself in the category of those bringing harm and wanted the team to have a safe space without faculty. But my absence was sorely felt, as I was told later. Where had I gone? Here was my biggest failure. I had struggled the whole project with when I should and could be present and when I should not and could not. Reading back through the blog posts, I feel the mentions of my absences most acutely.

What I hadn't understood fully was the power of my presence. I do not mean my physical presence, but rather my presence as the head of this project, its chief instigator, and cheerleader. Indeed, I often did not need to be physically present to have my presence felt, but in this case, my leaving felt like a desertion.

Ultimately, I had made both the team and my faculty colleagues more vulnerable than they should have been in the moment. And while a failure is a great teacher (Geertz 1983), I would do this very differently if I had the chance. In the aftermath, there were tears among the team and recriminations among the faculty, and in my way, I sought to repair all the relationships. I met with the faculty members over beer to explain what they hadn't fully understood was happening and to further plead for the power of the method in the era of reconciliation. It may have been that they felt they had been set up. It was a very tough moment, although I count all those present as good colleagues to this day.

Dealing with the rupture with the research team was a longer-term project, and it took time to find a clear path forward. In the interim, work continued, while we were all in pain.

Our Last Design Studio: Diplomacy between More than Two Worlds

The centrality of relationships and the value of relationality were the warp and woof of the Raising Spirit Project and learning this was hard-won in many instances. Here, I quote at length from a co-written piece by Amy and me that describes a design studio meant to repair relationships.

> We sat somewhat awkwardly around our oblong table in the Lair. The room felt unfamiliar despite the brown paper and markers on the table and the smell of coffee brewing. It was the first time our team had all come together since our design studio with the Anthropology Department. Many conversations had been had between individual team members in the weeks since the design studio. These conversations reflected the forms of difference we saw at the beginning of our project … among the settler students, the young Blackfoot students, and those working within the university. Yet they were also cross-cutting as we drew on the relationships built through a summer of intense design studio work. This foundation, built on a commitment to our relationships, allowed us to work through the disruption with a final design studio.
>
> Newberry guided us through a reconciliatory design studio: we used the talking circle to express our feelings and perceptions of the previous design studio; we used the brown paper and markers to abstract these

> further when words were difficult. This meeting, like all design studios before it, was a partial attunement. We realized we would never quite see that encounter in the same way, just as we would never come to a true reconciliation of values in our collaborative coding. More important, this design studio created an ethical space in which we were able to begin rebuilding relationships.
>
> Our attempts to recognize and reconcile notions of expertise within both Blackfoot and ethnographic contexts sometimes were met with refusal. Yet as we have noted, there have been productive moments of partial attunement and transformation. When asked by other anthropologists why this is a worthwhile method, we can point to its power to build strong relationships, which Tanya had encouraged us to see as central all along. Building relationships has always been central to both ethnographic and Indigenous ways of knowing. Recognizing the centrality of relationship is integral to a return to decolonizing the discipline. (Mack and Newberry 2020, 101)

Using the design studio process to address the problem of coding materials for the digital library produced the most telling moments in this project. This collaborative process that the team developed made a space for working together and alongside that illustrated other possibilities. For example, the possibility of new publics for the sharing of new forms of knowledge was opened in the era reconciliation. When the team worked to consider values together over pieces of brown paper, they expanded Indigenous forms of collaboration while simultaneously undermining two-world models of Indigenous and settler relations. Their work also demonstrates the possibility of a public shaped by the young (Nolas 2015). Even so, the continued doubling of young people through their participation in the project led to questions about the principle of non-interference in pluriversal futures to resist ethnographic recognition. I will return to these ideas below by way of a conclusion to this chapter, but first the limits of a two-world model of Indigenous and settler relations is considered.

Elder Willie Ermine (2007), working specifically on the divide between Indigenous and Canadian law, considers the role of ethics and the entangled history of Indigenous Peoples being understood through European knowledge practices that emphasize Western universality. He identifies the presence of an ethical space between: "The idea of the ethical space, produced by contrasting perspectives of the world, entertains the notion of a meeting place, or initial thinking about a neutral zone between entities or cultures. The space offers a venue to step out of our allegiances, to detach from the cages of our mental worlds and assume a position where human-to-human dialogue can occur. The ethical space offers itself as the theatre for cross-cultural conversation in pursuit of ethically engaging diversity and dispersed claims to the human order" (202). Importantly, Ermine grounds this in ways of knowing or "thought worlds"; his ethical space is a space between what we would now call ontological worlds but with political, legal, and ethical implications. As he says, "shifting our perspectives to recognize that the Indigenous-West encounter is about thought worlds may also remind us that frameworks or paradigms are required to reconcile these solitudes" (201). While Ermine calls for new paradigms, his concept of ethical space posits a two-world model with the possibility for a neutral space between.

The Raising Spirit team's approach to ethical space began with an emphasis on the ethical aspect of their work together, by which we meant a desire for respectful engagement across the difference at the centre of the project: the difference between Blackfoot and settler values. Yet, the acts of translation that took place in the space of the design studios conducted were crucial to the recognition and reproduction of many forms of differences. At the centre of this work was translation, but in this context, translation was not just the movement between the Blackfoot language and English. Certainly, language revitalization was one of Tanya's hopes for the digital storytelling library, and the recording of traditional stories told in Blackfoot at Opokaa'sin was an important part of this work. The research team worked with many Elders fluent in Blackfoot during the collaborative coding to link values with Blackfoot words identified by fluent Elders. Yet none of the young researchers was a Blackfoot speaker.

The translation that became the focus of the design studios was less about language and cultural values; instead, it was about the *value of culture*. As previous chapters have demonstrated, Blackfoot expertise is distributed across Blackfoot Territory, challenging any clear boundary around "cultural" knowledge and values. Initially, the design studio process was about eliciting forms of cultural contrast and difference. But over time, the process of coding collaboratively led us away from translation as the movement between two worlds and towards the making of new imaginaries and new possibilities for knowing alongside.

One of the most promising and perplexing problems with the design studio method in Raising Spirit concerned who was to be the public for this information. Who would witness the results of our coding work? The digital storytelling library itself seemed to have a clear audience: the young Indigenous people in Opokaa'sin's program who would use it as a form of language revitalization to support cultural resurgence and resilience as Tanya hoped. Yet, as the method evolved to include more and different people in the contemplation of differing values, the possible publics increased to include university students, Blackfoot Elders, and Indigenous and settler researchers and students. Indeed, the most powerful takeaway from the method for me was what happened over the brown paper as an opening up of possibility for thinking through the implications of differing values together beyond the project. Did the method work as a form of reconciliation work? Did these ways of provoking conversations provide a path for imagining different futures for young people in Canada, one that produced new publics for this kind of pluriversal future (Escobar 2017)? Here, thinking through Homi Bhabha's (1994) third space is helpful.

Bhabha (1994) uses the idea of enunciation to unsettle any ethnological category of culture to show that cultural difference emerges in spaces "where meanings and values are (mis)read or signs are misappropriated" (34) just as they were over the brown paper on the table in the Lair. He directs us to enunciation as the process by which culture becomes said and so "knowledge*able*" and "authoritative, and adequate to systems of cultural identification" (34). In other words, the third space is the space for enunciation of cultural difference and useable, authoritative knowledge, and this was the goal of much of the second phase of the Raising Spirit Project, especially the work done by the young researchers.

The role of translation in third spaces is taken up by Timothy Choy (2005) in a consideration of vernacular science and expertise in an incinerator project in Hong Kong. For Choy, translation is about the articulation of different forms of knowledge (drawing on Laclau and Mouffe 1985), a process through which a "contingent collectivity" is mobilized. And what better way to describe the people gathered around the brown paper at various points in the project? Such contingent collectivities are produced in third spaces: "True to the double significance of articulation, translation both voices claims and effects a kind of conjunction between domains that are not necessarily related. The act of translation reaches across distinct social worlds and asserts the relevance of one to the other" (Choy 2005, 14). Choy demonstrates how the work of articulation can generate relationships that are collaborative and collective even as they produce certain relational identities (12). For the Raising Spirit Project, these relational identities registered the complexities of being young, being an Elder, whether Blackfoot or settler, and being in touch with traditional teachings or learning about them through this project. Perhaps it is worth remembering here that one of the original goals of the photo-elicitation project was to facilitate the articulation of Blackfoot values, latent and suppressed. What actually happened was that our design studios made the space for a kind of conjunction between *multiple* social worlds, asserting their mutual relevance, in a discussion about possible values.

Over the course of the project, the team slowly came to realize that their collaborations through the design studio method aligned closely with Indigenous ways of knowing. This was partly a conscious choice, as when the team envisioned what happened at the table in the Lair as a kind of talking circle following the advice of Indigenous team members.[3] At other times, it was evident that an emphasis on the relationality of knowledge and its production in anthropology, both the ontological and the epistemological aspects engendered by the design studio process, was deeply resonant with what have been described as the relational elements of Indigenous research methods (Kovach 2021; Smith 1999; Wilson 2008). Indeed, the relationship-building produced through the project materials was what Tanya had told us from the beginning was the point of this project.

Even so, in our ethnographic blunderings, we ran the risk of failing to acknowledge the work of Indigenous methodologists and critical Indigenous studies scholars who have called for new approaches to research by and with Indigenous communities (e.g., Tuck et al. 2023). Recall that we had explicitly taken up Ermine's ethical space as the goal of the design studios. In fact, the team didn't talk about third spaces, but rather about how to create a respectful place *between worlds*. Amy's work on the ethics of research with Indigenous communities was especially important in shaping the design studio project, and this was work with Elder Reg Crowshoe.

But, in fact, most of our choices were driven by practical engagements with how to do the coding work collaboratively with young researchers and others rather than through a literature review on Indigenous methodologies. And this work had been shaded by the celebratory emphasis on design and collaboration coming out of STS and anthropology of design, a space markedly devoid of attention to Indigenous methodologies, much less the views of young people. Our approach to the coding problem had begun with reference to calls for experimentation and the use of design principles in ethnography. As it happens, the contrast between third spaces and ethical spaces identifies some very interesting tensions in the work of Indigenous and settler researchers alike. Not unexpectedly, these tensions were both diagnostic and productive. Although not exhaustive by any means, here I use the ideas that inform two-eyed seeing to consider this tension.

Two-eyed seeing has become central to many projects in education and health, in Canada especially (Bartlett et al. 2012; Reid 2020; Hogue and Bartlett 2014).[4] This approach has been elaborated and developed by an array of scholars. Here, for example, is a description of its use in a project on participatory archival research:

> In particular, the project's guiding principles were based in the Mi'kmaw worldview of *Etuaptmumk* (in English: Two-Eyed Seeing) as espoused by Mi'kmaw Elder Albert Marshall: an understanding which emphasises the importance of exploring difference and linking knowledge systems (Iwama et al. 2009). *Etuaptmumk* refers to learning to see (from one eye) the strengths of, or the best in, Indigenous knowledge systems. It also means seeing (from the other eye) the strengths of, or the best in, western knowledge. In doing so, we can arrive at more comprehensive understanding of any particular phenomena.... (Cullen and Castleden 2022, 2)

While two-eyed seeing is meant to produce the depth perception necessary for more comprehensive understanding, it is premised on a two-world model. While the principle is attentive to what can be produced by keeping both in mind, it simultaneously reproduces the boundaries and the distance between the two worlds. Recall again Choy's (2005), point that an act of translation presupposes an original distance between worlds even as it is involves moving between them. For Choy, "translation both voices claims and effects a kind of conjunction between domains that are not necessarily related. The act of translation reaches across distinct social worlds and asserts the relevance of one to the other" (11). In this, he sounds like Ermine. Perhaps the point I am making here is a minor one, but it does relate to the question of cultural expertise developed in the last chapter. For as Choy notes, "It is this fact of difference that allows the act of translation to serve as a kind of proof that circulation – a precondition of expertise – is in process" (1). By bringing it back to expertise, the space between becomes both that staging area for cultural difference but also for the articulation of knowledges as expertise. This is not about two worlds but many (de la Cadena and Blaser 2018; Escobar 2017).

A reminder here that the young Raising Spirit team had resisted and refused the idea of cultural expertise and that their collaborative work illustrated the patchy and distributed character of expertise and knowledge across the team, as well as across Blackfoot Territory. Our design studios underlined this understanding. What happened over brown paper was the articulation of other relationships to Blackfoot identity and expertise, unsettling any clear divide between town and reserve, old and young, Blackfoot and other forms of Indigenous identity, and between settler and Indigenous more generally.

Given the moment of this writing during a time of Indigenous resurgence and the reckoning with residential schools and what reconciliation might look like, it is awkward to question the two-world model and suggest a return instead to hybridity (Bhabha 1994) and circulation. Yet what the design studio process brought us to was less a two-world model and instead the possibility for multiple positions within the "contingent collectivity" at the table. Work in child and youth studies also underlines the multiple communities that the young move through, their relation to meaning making as knowledge production, and the methods that can engage them (e.g. Clark 2011; Cahill 2007; Leon and Rosen 2023) Daelman et al. 2020).

For the work of the young Raising Spirit researchers, it was the circulation of knowledge, distributed and patchy, that surfaced forms of difference. It was also circulation that dissolved them repeatedly. Perhaps this is the effect of starting from anthropology rather than Indigenous studies, but my emphasis here is less on respectful engagement – although I hope we achieved that. Instead, I have come to see the space produced through the design studios as a space for things to turn out differently for all. It is in such spaces that we can produce the possibilities for new publics, new enunciatory communities, and the enrolment of new allies that did not fit neatly in a two-world model. Taking inspiration from anthropologists, such as Marisol de la Cadena and Mario Blaser (2018) and Arturo Escobar (2017) working in other regions of the world, such collaborative work allows us to imagine new ways to be and to be together.

The political possibilities produced in these new publics and the enunciation of other identities seems to evoke the idea of a third space, although it seems out of favour to talk about hybridity in the era of Indigenous resurgence, when clear boundaries on status and identity are being emphasized. Yet, by seeing the ethical space as a third space, we open the space for more identities than Indigenous versus settler, Blackfoot and everyone else. We allow space for young Blackfoot people raised in the care of settler foster parents to craft their connection to being Indigenous and being Blackfoot in ways that do not diminish them.

In fact, some Indigenous scholars also trouble two-world models. Brian Noble (2002), working with Piikani Elder Reg Crowshoe, describes a Blackfoot notion of parallel worlds, one that reminds us of the conventional interpretation of the Two-Row Wampum Treaty as a model for Indigenous–settler relations based on staying in your own lane. But as Noble and Crowshoe share the words of The Old Man, who signed the treaty that governs Blackfoot Territory in 1877, they point to his emphasis on the need to engage with settlers to help them understand. Dwayne Donald (2009) makes a similar point when referring to the work of Indigenizing the curriculum in Alberta, where this project took place, and the pitfalls of purity produced through oppositional logics of third spaces. The space between is one not just of surfacing difference and treating each respectfully, it is about the work through difference that offers new futures.

Indeed, Richard Hill and Daniel Coleman (2019) recently used the Two-Row Wampum Treaty as a model for Indigenous–university relationships. The two-row wampum represents the treaty between the Haudenosaunee and the Dutch, which has been a long-standing model for relations between Indigenous and settler communities in Canada. Hill and Coleman advocate for the recognition that knowledge circulates in relationships (2019, 354). While the two-row wampum can be read as two worlds seen across a river, and as a "stay in your lane" ideology, there is the question of those who stand with a foot in both canoe and ship. Our design studio process troubled the river between as separation and directed us instead to the flow and circulation of multiple forms of difference – not in opposition and occasionally in alignment. Latour's' (2014) description of the need for diplomacy between different ontological worlds is apt here. He proposes "deontology" as way to pursue "a better way of refastening broken relations by recognizing another legitimate way of being" (2). For Latour, this is a reassertion of what anthropology has always been after: respectful, diplomatic recognition of difference without the need to change.

I pointed to the role of encounter in the making of cultural experts in the last chapter and return to it by here. "Encounters (everyday, or extraordinary) across partially connected (and also heterogenous) worlds may be sustained by conversations that draw from domains in which not all participants participate" (de la Cadena and Blaser 2018, 9). As with the attention to misunderstanding and mistranslation described above, the generative effects of moments of divergence and incommensurability have been noted (Strathern 2018a; Tsing 2015; Povinelli 2001). De la Cadena and Blaser draw on Strathern, who is drawing on the work Isabelle Stengers (2011) to understand divergence as *constituting* "the entities (or practices) as they emerge both in their specificity and with other entities or practices" (de la Cadena and Blaser 2018, 9). The similarity to Bhabha's description of what happens in third spaces is clear. More to the point here is that these moments of emergent difference, divergence, and incommensurability are the stuff of new worlds. "This mode of participation requires working at the site of divergence, where the coincidence among participants does not absorb their being who they are" (de la Cadena and Blaser 2018, 11). These are moments of pluriversal imagination as Escobar (2017) describes.

The encounters of the Raising Spirit team over brown paper in the lab were both everyday and extraordinary. Across these sessions, the team was working together through many moments of divergence, but also moments of partial attunement as multiple domains were engaged. Despite our missteps, our time in the churn of the river in-between changed us all and without diminishing the worlds that we each brought with us into the space.

Arguing for Non-interference in the Pluriverse

There are reasons to be suspicious of design-influenced approaches to ethnography that take place within and are shaped by the kind of elite spaces that are as white and as unwelcoming to the marginalized as the spaces and professions involved: corporate finance offices, science and technology labs, architectural firms, and so forth. In our design studios, the folks at the table were younger, more Indigenous, and more unsure of their role in the production of knowledge. The possibilities opened in the space of the design studio were the river between STS and Indigenous methodologies in a sense. This space was about ethical possibilities, including the possibility that these contingent collectivities might define another way to talk about the role of young people and what Indigenous folks and their others might usefully say to one another.

The utopian possibilities for other futures and other imaginaries that accompany some of the turn to collaboration and design in anthropology might be the refunctioning of ethnography hoped for by Holmes and Marcus (2008). But following on Latour, I wonder whether what we really need is a de-functioning of ethnography. This is not a call to burn down anthropology or reject our central interest in diplomatic relations with other ways of knowing and being, but rather an argument about accepting the limits of what can be known *ethnographically*.

Some have asserted a widely held principle of non-interference among Indigenous Peoples in North America (Wark et al. 2019), such as that enshrined in the conventional understanding of the Two-Row Wampum Treaty (Hill and Coleman 2019). Non-interference has also been suggested to represent a more general value against interference in the activities of another person, including the young: "This concept has been used to explain the reluctance of First Peoples to engage in a diverse range of behaviours deemed to be interfering or coercive, including addressing another person unless acknowledged, confronting or contradicting others, providing or requesting advice or assistance, and commenting on or imposing consequences on improper behaviour…." (Wark et al. 2019, 420). Non-interference has significant implications for political action by Indigenous Peoples, especially that organized around the idea of protection – whether the protection of children or the protection of cultural integrity. Yet, what was so very clear in work with the Raising Spirit team and the children and families at Opokaa'sin is that Indigenous Peoples in Canada and their children are always already interfered with. Indeed, the results of this interference, whether from residential schooling, the Sixties Scoop, or the foster care system, were one of the prompts for this project aimed at articulating Blackfoot values through the participation of young people themselves.

Demands for research participation by Indigenous young people is yet another form of interference. Dhillon (2017) outlines the effects of state demands for participation as a "vehicle for increasing Indigenous representation in youth directed social policy" as a "mechanism to recalibrate relations between the governing and governed" (21). Beyond the exercise of state violence, colonial rule is reproduced through "the ability to entice Indigenous peoples to *identify*, either implicitly or explicitly with the profoundly *asymmetrical* and *nonreciprocal* forms of recognition either imposed on or granted to them by the settler state and society" (Coulthard 2014, 25). Both Coulthard and Dhillon attend to how the politics of recognition drag Indigenous forms of governance into the established frame of the Canadian state, a process reminiscent of translation as described above. In other words, to make Indigenous forms of governance knowledgeable they must be recognized. Such recognition necessarily reproduces a two-world model.

Here, I am mindful of the warning from Fortun and Cherkasky (1998) that collaboration in the search for counternarratives can be nefarious: "we do want to retain the tension and sense of intrigue that the term collaboration invokes, as a reminder that collectivity is not only difficult to produce and strategize, but that it can also marginalize and alienate" (146). Collaboration produces double binds, as they note, an effect taken up in the next chapter. In its early phases, the Raising Spirit Project required a kind of ethnographic recognition from the young Indigenous members of the team, a recognition that demanded that they identify in ways that reproduced ethnological categories of culture. To be fair, such identifications were clearly what some traditionalists favoured. By the end of the project, the design studio process effectively broke that frame – as did our failures and blunders – directing us instead to the possibility of other worlds, other publics, other futures.

Our adaptation of a design approach to solve the problem of coding values in project materials traces a methodological move from participation and elicitation to a more fully collaborative contemplation of how we can engage in open discussions about values over a common table. In the process, we moved from a two-world model to the making of spaces for many kinds of relationships to values and a more open-ended sense of identity than first brought people to the table. But I am the one writing here, not the young Indigenous people involved in this project. So perhaps it is only my own hope when I describe the possibility for new worlds and new publics created in the space between that allows for the emergence of difference without harnessing it for governance or for catalogues of identity.

Refusing Recognition

The Raising Spirit Project was an unexpected experiment in ethnographic methods, one that came to be shaped significantly by collaborative design. The initial issue we confronted was how to code photographs for values across communities: the First Nations of the Blackfoot, those living in the city versus on the reserve, the young as well as Elders, those raised traditionally and those whose lives have been disrupted by residential schooling and foster care, and, ultimately, those who identify as Indigenous versus those understood to be settlers. The problem itself revealed the continuing colonial logic of coding as collection and analysis in qualitative research, drawing our attention to the space between object, image, or story and the values presumed to be articulated through them.

To solve the problem of coding, we turned to design approaches as they were being described and used in anthropology and ethnography. Because the project had always been understood to be a participatory one, the move to collaborative design just made sense. Ultimately, this shift changed the project and its goals fundamentally. What began as a technical fix for coding led to a complete repurposing of the design studio method that we were making and shaping collaboratively. We moved from thinking about collaboration as sharing values between worlds to open-ended conversations about values that challenged two-world approaches to Indigenous knowledge. The design studio process we improvised led the team to recognize how much of our emerging method resembled Indigenous ways of knowing, our work together also revealed an unexpected power to shape new spaces for translation and for the speaking or enunciation of different forms of knowledge, making it available for imagining what reconciliation might include and what other futures might be possible. For those of us most centrally involved in the work, we witnessed the possibility of new publics and new ways to "enrol allies" (Choy 2005).

Still, what to make of the refusals by young Indigenous researchers unwilling to claim their own expertise and to use these new public and pluriversal forms of culture enunciated there? Despite my hopes for what happened in the space of our collaborative coding in design studios, it is undeniable that this work put these young researchers in a double bind. The next chapter takes up the question of what happens when young people leave the table and the questions behind.

NOTES

1 Quirkos (https://www.quirkos.com/) is a coding program that Mikey had used in a previous SoTL project with me. A qualitative data software program offered through the university at that point, its limits for the Raising Spirit Project were quickly realized and it was never pursued further.

2 Amy is referencing an article by Joanne Rappaport (2008) that guided our thinking about co-conceptualization as an aspect of collaboration.

3 Running Wolf and Rickard (2003) describe the talking circle as typically credited to "Woodlands tribes in the Midwest" and as a parliamentary procedure for respectful sharing of ideas to reach consensus. It is widely used in Indigenous settings, and now health and educational settings as well.

4 The history of this concept begins with the teachings of the late spiritual leader, healer, and chief Charles Labrador of Acadia First Nation, Nova Scotia, especially these words: "Go into a forest, you see the birch, maple, pine. Look underground, all those trees are holding hands. We as people must do the same" (Kierans 2003; cited in Iwama et al. 2009, 3). Iwama et al. (2009, 3) describe the Institute for Integrative Science/Toqwa'tu'kl Kjijitaqnn and Health (IISH) at Cape Breton University as the "physical of 'Two-Eyed Seeing,' an Indigenist pedagogy, research, practice, and way of living that incorporates Western and knowledges (see IISH Web site)."

Chapter Six

Double-Bind Ethnography

"Sometimes – often in science and always in art – one does not know what the problems were till after they have been solved. So perhaps it will be useful to state retrospectively what problems were solved for me by double bind theory."
(Gregory Bateson, *Steps to An Ecology of Mind*, 1972, 271)

Bateson's words are a fitting introduction to this concluding chapter. It was only after the Raising Spirit Project ended and I struggled to shape what this book would be about and how to write it that I understood the problem at its heart. The double bind is that problem. To draw this messy consideration of a messy project to a close, I return to the threads developed across previous chapters that have led to seeing the double bind as a way to understand the limits and possibilities for what can be done ethnographically.

The patchy and distributed character of knowledge about Blackfoot culture was evident early in this project. As chapter 2 illustrated, the original goals of the photo-elicitation project shifted as young Blackfoot people became central to building a digital storytelling library. Their training in both university research and Blackfoot protocol was just one of many doublings they experienced. As chapter 3 shows, when positioned as para-ethnographers and asked to act as cultural experts, they accepted reluctantly and sometimes refused. It is easier perhaps to imagine Amy and Mikey and the other undergraduate anthropology students as culture experts in-the-making. Yet, the original method of photo-elicitation implied that Hudson, Tesla, and Taylor should be experts already. Asked to translate Blackfoot knowledge for the project, they were doubled as insiders with expertise who would also become ethnographers after being trained. They were expected to offer up vernacular forms of knowledge, but the need to align with Indigenous knowledge writ large, perhaps especially in the era of reconciliation, made them leery of making claims to cultural expertise. Their doubts were compounded by their age and the sense that such knowledge should best come from Elders. Their encounters in the field and in the lab did surface forms of vernacular knowledge, but they refused to claim any kind of authority as experts on Blackfoot culture. Their discomfort reflected the distributed and patchy character of knowledge and knowledge practices in Blackfoot Territory for many Blackfoot people, regardless of age.

Then, when asked to code the photographs and other materials amassed, the growing contradictions and tensions in their doubling through the original framing of the project led to methodological experimentation and improvisation. As chapter 4 outlines, the design studios were an experiment in collaborative coding, an improvisation that changed the project fundamentally. Rather than only seeking the identification of Blackfoot values, although some of that did happen, the team learnt how knowledge and values can circulate in Blackfoot Territory as a kind of pedagogy for all, as the roles of teacher and learner were surfaced in specific encounters. The spaces created by this work offered the possibility for new publics and the enunciation of other ways to be together in the era of reconciliation that challenges two-world models of relations between Indigenous and settler ways of knowing.

Even so, the effects of ethnographic recognition and refusal haunted the project until its end revealing the problems and possibilities of ethnography. Here in this final chapter, the question of the photographs that anchored the project brings together the two contradictory effects of the Raising Spirit Project: The photographs gathered relations, but they also put the young research team in a double bind. The consequences of that double bind remain uncertain.

An Unexpected Project: Gathering Photos

I did not expect to become an anthropologist of early childhood education, or that I would do so much work of this work in Blackfoot Territory, much less during the time of the Truth and Reconciliation Commission's reporting on the genocidal effects of residential schooling. This project has meant the exploration of a series of literatures from child and youth studies to Indigenous methodologies to the contemporary politics of Indigenous North America to design thinking and ethnographic experimentation to multimodality. Not since my dissertation have I covered so much ground, and I confess that my courage failed when I considered taking on the vast and vibrant field of visual anthropology. After all, I was drawn to photo-elicitation as a means to an end, not because I intended to analyse the photographs themselves. This work had brought me back to the early visual anthropology of Margaret Mead and Gregory Bateson (1942) in the study of children and childhood. Yet, our attempts to code the photographs for values took the project to a series of tensions and dilemmas at the heart of ethnography, perhaps especially with Indigenous Peoples in North America, that are highlighted through the role of photography. One further surprise awaited me as I began to try to describe this project and the photographs that began it: an unexpected return to the feminist materialism that shaped my original work in Java by recognizing the power of the photographs not as representations of values but as agentive objects in circulation that gather relations.

In fact, I had already been made aware of the power of the photograph as agentive object during my dissertation research. Arriving in Yogyakarta in 1992, before the advent of digital photography and cell phones, my partner and I had lugged camera and video equipment with us. Sadly, most was stolen at the Jakarta airport, and I was left with one old camera. Little did I know that the photographs produced (sometimes badly) by this old SLR camera would allow me to negotiate my way through our neighbourhood market (Newberry 2008). I had wanted to interview the market women as part of my consideration of women, economy, and community. They were understandably reluctant to talk about their work, which was based on the control of information and long-standing community relationships of trust with the women of the neighbourhood who were their customers. I did not fit into this calculation, and it was the promise to give them a photograph of themselves that won me the right to interview them. It was a striking moment for me. Most of these women were rural, poor, and uneducated, and in 1992, many had never seen a photographic image of themselves alone. Their delight was evident when they grabbed for the developed photograph as I extended it to them. To me, the image captured was not the point. Rather it was the relationship produced through the photo itself and its movement from my hand to theirs that made this aspect of my work possible. In much the same way, the photographs taken at the Raising Spirit project served to connect people and places across the project. The photographs gathered the relations that made this project possible.

The Raising Spirit Project had begun with photographs. In conceptualizing the photo-elicitation work for the first phase of the project, I had drawn on Karl Heider's (1975) use of auto-ethnography understood as a routine-eliciting technique to get at the Dani people's own account of "what people do" (3; Newberry 2021). By modifying photo-elicitation to be the routine-eliciting technique for community-based participatory action research, 8,000 photographs of everyday moments of raising children were taken by Opokaa'sin caregivers. Yet, the use of these photographs in photo-elicitation interviews with the photographer-participants was only the beginning of their life in the project.

The photographs also became prompts in a series of other interviews with powwow participants, Elders, community workers, and university students. They were used to guide conversations with young people at Opokaa'sin. Artwork was made in response to them. They were shared at community consultations and in public exhibits. They were sorted and collated at various points in the project, and they were coded for the values represented. Ultimately, they became embedded in the digital storytelling library on the Thing Link platform, along with the interviews, videos, photographs taken of the project itself, and Blackfoot terms. The original photographs anchored all this work, and issues with their interpretation led to the experiments in methods that characterized the second phase of the project.

It's strange, then, that a book about a project so centrally concerned with photographs includes almost none. That decision stems, in part, from the original principles of the project. Tanya and I had begun our collaboration to devise a way to facilitate the articulation of values held by Blackfoot and Indigenous Peoples embedded in the raising of children. Our pilot in Blackfoot Territory was meant to be used in a second phase in central Java, Indonesia, where my own work began. The goal for both projects was how to articulate existing, vernacular child-rearing expertise within subordinated groups. As it happens, the questions – theoretical, methodological, and ethical – that emerged across the project's run fully captured my imagination and research energy, and I have not returned to fieldwork in Java.[1]

Our other starting principle was that the work done was to support Opokaa'sin's mission. We understood these photographs as "belonging" to Opokaa'sin, but this general principle was troubled in various ways.[2] The university researchers, by which I mean myself, Erin, and Amy, were worried about the use of images of young and Indigenous people on platforms that would be publicly accessible. We were strongly guided by the Tri-Agency Council policies on human subject research (https://ethics.gc.ca/) and the need to protect those consulted during our work.[3] Yet, as Amy learnt through ethics workshops at Opokaa'sin and in consultation with the First Nations Information Governance Committee's principles of ownership, control, access, and possession (OCAP; https://fnigc.ca/ocap-training/; and see Walter and Suina 2019; Walter et al. 2020), other principles were at play. The private ownership of intellectual property is a value imposed on Indigenous communities. Instead, Indigenous knowledge is often understood to be a resource for the whole community, as Amy learnt in her workshop training with Piikani Elder Reg Crowshoe. Certainly, Tanya's feeling was that the sharing of these images of family life was meant for all those Opokaa'sin serves.

The question of "ownership" was only one complication in the sharing and display of the photographs. A final exhibition for the project called Elders of the Future was organized by settler graduate students under the supervision of Dr. Kristine Alexander. This final exhibition at our local arts organization and performance space incorporated examples from the project including the brown paper design studio work. It also included artwork produced by Indigenous young people specifically for inclusion in the digital storytelling library, as well as original artwork. The making of the exhibit involved work with a local settler curator who helped train young Indigenous people on all the elements of mounting such an exhibit, from choosing some of the work to be displayed to matting artwork to designing and arranging the displays.

The research team discussed using the metaphor of bundle transfer in this final exhibition to mark the transfer of the digital storytelling library to Opokaa'sin's full control. Bundle transfers are a set of longstanding practices among Blackfoot peoples (Bastien 2004; Crowshoe and Manneschmidt 2002; Ladner 2003; Wissler 1927; Noble 2002, 2007; Zedeño 2008) and other Indigenous Peoples of the plains of North America (Lowie 1956). This choice of the bundle transfer as a metaphor along with the solicitation of the voice of young people through creative work locates two key tensions in the Raising Spirit Project: the use of a Blackfoot metaphor to understand the production of knowledge and the focus on young people's voices as the access to that knowledge. In the first instance, the use of the Blackfoot concept of bundle transfer touches on the tension between the vernacular knowledge of local people, including young people, and the building of an Indigenous canon, a tension at the heart of para-expertise. In the second instance, asking young people to share their worlds, their ideas, and their experiences is a request to translate them into an existing form for ready recognition by others. As we learnt, this request for ethnographic recognition produces a double find.

Bundled Expectations

Initially, by drawing upon the idea of the transfer of bundles to describe the transfer of the digital storytelling library, we had wanted to recognize this production of knowledge about Blackfoot values in local terms. Yet our discomfort with using bundle transfers, a sacred practice, to describe this grew across the run of the project as the era of Indigenous resurgence, reconciliation, and racial reckoning gained momentum in North America. The transfer of materials through bundles is part of a set of sacred practices in Blackfoot Territory. These bundles are not just understood as material items but as living beings and as channels for connections to other beings. Their transfer means a transfer of rights, including rights to knowledge (Bastien 2004). We had intended a kind of respectful acknowledgement of these practices, and the anthropologists in the group readily accepted the library as a living thing that channelled exchanges that would build and sustain relations, as bundles do.

It is a long-standing practice in anthropology to take a term of local significance to abstract and generalize it to describe similar patterns and practices in other spaces. Yet, this practice has received significant challenges in recent years. In a controversy at the journal *Hau,* a group of scholars from New Zealand challenged the journal's use of the Māori term "hau," so well-known to anthropologists from the work of Marcel Mauss, as its name (ASAA/NZ 2018). In a second letter on the controversy, the Mahi Tahi collective responded to the journal's editor's initial response:

> You are right that the word, hau, is indeed common parlance in anthropology, and it's worth our whole discipline reflecting on the process by which concepts can get so removed from the communities that generate them. After all, for a journal that sees the generative potential of ethnography for developing theory, taking a century old, third hand, western account, without any further reference to that living, changing, intellectually engaged social world, is simply bad ethnography. It also assumes anthropologists are the only ones who can extrapolate wisdom from the raw building blocks of someone else's "culture," that we are accountable only to our own intellectual circles. (ASAA/NZ 2018; and see Stewart 2017)

In this context, describing the move of the library to Opokaa'sin as a bundle transfer seemed problematic. The question about the use of local, vernacular knowledge for generalized anthropological concepts loops back here to the tension between indigenous and Indigenous knowledge introduced earlier. Some of anthropology's most powerful analytical tools are derived from local, vernacular, indigenous knowledge: hau, totem, taboo. As the Mahi Tahi collective reaction describes, this is often done without sufficient acknowledgement of local specificity and the living, changing meanings of such terms. Just as importantly, while most are now more aware of the problems of appropriation, the flow of concepts is now being reversed as an Indigenous canon is built and shared. Indigenous scholars themselves now offer concepts like braiding sweetgrass, weaving, storytelling, and ceremony (Kimmerer 2013; Smith 2019; Pratt 2019; Kovach 2021) as methods useful beyond local contexts.

Here, I argue that avoiding the use of concepts like hau and practices like the Blackfoot bundle transfers can actually serve as a disavowal of what we have learnt from Indigenous ways of knowing. That is to say, the reciprocal nature of the relations produced and reproduced through the Raising Spirit Project hinged on the role of circulation and redistribution in the production of knowledge. Rather than avoiding the use of this knowledge, we must instead acknowledge our responsibility by staying in relation to its production and use. Anthropological knowledge often *is* Indigenous knowledge – but washed clean in the colonial washing machine and generalized to other cases. Reversing this move towards abstraction by respecifying the practice of transferring bundles in Blackfoot Territory offers a way to understand what the photographs did in the project. As it happens, bundle transfers as a practice capture this very well indeed.

In keeping with the values that have driven the writing of this book, I offer no comprehensive analysis of these practices here. Rather, I note that the practice of transferring rights through the transfer of bundles is widely understood to open and continue channels of exchange and relationship-building between individuals and groups. Indeed, these practices are not only a part of sacred Indigenous canon protected by Elders, but it is also a well-known form of vernacular knowledge used in a variety of circumstances. Blackfoot Peoples understand what is being described. Here, I want to draw attention to how this understanding of bundles can reframe what the photographs did during the Raising Spirit Project by focusing on their work as objects.

María Nieves Zedeño (2008), an archaeologist who has done extensive work with Blackfeet Peoples in Montana, has identified three key aspects of the Blackfoot bundle system, based on Algonquian linguistics and previous work by Wissler (1927). It is her attention to the bundles as "object-persons" and the role of transfer as "the ability of animating power to move from objects to humans and vice versa" (Zedeño 2008, 366) that are helpful here for thinking through what the photographs did in the Raising Spirit Project.

Across Blackfoot Territory, people were gathered across encounters to consider the photographs from the project. Knowledge was circulated and transferred in and through them to build relations that reached across apparent community divides. The photographs acted to bring people and ideas together. They facilitated the circulation of knowledge and understanding as a kind of relational transfer that was both Blackfoot and more. The photographs made possible diplomatic relations between ways of knowing as a form of the deontology that Latour (2013) describes. Even more, whether at Opokaa'sin, at the university, or on the reserve, the photographs surfaced the potential (Elyachar 2010) for forms of recognition that could exceed colonizing frames in the space created through the design studios.

This extension beyond and through the photographs as more than objects was evident in other aspects of the project, which I have come to describe as a multimodal, an approach being taken up in ethnography and design work (Collins et al. 2017; Pink 2011; Dicks et al. 2006) as well as with the young (Varvantakis and Nolas 2019; Johnson et al. 2012; Clark 2011). As with many of the most important aspects of the Raising Spirit Project, its multimodal character was something of a surprise, a powerful if unexpected outcome. The public exhibits of the materials at the local mall and in a local arts organization were evidence of this, as was the artwork produced through interviews with the very young and by middle and high school students for inclusion in the digital storytelling library and the exhibits. Taking inspiration from Walley's (2015) transmedia work on the Point Zero project in a deindustrializing town in Michigan, we had encouraged community members to contribute their own photographs to the library to encourage a sense of engagement, to promote sustainability, and to show that the library offered a medium for community reflection and curation. We did this only once, and although it was not as successful as we might have hoped because of scanner malfunctions, it served as another moment for community consultation about the project and its goals.

The media produced, used, and adapted for this project were multiple, sometimes overlapping and reinforcing, and sometimes jarringly discordant. This book, for example, appears as sole-authored and yet it relies on the digital blogs of the young researchers. Indigenous young people produced art, sometimes in university spaces, and occasionally at odds with their own desires. Rolls of brown paper carried the scribblings of the people gathered at various times during the project, to reflect, to seek correspondence and attunement, but also to reject, to refuse, and to reconsider. If the photographs gathered relations, the various media were the other channels that allowed for the transfer and circulation of distributed knowledge to find expression in collaborative spaces, perhaps especially through the design studios process.

In the design studios, a space for reinvention and reimagination was produced through the gathering of people, ideas, and hopes over the photographs. In this space, it was less what was depicted in the photograph than the relationships realized through considering them together. Various groups gathered over the photographs and sheets of brown paper for the collaborative work of interpretation contemplated values. These were values understood to be evident in how children are raised, and while not considered here in depth, this understanding of values has a particular temporal weight. How we raise children immediately connects us to ideas of tradition and how things have "always been done," a sense of historical endurance and stability. And yet, at the same time, the figure of the child has been understood to represent futurity (Edelman 2004; Tuck and Gaztembide-Fernández 2013; Stirling 2022). The era of reconciliation has highlighted the violent rupture in these temporalities. "Traditional" practices were explicitly targeted for interruption and therefore destruction. The TRC and its final reports (2015a, 2015b) direct us to the genocidal effects of this. The Raising Spirit Project was less a catalogue of that damage than an assertion of presence and a contemplation of "where to now?" In fact, the photographs did what Tanya hoped: They illustrated survivance (Vizenor 2008; Sabzalian 2018). This was evident in conversations around them in reserve offices, in interviews with Elders, and over lengths of brown paper. The photographs gathered people from various backgrounds in this contemplation, producing relationality across difference, or perhaps because of and in terms of forms of difference: young, old, university-based, community-based, settler, and Indigenous.

Elizabeth Edwards's work on the photography complex (2012) is helpful here. She follows Alfred Gell in highlighting the "practical mediatory role" of the photograph "in the social process" (Gell 1998, 6, cited in Edwards 2008, 27; and see Collier 1957). As she describes, "this places photographs in subjectivities and emotional registers that cannot be reduced to the visual apprehension of an image," but instead positions them as "relational objects" (Edwards 2008, 27). Such a relational object can "entangle the photographic image" and has the "capacity to mobilize new material realities" (Edwards 2012, 223). The agency of the photograph itself is activated by "networks of humans and nonhumans, people and things" (Edwards 2012, 223).

The photography complex is a distributed one that reaches beyond the object itself (Edwards 2012). As Doucet (2008) suggests, Karen Barad's attention to entanglement helps blur any division between a photographic object and its subjective interpretation. Barad's agential realism directs us towards a relational understanding of things entangled with humans and non-humans. These descriptions resonate very strongly with how bundles are understood in Blackfoot Territory, and with what Zedeño (2008) describes as the Blackfoot ontology demonstrated through their transfers. Drawing on Barad's (1998, 2007; Doucet 2018; and see Daelman et al. 2020 and Huf and Kluge 2021 in relation to work with children) approach to entanglement is helpful then in two senses. First, entanglement would suggest that rather than seeing the photographs as objects that circulate, it is more productive to see how circulation is effected through entanglements with the photographs as active participants. At the same time, the entanglement of materialist theory with Indigenous ways of knowing is also evident. While the return to materialism is a welcome one, there is a risk again of failing to notice how these ideas mirror and draw upon Indigenous forms of knowledge.

Whether understood from the perspective of agential realism and the new materialism or a Blackfoot ontology, what the Raising Spirit Project showed was that not only did the photographs circulate, but they also gathered people in relations.

Voicing Concerns

The shift in methodology from seeking to interpret the values represented by the photographs taken to acknowledging the relationality built through their circulation was a defining feature of the Raising Spirit Project. This shift was prompted by a series of refusals by the research team. These refusals to be doubled loop back to the question of voice raised in chapter 1.

The participation of young Indigenous, primarily Blackfoot, people in the Raising Spirit Project included interpreting the original photographs, making art in response to them, designing art for their digital storytelling library, and mounting the exhibits. Their incorporation followed from the participatory aspect of the project from its inception, influenced by my own interest in community-based participatory research. Work with visual images, art, and photography is common in research with young people (e.g., Luttrell 2010; Clark 1999). Although not designed as a photo-voice project, the goal of working with young Indigenous people shares an emphasis on the right to be heard (Thomson 2008) associated with photo-voice and the emancipatory potential of describing one's own reality in stories than can clarify oppression. Photo-voice has been popular in research with young people (Varvantakis et al. 2019; Shaw 2021; Johnson 2011; Johnson et al. 2012; Wilson et al. 2007; Clark 1999; Evans-Agnew and Rosemberg 2016). Yet as

Cooper notes (2022), the idea of a transparent window onto the experience of the young is a troubling one (and see Spyrou 2011; Sæther et al. 2024). In terms of work with Indigenous communities, Heather Castleden et al. (2008) provide a review of both photo-voice and its role in community-based participatory action research (CBPR) for a project with Huu-ay-aht First Nation First Nation in British Columbia. While they conclude that a modified photo-voice approach can balance power in the research relationship, more recent critiques of this method have emerged (Abma et al. 2022; Shankar 2019; Wasson 2000; Cooper 2017; Milne 2016).

I began this book with a question about how and where to locate my voice in this sprawling project and to register the changes in approaches to ethnography since my own initial fieldwork. My time working in child and youth studies and on the Raising Spirit Project specifically has only increased my concerns. As I have written elsewhere, it is a terrible burden to ask young people to make their worlds transparent and available to us (Newberry 2017b), a conclusion that aligns with Dhillon's (2017) work on the tyranny of participation for young people (and see Cooke and Kothari 2001; Hartung 2017). Perhaps it is no wonder that our requests were often refused. These refusals were often prompted by the request to interpret and translate the photographs. What became clear across the project was that these requests put young people in a double bind.

For our public exhibits and in my thinking about writing a book such as this, that question remained at the forefront. Who and how to choose a selection of photographs that truly captured the scope of the project? At the heart of this concern was who was to have the power to interpret them. Who should describe what values were represented in the photographs? As suggested in the last chapter, the interpretive chain from image to Indigenous or specifically Blackfoot value can be elided through coding (Tuck and Yang 2014b) and the process of abstraction (Strathern 2005; Riles 2000a) for interpretation. The long history of photography's role in the colonial gaze (Said 1978; Alloula 1986; Lonetree 2019; Lydon 2010; Glass 2009; Lien and Nielssen 2021; Williams 2003) intensified my concern about their interpretation. The possibility for representational violence is compounded when subjects are both young and Indigenous, risking and reinforcing the continuing conflation of the savage with the child, a long-standing trope in the West (Rollo 2018a). There was real danger in displaying images that would reinforce the chains of implicature in that logic.

My own initial response to the photographs was evidence of this danger. When I first looked at them, I thought to myself, "These are boring!" What did I expect? Something out of the ordinary, something extraordinary, something "other"? I am not proud of my reaction, but I offer it here to illustrate the slippery endurance of the colonizing gaze that would turn children and practices of child-rearing into avatars of the romance of Indigenous life (Deloria 1994). I need only have remembered Tanya's goal in wanting these photographs: to show that Blackfoot and other Indigenous families in southern Alberta were going about the mundane practice of raising their children and doing a fine job of it. The ordinariness of the images in the photographs was the point (and see Sæther et al. 2024). And the circulation, and recirculation, of the photographs in the project spoke to needs in the Blackfoot community. As I had written elsewhere,

> Photographs of Indigenous people in North America have been a particularly powerful point of contention in terms of representation (Glass 2009). Although in this case, Indigenous, primarily Blackfoot caregivers, were making choices about what to photograph, the underlying logic of the initial project had been to locate and elicit a tradition of values still practiced despite violent disruption. This logic of lost tradition was not only my own, but that of our Indigenous collaborators. My recognition of the colonizing implications of choosing photo-elicitation was slow in coming in part because of the entangled character of photographs with memory, and with the anticipation of the re-appropriation of memory by Indigenous peoples whose images have been captured and collected for so long (Seesequasis 2019). The goal of preservation was driven by the felt sense by many of our Blackfoot collaborators that histories of childrearing practices were still being erased through foster care and a broken child-care system....
>
> The repatriation (and digitization) of photographs from museums and archives (Lydon 2010; Seesequasis 2019) to their original communities is part of yet one more return to decolonizing anthropology. Attention to the resignification of the photographs after return transfers has been considered as well (Glass 2009). Hulleah Tsinhnahjinnie (1998, 42), a Seminole/Muscogee/Dine' photographer, describes the beautiful day when she decided to "take responsibility to reinterpret images of Native people." (Newberry 2021, 39)

Attention to the repatriation and reinterpretation of photographs by Indigenous Peoples has grown (Lonetree 2019; Lydon 2007, 2010; Lien and Nielssen 2021; cf. Chambers and Blood 2009). Despite the clear colonial legacy of photography, "such images have nonetheless rich potential for appropriation and repossession by Native subjects"

(Owens 2003, cited in Lonetree 2019, 35). And it is interesting here to return to the idea of circulation and redistribution in the production of knowledge and expertise as images move from archives and museums back into the hands of Indigenous Peoples themselves.

Following Jane Lydon (2019), Lonetree notes how reworking the archive can assert a historical presence (35). She uses a set of photographs of her own Ho-Chunk family to demonstrate "survivance," Vizenor's (2008) portmanteau term of Indigenous survival and resistance. Lonetree's assertion that "the survival of our families and the visual images conveying the ongoing presence of our families is *anything but ordinary*" (Lonetree 2019, 43) is a powerful challenge to my initial reaction to the photographs. As she notes, demonstrating such presence in the nineteenth century was powerful "because the official government policy at this time was one of assimilation" (43). The photographs taken for the Raising Spirit Project likewise are assertions of ongoing presence and survivance, their collection driven by Tanya's goal to simply demonstrate that Blackfoot and Indigenous families were successfully raising their children.

Even so, the effects of the repatriation and reinterpretation of images are not straightforward. For example, in his elicitation work with colonial photographs in The Gambia, Liam Buckley (2014) found that his interlocutors responded with attention not to the effects of colonialism, but to the aesthetics of the photographs in the now, confounding his expectations about what the photographs would do. In Blackfoot Territory, presumptions about what photographs can do have continued the power of photography to colonize. Projects done in conjunction with British museums have offered photographs of cultural properties to Blackfoot Peoples rather than the return of the goods themselves (Brown and Peers 2006; Lydon 2007; and see Milun 2001), highlighting the continuing preservationist, natural history approach of museums regarding the "things" they have collected. One wonders why museums don't return the property and keep the images themselves. To do so would be much more in keeping with the Blackfoot idea of the transfer of bundles, the idea we took up for the final exhibition of the project.

The role of the photographs in Raising Spirit was central. Our methodological experiments with collaborative coding in the second half of the project were a response to the refusals of young Indigenous people to interpret their meanings as experts. The photographs presented an ethnographic double bind that was never resolved in the project. It was never clear who should interpret them. Green (2014, 8) recounts one of Bateson's attempt to describe the double bind in this way: A Zen Buddhist master "holds a stick over the head of the student and says,

'If you say this stick is real, I will strike you with it; if you say it is not real, I will strike you with it; if you say nothing I will strike you with it.'" The exhortation to interpret the photographs was equally unsolvable, especially for the young researchers. By offering an interpretation, they claimed an expertise they did not believe they held. Yet, if they left the interpretation to the settlers, they denied relationship to their own cultural background. What then to do?

The Double Bind

Gregory Bateson's double bind theory crafted in the 1950s to understand the nature of schizophrenia (Bateson et al. 1956; Bateson 1972) has seen something of a renaissance in recent years (Fortun and Cherkasky 1998; Green 2014; Chaney 2017). This renaissance appears nearly contemporaneously with another return, this one to Frantz Fanon and the question of double consciousness (Coulthard 2014). Perhaps this is unsurprising given the return as well to the question of decolonization in scholarship, including in anthropology. The demands for doubling made upon Indigenous young people in the Raising Spirit Project extend and complicate these ideas, even as it offers a way to bring together some of what was learnt through the project. Here, I take inspiration from Bateson's attention to transcontextual tangles as central to the double bind.

For Bateson, the problem of the double bind was one of communication. It was not just that the ends or the means contradicted one another, it was that *the message was refuted by its context* (Chaney 2017, 5; emphasis added). Bateson's attention was to how the messages delivered were denied by their medium of communication; for example, a mother declares her love as she pushes the child away. Leaving aside the troubling assertion of schizophrenia's causes lying in deficient mother love, Bateson presents the double bind as a problem of reconciling contradictory codes, which is relevant here following on the coding dilemmas described in the last chapter.

For Bateson, "the context was imperative; the message ordered the listener to ignore the context" (Chaney 2017, 5). Focusing, for example, on the double bind of a child who is punished for correctly demonstrating his or her fear of punishment, Bateson suggested that this was a "*a child who might learn not to know what he or she knows.* That was a child caught in a double bind" (Bateson 1972, 248; emphasis added). Bateson's explication of the problem of schizophrenia as a transcontextual one resonates with the translational encounters identified in chapter 3. The young Indigenous researchers in the Raising Spirit Project seemed to have learnt "not to know what they know," or at least not to trust it. By asking for their cultural expertise in the context of a research project and not in the context of the relations that they themselves sought to take part in as they learnt more Blackfoot knowledge, we were producing a transcontextual tangle and a double bind.

It was not just the double bind of the expectation that they could provide easy and authentic knowledge that had been suppressed and erased, even as they were being trained in both ethnographic research methods and appropriate Indigenous protocol. It was that the medium into which they were to translate their knowledge was made up of some of the standard modalities of ethnographic research: interviews, field notes, and coding. Their expertise-in-the-making was meant to lead to forms of ethnographic recognition – that is, it was to be translated into recognizable ethnographic research.

Bateson suggests that schizophrenia is a problem of "transforms" in the mind (in a simplified sense, how the human mind moves from experience to representation and back again) and the rules that guide these transforms. "We are talking then about some sort of tangle in the rules for making the transforms and about the acquisition or cultivation of such tangles" (1972, 272). He then proposes the term "transcontexual" to cover the "genus of syndromes" that derive from these tangles, and he notes that someone might be enriched by these transcontextual gifts while others are impoverished. "Within its terms there is nothing to determine whether a given individual shall be a clown, a poet, a schizophrenic or some combination of these" (ibid.).

The Raising Spirit Project demonstrated the limits of some of the progressive hopes for collaboration and co-conceptualization through ethnography. Do photo-elicitation and para-ethnography position the young researchers as co-experts? Or did these methods require a kind of ethnographic recognition that required a doubling that reproduces the "original distance between those worlds" (Choy 2005, 11), one where university researchers are in a position of equality and one where young Indigenous researchers are merely para? The contextual refutation of Indigenous knowledge was highlighted through their refusals. As Simpson (2016) says, "let's not pretend that there is an even playing field for interpretation" (328). In fact, there may be a proliferation, "a tripleness, a quadrupleness, to consciousness" (A. Simpson 2014, 8).

Positioning the young researchers as cultural experts put them transcontextual tangles that led to just such a proliferation. In fact, the initial design of the project was designed around their doubleness. It was their refusals that led to improvising a method to collaboratively code together through the design studio process. The possibility for a diplomatic space between was opened from which to enunciate new imaginaries and new publics that did not relegate anyone involved to one identity or the other: young, older, university-based, community-based, Blackfoot, and other. The poetic and hopeful were the transcontexual gifts that emerged in the design studio space. And yet to ignore the distress and the refusals that were also produced would be to misunderstand as much as we had learnt. The refusals produced through the project prompt important questions about the possibilities and limits of ethnography in the era of resurgence and reconciliation.

Stubbornly Entangled

Perhaps it is only serendipitous that Bateson was interested in tangles while Barad is interested in entanglement. Transcontextual tangles and entangled translations – these are two different ways to describe the double bind of the young Raising Spirit researchers. The doubling began with positioning them as translators between different cultures, different ways of knowing, based on an assumption that they were already experts on Blackfoot culture. Repeatedly, their work interviewing Elders, coding photographs. and debriefing after field trips required the kind of doubling through translation described by Susan Gal (2015). The translational encounters they experience during the project required a doubled voice, both "foreign and domestic," as they were asked to "take on a different voice and role than they would with coexperts" (233). Yet they weren't entirely comfortable with the idea of being an expert at all, and like other young people involved in the project, sometimes they refused.[4]

Doubling was a thread across the arc of the project that traces the continuing desire for the ethnographic recognition of cultural expertise. Such recognition was at the root of the methods we began with, from photo-elicitation with participant-caregivers to the framing of the young researchers as para-ethnographers to their work as participant-researchers in summer camps. They were asked to help the settler researchers understand everything from how to offer tobacco to how to dress for the Sundance. But they were not just meant to be cultural experts; they were also meant to provide the voices of the young to the project. The assumption that the young will provide perspectives "other" than adult ones is central to child and youth studies (Cooper 2022). Davies (1982) identifies this in relation to schooling particularly. Children, upon entering school, inhabit a double world: one of children and one of adults. In response to the strangeness they encounter, they create their own rules, which are the basis of a separate *culture*. Alison Clark (2011) describes young people's work as cultural brokers in multiple language communities. Other child and youth scholars attend to the questions of how the voices of the young are translated and understood, whether in research or otherwise (Lundy and McEvoy 2011; Kellett 2010; Spyrou 2011). This double voicing by the young is not conventionally described as double consciousness, but the relevance of that connection was clear in the Raising Spirit Project. The research encounters depended on doubled consciousness and on an awareness of their position in two worlds, one dominating and one dominated. This was only compounded through age-related forms of difference.

Forms of doubled consciousness are central to the space between worlds (Fanon 1967; Du Bois 1965; Bhabha 1994) along with their pain and possibility. We had hoped to produce a third space as one of ethical engagement, but in fact, we were requiring and depending on the doubling of the young researchers. These moments were surfaced in a collaborative space created to engender design thinking and co-conceptualization as the kind of transition work in ethnography that many have been calling for (Tsing 2015; Escobar 2017; Rabinow et al. 2008; Doucet 2018). Despite the hopes for the emergence of a diplomatic relationality in such spaces that moves beyond any colonized binary, it was a space refused by some.

Amy and I have described the refusals we encountered elsewhere (Mack and Newberry 2020). Rather than rehearse the full argument here, I expand on our initial insights to identify the power of both the pain and possibility evident most potently in how the photographs changed our methods. At the time we wrote together about the refusals we saw during the project, we were responding to a rise in interest in this topic (Ortner 1995; A. Simpson 2016, 2017; McGranahan 2016a, 2016b; Tuck and Yang 2014a, 2014b), particularly in relation to ethnographic work. We too wondered what could be learnt at the point of refusal (A. Simpson 2016). Could refusal be generative? Can it mean more than just a "no," but instead become a starting place for "other qualitative analyses and interpretations of data" (Tuck and Yang 2014b, 812)?

Dilemmas in how to code the photographs in the Raising Spirit Project led to methodological changes that ultimately produced a reconceptualization of what the photographs could do. This changed the work from translation and interpretation of Blackfoot values represented in the photographs to collaborations through the photographs as agentive objects that gathered people in relations. The photographs were entangled not only with all the people asked to contemplate them, but also with the effects of histories of representation and ethnographic recognition for Indigenous Peoples in North America. Returning to Andrea Doucet's (2018) work on family photographs, she advocates attending "to images as a set of practices whose content and meaning are in turn made within practices, including the specific research practices wherein the photos are viewed and discussed" (739). Our ethnographic experimentation with collaborative design surfaced the role of these photographs in producing forms of relationality that were not limited to colonial forms but offered the possibility of other futures imagined and practised together.

What this book has centrally concerned is ethnography, the forms of expertise it implies and demands, the patchy forms of knowledge upon which it depends, its need for a decolonizing fix, and its openness to experimentation as one way to "refunction" it (Holmes and Marcus 2008; Rabinow et al. 2008). Reconsidering the central method of anthropology is not just a methodological question but a political and ethical one, perhaps especially in a time of Indigenous resurgence and racial reckoning. Drawing on Lorraine Code (2006), as Doucet (2018) does on work between settler and Indigenous researchers in Canada, it is when we move beyond questions of representation that we can ask instead "whether a knowledge-making practice leads to just and cohabitable worlds" (Doucet 2018, 749).

It is here that the refusal of the double bind becomes hopeful, a source of poetry rather than schizophrenia. Refusal redistributes. The young Indigenous researchers walked away from this project in significant ways: because they needed to finish school, start families, and find jobs, but mostly importantly, because this medium doesn't interest them, nor necessarily support the forms of knowledge they care about as work on the Raising Spirit Project showed. Even so, the photos remain, and they circulate through their use by Opokaa'sin, but not in my world. In fact, the effects of the project are in many ways quite opaque to me. They continue to circulate and redistribute the potential for knowledge production about values, but the work of the photographs now takes place outside the frame of ethnographic recognition. That is the generative power of refusal.

NOTES

1 In fact, this project with Tanya has led to two further projects, both centrally concerned with question of economic empowerment among Blackfoot women.

2 I retained a hard drive with the information collected as a backup. The only other material that I kept was the brown paper as a record of the design studio process and the working notes on them.
3 The three agencies referred to here that guide research in Canada are the Social Sciences and Humanities Research Council, the Canadian Institutes of Health, and the Natural Sciences and Engineering Council.
4 This discussion draws heavily on Mack and Newberry (2020).

After Raising Spirit

It is entirely fitting that my return to write an epilogue about the Raising Spirit Project has led to more refusals. To update readers on what has happened with the contributors and collaborators since the project in September 2017, I reached out to each of them to ask them to contribute some words describing where they are now and the effects of project on them. Not surprisingly, those who remained in university settings responded with achievements and descriptions of what the project meant for them. For those whose lives took them elsewhere, there was agreement – "yes, yes, of course, help out" – and then … nothing. It's reassuring in a way to have my argument that books like this have limited value in their lives borne out so completely. Seeking to extract updates from them now is not in keeping with the central teaching of this project. Still, for the readers who might want to know what happened next, I can offer some updates.

Amy Mack is now Dr. Amy Mack. She completed a PhD in anthropology at the University of Alberta on the resurgence of far-right extremism in Canada and on social media. Completing a postdoctoral fellowship at the Center for Research on Extremism at the University of Oslo at the time of this writing, she writes that "the lessons I learned from Raising Spirit – about connection to land, responsibility to kin, and community-based research – informs how I do my current work on rural radicalization in southern Alberta." Amy has developed an impressive international network, even as she remains committed to community-engaged research in her new role as a Canada Research Chair, Tier I, at the University of Lethbridge.

Dr. Erin Spring is a new Associate Dean of Undergraduate Education at the Werklund School of Education, University of Calgary. She sees her time as a postdoctoral fellow at the Institute for Child and Youth Studies and her involvement in Raising Spirit as having profoundly reshaped her trajectory as a scholar. It's worth quoting her description at length here:

> While I still love the traditional parts of my job – the writing, the reading, the research – it is no longer enough for me to sit alone in my office with the door closed. I need to do my work with people alongside me. When working on the Raising Spirit project, I shared an office with colleagues at different stages of their careers: professors, graduate and undergraduate students, and young people still in high school. We came together as aspiring allies and faced big problems together. We made mistakes. We shared moments and experiences of profound joy. None of us were experts at everything, but we brought our own stories and versions of expertise to the lair's table, or out on the land, and were put in conversation with one another. I continue to carry these conversations with me everywhere I go.

Tanya Pace Crosschild is currently on a temporary leave from Opokaa'sin to work with Kainai Children Services on their response to the devolution from the federal government of foster care and other services for Blackfoot children. Her commitment to young people remains central, and as with her work at Opokaa'sin, her wisdom, her strength of purpose, and the clarity of her vision are inspiring and deeply influential. She models leadership for many of us through her sustained practice of relationality and community engagement.

Mikey Lewis has begun a graduate program in child and youth studies at Brock University, after graduating with honours from the University of Lethbridge. They describe the Raising Spirit Project as deeply impactful for them both as a researcher and as a person. "It informed my politics, exposed me to arts-based methodologies and youth-centred research, and taught me what it means to lean into discomfort as a place of potential growth."

Taylor Little Mustache went on to complete her teaching degree and to return for her master's in educational leadership at the Faculty of Education at the University of Lethbridge, following her sister and mother to the "big school." She has taught on both the Piikani and Kainai Reserves, even as she has taken on the care of her nephews following her sister's death.

Tesla Heavy Runner has become a mother to young Arthur. Although she has returned to work occasionally for Opokaa'sin, her commitment now is to her young family.

Hudson Eagle Bear has suffered traumatic losses of family members and has spent time searching for his place in the world. Still, he remains committed to learning and living Blackfoot values. I am always heartened by his Facebook "hello, it's a good day" to friends and families.

And the library? According to Tanya, "Opokaa'sin is still using the library and it has taken on a life of its own! We are still adding to it and extracting Blackfoot value lessons for our children!"

As I contemplated how hard I should push for updates from my former research team and from Opokaa'sin, I remembered again that this book is meant to help people understand the possibilities and limitations of ethnography in a world that requires much more truth and much more work towards reconciliation. I do not mistake it for describing what is meaningful for Blackfoot Peoples. That is for them to do. We will all be the better for it.

Bibliography

Abebe, Tatek, Anandini Dar, and Ida M. Lyså. 2022. "Southern Theories and Decolonial Childhood Studies." *Childhood* 29, no. 3 (August): 255–75. https://doi.org/10.1177/09075682221111690.

Abma, Tineke, Marieke Breed, Sarah Lips, and Janine Schrijver. 2022. "Whose Voice Is It Really? Ethics of Photovoice with Children in Health Promotion." *International Journal of Qualitative Methods* 21 (January): 1–10. https://doi.org/10.1177/16094069211072419.

Adriany, Vina, and Jan Newberry. 2022. "Neuroscience and the Construction of a New Child in Early Childhood Education in Indonesia: A Neoliberal Legacy." *Current Sociology* 70, no. 4 (July): 475–643. https://doi.org/10.1177/0011392120985875.

Adriany, Vina, and Kurniawan Saefullah. 2015. "Deconstructing Human Capital Discourse in Early Childhood Education in Indonesia." In *Global Perspectives on Human Capital in Early Childhood Education: Reconceptualizing Theory, Policy, and Practice*, edited by Theodora Lightfoot-Rueda and Ruth Peach, 159–79. Palgrave Macmillan. https://doi.org/10.1057/9781137490865_9.

Agrawal, Arun. 1995. "Dismantling the Divide Between Indigenous and Scientific Knowledge." *Development and Change* 26, no. 3 (July): 413–39. https://doi.org/10.1111/j.1467-7660.1995.tb00560.x.

– 2009. "Why 'Indigenous' Knowledge?" *Journal of the Royal Society of New Zealand* 39, no. 4 (December): 157–8. https://doi.org/10.1080/03014220909510569.

Ahenakew, Cash. 2016. "Grafting Indigenous Ways of Knowing onto Non-Indigenous Ways of Being: The (Underestimated) Challenges of a Decolonial Imagination." *International Review of Qualitative Research* 9, no. 3 (November): 323–40. https://doi.org/10.1525/irqr.2016.9.3.323.

Ahmed, Sara. 2017. *Living a Feminist Life*. Duke University Press Books.

Akama, Yoko, Sarah Pink, and Shanti Sumartojo. 2018. *Uncertainty and Possibility: New Approaches to Future Making in Design Anthropology*. Routledge. https://doi.org/10.4324/9781003087274.

Alderson, Priscilla. 2001. "Research by Children: Rights and Methods." *International Journal of Social Research Methodology: Theory and Practice* 4 (2): 139–53. https://doi.org/10.1080/13645570120003.

Alexander, Kristine, Ashley Henrickson, Amy Mack, et al. 2018. "Translating Encounters: Connecting Indigenous Young People with Higher Education through a Transmedia Project." *Journal of Community Engagement and Higher Education* 10 (1): 61–71.

Alfred, Taiaiake. 2015. "Cultural Strength: Restoring the Place of Indigenous Knowledge in Practice and Policy." *Australian Aboriginal Studies*, no. 1, 3–11.

Alloula, Malek. 1986. *The Colonial Harem*. Translated by Myrna Godzich and Wlad Godzich. Manchester University Press. https://doi.org/10.5749/j.ctttth83.

Alonso Bejarano, Carolina, Lucia López Juárez, Mirian A. Mijangos García, and Daniel M. Goldstein. 2019. *Decolonizing Ethnography: Undocumented Immigrants and New Directions in Social Science*. Duke University Press. https://doi.org/10.1215/9781478004547.

Andersen, Chris. 2009. "Critical Indigenous Studies: From Difference to Density." *Cultural Studies Review* 15, no. 2 (September): 80–100. https://doi.org/10.5130/csr.v15i2.2039.

Anker, Kirsten. 2017. "Reconciliation in Translation: Indigenous Legal Traditions and Canada's Truth and Reconciliation Commission." *Windsor Yearbook of Access to Justice* 33 (2): 15–43. https://doi.org/10.22329/wyaj.v33i2.4842.

Ardener, Shirley. 2005. "Ardener's 'Muted Groups': The Genesis of an Idea and Its Praxis." *Women and Language* 28, no. 2 (Fall): 50–4.

Asad, Talal, ed. 1973. *Anthropology & the Colonial Encounter*. Humanities Press.

Astuti, Rita. 2017. "On Keeping up the Tension between Fieldwork and Ethnography." *HAU: Journal of Ethnographic Theory* 7, no. 1 (Spring): 9–14. https://doi.org/10.14318/hau7.1.003.

Awosoga, Olu, Jeff Meadows, and Jan Newberry. 2020. "Trying Team-Based Learning in Two Classrooms." *Transformative Dialogues: Teaching and Learning Journal* 13, no. 1 (Summer): 34–52.

Ballestero, Andrea, and Brit Ross Winthereik, eds. 2021. *Experimenting with Ethnography: A Companion to Analysis*. Duke University Press. https://doi.org/10.1515/9781478091691.

Barad, Karen. 1998. "Getting Real: Technoscientific Practices and the Materialization of Reality." *Differences: A Journal of Feminist Cultural Studies* 10 (2): 87–128. https://doi.org/10.1215/10407391-10-2-87.

– 2007. *Meeting the Universe Halfway: Quantum Physics and the Entanglement of Matter and Meaning*. Duke University Press. https://doi.org/10.1215/9780822388128.

Barcham, Manuhuia. 2021. “Towards a Radically Inclusive Design – Indigenous Story-Telling as Codesign Methodology.” *CoDesign* 19, no. 1 (March): 1–13. https://doi.org/10.1080/15710882.2021.1982989.

Bartlett, Cheryl, Murdena Marshall, and Albert Marshall. 2012. “Two-Eyed Seeing and Other Lessons Learned within a Co-Learning Journey of Bringing Together Indigenous and Mainstream Knowledges and Ways of Knowing.” *Journal of Environmental Studies and Sciences* 2, no. 4 (August): 331–40. https://doi.org/10.1007/s13412-012-0086-8.

Bartmes, Natalie, and Shailesh Shukla. 2020. “Re-Envisioning Land-Based Pedagogies as a Transformative Third Space: Perspectives from University Academics, Students, and Indigenous Knowledge Holders from Manitoba, Canada.” *Diaspora, Indigenous, and Minority Education* 14, no. 3 (July–September): 146–61. https://doi.org/10.1080/15595692.2020.1719062.

Bastien, Betty. 2004. *Blackfoot Ways of Knowing: The Worldview of the Siksikaitsitapi*. Edited by Jurgen W. Kremer and Betty Bastien. Cagary: University of Calgary Press. https://library.oapen.org/bitstream/20.500.12657/57435/1/9781552387450.pdf.

Bateson, Gregory. 1972. *Steps to an Ecology of Mind: Collected Essays in Anthropology, Psychiatry, Evolution, and Epistemology*. Jason Aronson. First Published 1972 by Chandler Publishing Company.

Bateson, Gregory, Don Jackson, Jay Haley, and John Weakland. 1956. “Towards a Theory of Schizophrenia.” *Behavioral Science* 1 (4): 251–64. https://doi.org/10.1002/bs.3830010402.

Bateson, Gregory, and Margaret Mead. 1942. *Balinese Character: A Photographic Analysis*. New York Academy of Sciences.

Battiste, Marie. 2005. “Indigenous Knowledge: Foundations for First Nations.” *WINHEC: International Journal of Indigenous Education Scholarship*, no. 1 (January): 1–7. https://journals.uvic.ca/index.php/winhec/article/view/19251.

Bear Chief, Roy, Peter Choate, and Gabrielle Lindstrom. 2022. “Reconsidering Maslow and the Hierarchy of Needs from a First Nations’ Perspective.” *Aotearoa New Zealand Social Work* 34 (2): 30–41. https://doi.org/10.11157/anzswj-vol34iss2id959.

Becke, Sophia Daphne, Stephan Bongard, and Heidi Keller. 2019. “Attachment as a Collective Resource: Attachment Networks During Middle Childhood in a Cameroonian Clan.” *Journal of Cross-Cultural Psychology* 50, no. 2 (February): 200–19. https://doi.org/10.1177/0022022118814686.

Behar, Ruth. 1996. *The Vulnerable Observer: Anthropology That Breaks Your Heart*. Beacon Press.

Behar, Ruth, and Deborah Gordon, eds. 1995. *Women Writing Culture*. University of California Press. https://doi.org/10.1525/9780520916814.

Bhabha, Homi K. 1994. *The Location of Culture*. Routledge.

Bignante, Elisa. 2010. "The Use of Photo-Elicitation in Field Research: Exploring Maasai Representations and Use of Natural Resources." *EchoGéo*, no. 11 (November). https://doi.org/10.4000/echogeo.11622.

Bluebond-Langner, Myra, and Jill Korbin. 2007. "Challenges and Opportunities in the Anthropology of Childhoods: An Introduction to 'Children, Childhoods, and Childhood Studies.'" *American Anthropologist* 109, no. 2 (June): 241–6. https://doi.org/10.1525/aa.2007.109.2.241.

Boyer, Dominic. 2008. "Thinking through the Anthropology of Experts." *Anthropology in Action* 15, no. 2 (June): 38–46. https://doi.org/10.3167/aia.2008.150204.

Brendtro, Larry, Martin Brokenleg, and Steve Van Bockern. 1990. *Reclaiming Youth at Risk: Our Hope for the Future*. 1st ed. Solution Tree Press. https://doi.org/10.1007/BF00757202.

Brendtro, Larry, Martin Brokenleg, Steve Van Bockern, and George Blue Bird. 1991. "The Circle of Courage." *Beyond Behavior* 2, no. 2 (Winter): 5–12. https://www.jstor.org/stable/44707005.

Briggs, Charles, and Richard Bauman. 1999. "'The Foundation of All Future Researches': Franz Boas, George Hunt, Native American Texts, and the Construction of Modernity." *American Quarterly* 51, no. 3 (September): 479–528. https://www.jstor.org/stable/30042181.

Brown, Allison K. 2016. "Co-Authoring Relationships: Blackfoot Collections, UK Museums, and Collaborative Practice." *Collaborative Anthropologies* 9, no. 1–2 (Fall–Spring): 117–48. https://doi.org/10.1353/cla.2016.0013.

Brown, Allison K., and Laura Peers. 2006. *Pictures Bring Us Messages: Sinaakssiiksi Aohtsimaahpihkookiyaawa: Photographs and Histories from the Kainai Nation*. Toronto: University of Toronto Press. https://doi.org/10.3138/9781442627239.

Brown, Shae L., Lisa Siegel, and Simone M. Blom. 2020. "Entanglements of Matter and Meaning: The Importance of the Philosophy of Karen Barad for Environmental Education." *Australian Journal of Environmental Education* 36, no. 3 (November): 219–33. https://doi.org/10.1017/aee.2019.29.

Buckley, Liam. 2014. "Photography and Photo-Elicitation after Colonialism." *Cultural Anthropology* 29, no. 4 (November): 720–43. https://doi.org/10.14506/ca29.4.07.

Burman, Erica. 2007. *Developments: Child, Image, Nation*. 1st ed. Routledge.

Burow, Paul Berne, Samara Brock, and Michael R. Dove. 2018. "Unsettling the Land: Indigeneity, Ontology, and Hybridity in Settler Colonialism." *Environment and Society* 9, no. 1 (September): 57–74. https://doi.org/10.3167/ares.2018.090105.

Butler, Judith. 2015. *Notes Toward a Performative Theory of Assembly*. Harvard University Press. https://doi.org/10.4159/9780674495548.

Byrd, Jodi, Eve Tuck, Maya Caspari, Ruth Daly, and Rebecca Macklin. 2024. "'On Being Committed to Indigenous Feminist Interventions': Jodi Byrd and Eve Tuck in Conversation." *Parallax* 29, no. 2 (April): 229–47. https://doi.org/10.1080/13534645.2023.2271735.

Cahill, Caitlin. 2007. "Doing Research *with* Young People: Participatory Research and the Rituals of Collective Work." *Children's Geographies* 5 (3): 297–312. https://doi.org/10.1080/14733280701445895.

Carr, Summerson. 2010. "Enactments of Expertise." *Annual Review of Anthropology* 39: 17–32. https://www.jstor.org/stable/25735097.

Castleden, Heather, Theresa Garvin, and Huu-ay-aht First Nation. 2008. "Modifying Photovoice for Community-Based Participatory Indigenous Research." *Social Science & Medicine* 66, no. 6 (March): 1393–405. https://doi.org/10.1016/j.socscimed.2007.11.030.

Cattelino, Jessica R., and Audra Simpson. 2022. "Rethinking Indigeneity: Scholarship at the Intersection of Native American Studies and Anthropology." *Annual Review of Anthropology* 51 (October): 365–81. https://doi.org/10.1146/annurev-anthro-101819-110339.

Chambers, Cynthia M., and Narcisse J. Blood. 2009. "Love Thy Neighbour: Repatriating Precarious Blackfoot Sites." *International Journal of Canadian Studies*, no. 39–40: 253–79. https://doi.org/10.7202/040832ar.

Chaney, Anthony. 2017. *Runaway: Gregory Bateson, the Double Bind, and the Rise of Ecological Consciousness*. The University of North Carolina Press. https://doi.org/10.5149/northcarolina/9781469631738.001.0001.

Chapman, Owen, and Kim Sawchuk. 2012. "Research-Creation: Intervention, Analysis and 'Family Resemblances.'" *Canadian Journal of Communication* 37, no. 1 (April): 5–26. https://doi.org/10.22230/cjc.2012v37n1a2489.

Cheney, Kristen E. 2011. "Children as Ethnographers: Reflections on the Importance of Participatory Research in Assessing Orphans' Needs." *Childhood* 18 (2): 166–79. https://doi.org/10.1177/0907568210390054.

– 2018. "Decolonizing Childhood Studies: Overcoming Patriarchy and Prejudice in Child-Related Research and Practice." In *Reimagining Childhood Studies*, edited by Spyros Spyrou, Rachel Rosen, and Daniel Thomas Cook, 91–104. Bloomsbury Publishing Academic.

Chin, Elizabeth. 2017. "On Multimodal Anthropologies from the Space of Design: Toward Participant Making." *American Anthropologist* 119, no. 3 (September): 541–6. https://doi.org/10.1111/aman.12908.

Choy, Timothy K. 2005. "Articulated Knowledges: Environmental Forms after Universality's Demise." *American Anthropologist* 107, no. 1 (March): 5–18. https://doi.org/10.1525/aa.2005.107.1.005.

Christensen, Pia Haudrup. 2004. "Children's Participation in Ethnographic Research: Issues of Power and Representation." *Children and Society* 18, no. 2 (April): 165–76. https://doi.org/10.1002/chi.823.

Cisneros, Nora Alba. 2018. "'To My Relations': Writing and Refusal toward an Indigenous Epistolary Methodology." *International Journal of Qualitative Studies in Education* 31, (3): 188–96. https://doi.org/10.1080/09518398.2017.1401147.

Clark, Alison. 2011. "Multimodal Map Making with Young Children: Exploring Ethnographic and Participatory Methods." *Qualitative Research* 11, no. 3 (June): 311–30. https://doi.org/10.1177/1468794111400532.

Clark, Cindy Dell. 1999. "The Autodriven Interview: A Photographic Viewfinder into Children's Experience." *Visual Sociology* 14 (1): 39–50. https://doi.org/10.1080/14725869908583801.

Clifford, James. 1983. "On Ethnographic Authority." *Representations* 2:118–46. https://doi.org/10.2307/2928386.

– 1997. *Routes: Travel and Translation in the Late Twentieth Century.* Harvard University Press.

– 2011. "Response to Orin Starn: 'Here Come the Anthros (Again): The Strange Marriage of Anthropology and Native America.'" *Cultural Anthropology* 26, no. 2 (May): 218–24. https://doi.org/10.1111/j.1548-1360.2011.01096.x.

Clifford, James, and George E. Marcus. 1986. *Writing Culture: The Poetics and Politics of Ethnography.* University of California Press.

Code, Lorraine. 2006. *Ecological Thinking: The Politics of Epistemic Location.* Oxford University Press. https://doi.org/10.1093/0195159438.001.0001.

Coghlan, David, and Mary Brydon-Miller, eds. 2014. *The SAGE Encyclopedia of Action Research.* 1st ed. SAGE. https://doi.org/10.4135/9781446294406.

Collier, John. 1957. "Photography in Anthropology: A Report on Two Experiments." *American Anthropologist* 59, no. 5: 843–59. https://doi.org/10.1525/aa.1957.59.5.02a00100.

Collins, Samuel Gerald, Matthew Durington, and Harjant Gill. 2017. "Multimodality: An Invitation." *American Anthropologist* 119, no. 1 (March): 142–53. https://doi.org/10.1111/aman.12826.

Cook-Sather, Alison. 2007. "Resisting the Impositional Potential of Student Voice Work: Lessons for Liberatory Educational Research from Poststructuralist Feminist Critiques of Critical Pedagogy." *Discourse: Studies in the Cultural Politics of Education* 28, no. 3 (September): 389–403. https://doi.org/10.1080/01596300701458962.

Cooke, Bill, and Uma Kothari, eds. 2001. *Participation: The New Tyranny?* Zed Books. https://go.exlibris.link/ZNfv1Sf2.

Cooper, Victoria. 2017. "Lost in Translation: Exploring Childhood Identity Using Photo-Elicitation." *Children's Geographies* 15, no. 6 (December): 625–37. https://doi.org/10.1080/14733285.2017.1284306.

– 2022. "Child Focused Research: Disconnected and Disembodied Voices." *Childhood* 30, no. 1 (February): 71–85. https://doi.org/10.1177/09075682221132084.

Coppock, Vicki. 2011. "Children as Peer Researchers: Reflections on a Journey of Mutual Discovery." *Children and Society* 25, no. 6 (November): 435–46. https://doi.org/10.1111/j.1099-0860.2010.00296.x.

Corntassel, Jeff, and Tiffanie Hardbarger. 2019. "Educate to Perpetuate: Land-Based Pedagogies and Community Resurgence." *International Review of Education* 65, no. 1 (February): 87–116. https://doi.org/10.1007/s11159-018-9759-1.

Coulthard, Glen Sean. 2014. *Red Skin, White Masks: Rejecting the Colonial Politics of Recognition*. University of Minnesota Press. https://www.jstor.org/stable/10.5749/j.ctt9qh3cv.

Coulthard, Glen Sean, and Leanne Betasamosake Simpson. 2016. "Grounded Normativity/Place-Based Solidarity." *American Quarterly* 68, no. 2 (June): 249–55. https://doi.org/10.1353/aq.2016.0038.

Crabtree, Andy. 2004. "Taking Technomethodology Seriously: Hybrid Change in the Ethnomethodology–Design Relationship." *European Journal of Information Systems* 13, no. 3 (September): 195–209. https://doi.org/10.1057/palgrave.ejis.3000500.

Crane, Todd A. 2014. "Bringing Science and Technology Studies into Agricultural Anthropology: Technology Development as Cultural Encounter between Farmers and Researchers." *Culture, Agriculture, Food and Environment* 36, no. 1 (June): 45–55. https://doi.org/10.1111/cuag.12028.

Crenshaw, Kimberlé. 2017. *On Intersectionality: Essential Writings*. New Press.

Crowshoe, Reg, and Sybille Manneschmidt. 2002. *Akak'stiman: A Blackfoot Framework for Decision-Making and Mediation Processes*. University of Calgary Press. https://doi.org/10.1515/9781552382776.

Cullen, Declan, and Heather Castleden. 2022. "Two-Eyed-Seeing/Etuaptmumk in the Colonial Archive: Reflections on Participatory Archival Research." *Area* 55, no. 3 (September): 340–47. https://doi.org/10.1111/area.12786.

Daelman, Silke, Elisabeth De Schauwer, and Geert Van Hove. 2020. "Becoming-with Research Participants: Possibilities in Qualitative Research with Children." *Childhood* 27 (4): 483–97. https://doi.org/10.1177/0907568220927767.

Dan-Cohen, Talia. 2019. "Writing Thin." *Anthropological Quarterly* 92, no. 3 (Summer): 903–17. https://doi.org/10.1353/anq.2019.0042.

Dattatreyan, Ethiraj Gabriel, and Isaac Marrero-Guillamón. 2019. "Introduction: Multimodal Anthropology and the Politics of Invention." *American Anthropologist* 121, no. 1 (March): 220–8. https://doi.org/10.1111/aman.13183.

Davies, Bronwyn. 1982. *Life in the Classroom and Playground: The Accounts of Primary School Children*. Routledge Library Editions: Sociology of Education.

de la Bellacasa, María Puig. 2012. "'Nothing Comes Without Its World': Thinking with Care." *The Sociological Review* 60, no. 2 (May): 197–216. https://doi.org/10.1111/j.1467-954X.2012.02070.x.

de la Cadena, Marisol, and Mario Blaser, eds. 2018. *A World of Many Worlds*. Duke University Press. https://doi.org/10.1515/9781478004318.

de la Cadena, Marisol, Marianne E. Lien, Mario Blaser, et al. 2015. "Anthropology and STS: Generative Interfaces, Multiple Locations." Edited by Marisol de la Cadena and Marianne E. Lien. *HAU: Journal of Ethnographic Theory* 5, no. 1 (Spring): 437–75. https://doi.org/10.14318/hau5.1.020.

Deloria, Phillip Joseph. 1994. "Playing Indian: Otherness and Authenticity in the Assumption of American Indian Identity." PhD diss., Yale University.

Deloria, Vine Jr. 1969. *Custer Died for Your Sins: An Indian Manifesto*. University of Oklahoma Press.

Dempsey, Hugh A. 2019. "Blackfoot Nation." In *The Canadian Encyclopedia*. Historica Canada. http://www.thecanadianencyclopedia.ca/.

Dewantara, Ki Hadjar. 1967. "Some Aspects of National Education and the Taman Siswa Institute at Jogjakarta." *Indonesia*, no. 4, 150–68. https://doi.org/10.2307/3350909.

Dhillon, Jaskiran. 2017. *Prairie Rising: Indigenous Youth, Decolonization, and the Politics of Intervention*. University of Toronto Press.

Dicks, Bella, Bambo Soyinka, and Amanda Coffey. 2006. "Multimodal Ethnography." *Qualitative Research* 6 (1): 77–96. https://doi.org/10.1177/1468794106058876.

Donald, Dwayne Trevor. 2009a. "The Curricular Problem of Indigenousness: Colonial Frontier Logics, Teacher Resistances, and The Acknowledgment of Ethical Space." In *Beyond "Presentism,"* 23–41. Leiden: Brill. https://doi.org/10.1163/9789460910012_004.

– 2009b. "Forts, Curriculum, and Indigenous Métissage: Imagining Decolonization of Aboriginal-Canadian Relations in Educational Contexts." *First Nations Perspectives* 2, no. 1: 1–24.

Dorrow, Sara, and Amy Swiffen. 2009. "Blood and Desire: The Secret of Heteronormativity in Adoption Narratives of Culture." *American Ethnologist* 36, no. 3 (August): 563–73. https://www.jstor.org/stable/40389809.

Doucet, Andrea. 2018. "Decolonizing Family Photographs: Ecological Imaginaries and Nonrepresentational Ethnographies." *Journal of Contemporary Ethnography* 47, no. 6 (December): 729–57. https://doi.org/10.1177/0891241617744859.

Du Bois, W.E.B. 1965. *The World and Africa: An Inquiry into the Part Which Africa Has Played in World History*. International Publishers.

Durrani, Mariam. 2019. "Upsetting the Canon." *Anthropology News* 60, no. 2 (March/April): e48–52. https://doi.org/10.1111/AN.1134.

Edelman, Lee. 2004. *No Future: Queer Theory and the Death Drive*. Duke University Press. https://doi.org/10.1215/9780822385981.

Edwards, Elizabeth. 2008. "Photographs and the Sound of History." *Visual Anthropology Review* 21, no. 1–2 (March): 27–46. https://doi.org/10.1525/var.2005.21.1-2.27.

– 2012. "Objects of Affect: Photography Beyond the Image." *Annual Review of Anthropology* 41:221–34. http://www.jstor.org/stable/23270708.

Ellen, Roy. 2004. "From Ethno-Science to Science, or 'What the Indigenous Knowledge Debate Tells Us About How Scientists Define Their Project.'" *Journal of Cognition and Culture* 4 (3–4): 409–50. https://doi.org/10.1163/1568537042484869.

Elyachar, Julia. 2010. "Phatic Labor, Infrastructure, and the Question of Empowerment in Cairo." *American Ethnologist* 37, no. 3 (August): 452–64. https://www.jstor.org/stable/40784608.

Ermine, Willie. 2007. "The Ethical Space of Engagement." *Indigenous Law Journal* 6 (1): 193–204. https://ilj.law.utoronto.ca/sites/ilj.law.utoronto.ca/files/media/ilj-6.1-ermine.pdf.

Escobar, Arturo. 2008. *Territories of Difference: Place, Movements, Life, Redes*. Duke University Press. https://doi.org/10.1215/9780822389439.

– 2017. *Designs for the Pluriverse*. Duke University Press.

Evans-Agnew, Robin A., and Marie-Anne S. Rosemberg. 2016. "Questioning Photovoice Research: Whose Voice?" *Qualitative Health Research* 26, no. 8 (July): 1019–30. https://doi.org/10.1177/1049732315624223.

Faier, Lieba, and Lisa Rofel. 2014. "Ethnographies of Encounter." *Annual Review of Anthropology* 43:363–77. https://www.jstor.org/stable/43049580.

Fanon, Frantz. 1967. *Black Skin, White Masks*. Translated by C.L. Markmann. Reprint, Grove Press.

Ferzacca, Steve. 2001. *Healing the Modern in a Central Javanese City*. Carolina Academic Press.

Field, Les W. 1999. "Complicities and Collaborations: Anthropologists and the 'Unacknowledged Tribes' of California." *Current Anthropology* 40, no. 2 (April): 193–210. https://doi.org/10.1086/200004.

Fisher, Caitlin. 2015. "Mentoring Research-Creation: Secrets, Strategies, and Beautiful Failures." *RACAR: Revue d'art Canadienne Canadian Art Review* 40, no. 1 (August): 1–110. https://id.erudit.org/iderudit/1032752ar.

Fleur-Lobhan, Carolyn. 2008. "Collaborative Anthropology as Twenty-First-Century Ethical Anthropology." *Collaborative Anthropologies* 1:175–82. https://doi.org/10.1353/cla.0.0000.

Fortun, Kim. 2001. *Advocacy after Bhopal: Environmentalism, Disaster, New Global Orders*. University of Chicago Press. https://doi.org/10.7208/chicago/9780226257181.001.0001.

– 2005. "Scientific Imaginaries and Ethical Plateaus in Contemporary U.S. Toxicology." *American Anthropologist* 107, no. 1 (March): 43–54. https://doi.org/10.1525/aa.2005.107.1.043.

Fortun, Kim, and Todd Cherkasky. 1998. "Counter-Expertise and the Politics of Collaboration." *Science as Culture* 7 (2): 145–72. https://doi.org/10.1080/09505439809526499.

Fox, Richard Gabriel. 1991. *Recapturing Anthropology: Working in the Present*. School of American Research Press.

Frake, Charles O. 1961. "The Diagnosis of Disease among the Subanun of Mindanao." *American Anthropologist* 63, no. 1 (February): 113–32. https://doi.org/10.1525/aa.1961.63.1.02a00070.

Fraser, Nancy. 2007. "Special Section: Transnational Public Sphere: Transnationalizing the Public Sphere: On the Legitimacy and Efficacy of Public Opinion in a Post-Westphalian World." *Theory, Culture & Society* 24 (4): 7–30. https://doi.org/10.1177/0263276407080090.

Gal, Susan. 2015. "Politics of Translation." *Annual Review of Anthropology* 44 (October): 225–40. https://doi.org/10.1146/annurev-anthro-102214-013806.

Garfinkel, Harold. 2023. "Studies in Ethnomethodology." In *Social Theory Re-Wired: New Connections to Classical and Contemporary Perspectives*, edited by Wesley Longhofer and Daniel Winchester, 58–66. Routledge. https://doi.org/10.4324/9781003320609-8.

Gaudry, Adam, and Danielle Lorenz. 2018. "Indigenization as Inclusion, Reconciliation, and Decolonization: Navigating the Different Visions for Indigenizing the Canadian Academy." *AlterNative: An International Journal of Indigenous Peoples* 14, no. 3 (September): 218–27. https://doi.org/10.1177/1177180118785382.

Geertz, Clifford. 1983. *Local Knowledge: Further Essays in Interpretive Anthropology*. New York: Basic Books.

– 1996. *After the Fact: Two Countries, Four Decades, One Anthropologist*. Harvard University Press.

Gell, Alfred. 1998. *Art and Agency: An Anthropological Theory*. Clarendon Press. https://doi.org/10.1093/oso/9780198280132.001.0001.

Glass, Aaron. 2009. "A Cannibal in the Archive: Performance, Materiality, and (In)Visibility in Unpublished Edward Curtis Photographs of the Kwakwaka'wakw Hamat'sa." *Visual Anthropology Review* 25, no. 2 (Fall): 128–49. https://doi.org/10.1111/j.1548-7458.2009.01038.x.

Gough, Kathleen. 1993. "'Anthropology and Imperialism' Revisited." *Anthropologica* 35 (2): 278–89. https://doi.org/10.2307/25605745.

Graveline, Fyre Jean. 2000. "Circle as Methodology: Enacting an Aboriginal Paradigm." *International Journal of Qualitative Studies in Education* 13, no. 4 (November): 361–70. https://doi.org/10.1080/095183900413304.

Green, Sarah. 2014. "Anthropological Knots: Conditions of Possibilities and Interventions." *HUA: Journal of Ethnographic Theory* 4, no. 3 (Winter): 1–21. https://doi.org/10.14318/hau4.3.002.

Grosz, Elizabeth. 2004. *The Nick of Time: Politics, Evolution, and the Untimely.* Duke University Press. https://doi.org/10.1515/9780822386032.

Gudeman, Stephen, and Alberto Rivera. 1990. *Conversations in Colombia: The Domestic Economy in Life and Text*. Cambridge University Press. https://doi.org/10.1017/CBO9780511558009.

Günel, Gökçe, Saiba Varma, and Chika Watanabe. 2020. "A Manifesto for Patchwork Ethnography." *Society for Cultural Anthropology*, 20 June. https://culanth.org/fieldsights/a-manifesto-for-patchwork-ethnography.

Gunn, Wendy, Ton Otto, and Rachel Charlotte Smith, eds. 2013. *Design Anthropology: Theory and Practice*. Routledge. https://doi.org/10.4324/9781003085195.

Gupta, Akhil, and James Ferguson. 1997. *Anthropological Locations: Boundaries and Grounds of a Field Science*. University of California Press.

Habermas, Jürgen. 1989. *The Structural Transformation of the Public Sphere: An Inquiry into a Category of Bourgeois Society.* MIT Press.

Hagen, Joel B. 1992. *An Entangled Bank: The Origins of Ecosystem Ecology.* Rutgers University Press. https://doi.org/10.36019/9780813566191.

Haig-Brown, Celia. 2008. "Working a Third Space: Indigenous Knowledge in the Post/Colonial University." *Canadian Journal of Native Education* 31 (1): 253–67. https://www.proquest.com/scholarly-journals/working-third-space-indigenous-knowledge-post/docview/230304425/se-2.

Haraway, Donna Jeanne. 1991. *Simians, Cyborgs, and Women: The Reinvention of Nature.* Routledge.

– 2010. "When Species Meet: Staying with the Trouble." *Environment and Planning D: Society & Space* 28, no. 1 (February): 53–5. http://dx.doi.org/10.1068/d2706wsh.

– 2016. *Staying with the Trouble: Making Kin in the Chthulucene.* Duke University Press. https://doi.org/10.2307/j.ctv11cw25q.

Harper, Douglas. 1986. "Meaning and Work: A Study in Photo Elicitation." *Current Sociology* 34 (3): 24–46. https://journals.sagepub.com/doi/10.1177/001139286034003006.

Harrison, Faye V. 1992. "Decolonizing Anthropology Moving Further toward an Anthropology for Liberation." *Anthropology News* 33, no. 3 (March): 24. https://doi.org/10.1111/an.1992.33.3.24.

Hartung, Catherine. 2017. *Conditional Citizens: Rethinking Children and Young People's Participation*, vol. 5. Springer Singapore. https://doi.org/10.1007/978-981-10-3938-6.

Heider, Karl G. 1975. "What Do People Do? Dani Auto-Ethnography." *Journal of Anthropological Research* 31, no. 1 (Spring): 3–17. https://doi.org/10.1086/jar.31.1.3629504.

Hennessy, Kate. 2010. "Repatriation, Digital Technology, and Culture in a Northern American Athapaskan Community." PhD diss., The University of British Columbia. https://doi.org/ 10.14288/1.0071074.

Heritage, John. 1984. *Garfinkel and Ethnomethodology.* Polity Press.

Hill, Richard W., and Daniel Coleman. 2019. "The Two Row Wampum-Covenant Chain Tradition as a Guide for Indigenous-University Research Partnerships." *Cultural Studies ↔ Critical Methodologies* 19, no. 5 (October): 339–59. https://doi.org/10.1177/1532708618809138.

Hogue, Michelle, and Cheryl Bartlett. 2014. "Two-Eyed Seeing: Creating a New Liminal Space in Education." *Education Canada* 54 (3): 25–7.

Holmes, Douglas R., and George E. Marcus. 2006. "Fast Capitalism: Para-Ethnography and the Rise of the Symbolic Analyst." In *Frontiers of Capital: Ethnographic Reflections on the New Economy.* Duke University Press. https://doi.org/10.2307/j.ctv11smt25.5.

– 2007. "Cultures of Expertise and the Management of Globalization: Toward the Re-Functioning of Ethnography." In *Global Assemblages: Technology, Politics, and Ethics as Anthropological Problems,* edited by Aihwa Ong and Stephen J. Collier, 235–52. Blackwell.

– 2008. "Collaboration Today and the Re-Imagination of the Classic Scene of Fieldwork Encounter." *Collaborative Anthropologies* 1:81–101. https://doi.org/10.1353/cla.0.0003.

Huf, Christina, and Markus Kluge. 2021. "Being (with) Batman – Entangled Research Relations in Ethnographic Research in Early Childhood Education and Care." *Ethnography and Education* 16 (3): 248–62. https://doi.org/10.1080/17457823.2021.1903961.

Hunt, Sarah. 2014. "Ontologies of Indigeneity: The Politics of Embodying a Concept." *Cultural Geographies* 21, no. 1 (January): 27–32. https://www.jstor.org/stable/10.2307/26168539.

Ingold, Tim. 2015. *The Life of Lines.* Routledge. https://doi.org/10.4324/9781315727240.

Innes, Robert Alexander. 2013. *Elder Brother and the Law of the People: Contemporary Kinship and Cowessess First Nation,* vol. 17. University of Manitoba Press. https://doi.org/10.1515/9780887554377.

Iwama, Marilyn, Murdena Marshall, Albert Marshall, and Cheryl Bartlett. 2009. "Two-Eyed Seeing and the Language of Healing in Community-Based Research." *Canadian Journal of Native Education* 32 (2): 3–116. https://www.proquest.com/scholarly-journals/two-eyed-seeing-language-healing-community-based/docview/756676629/se-2.

Jacobs, Beverly. 2008. "Response to Canada's Apology to Residential School Survivors." *Canadian Women Studies* 26 (3–4): 223–5. https://cws.journals.yorku.ca/index.php/cws/article/view/22138.

James, Allison. 2007. "Giving Voice to Children's Voices: Practices and Problems, Pitfalls and Potentials." *American Anthropologist* 109, no. 2 (June): 261–72. https://doi.org/10.1525/aa.2007.109.2.261.

James, Allison, Chris Jenks, and Alan Prout. 1998. *Theorizing Childhood*. Teachers College Press.

Jobson, Ryan Cecil. 2020. "The Case for Letting Anthropology Burn: Sociocultural Anthropology in 2019." *American Anthropologist* 122, no. 2 (June): 259–71. https://doi.org/10.1111/aman.13398.

Johnson, Ginger A. 2011. "A Child's Right to Participation: Photovoice as Methodology for Documenting the Experiences of Children Living in K Enyan Orphanages." *Visual Anthropology Review* 27 (2): 141–61. https://doi.org/10.1111/j.1548-7458.2011.01098.x.

Johnson, Ginger A., Anne E. Pfister, and Cecilia Vindrola-Padros. 2012. "Drawings, Photos, and Performances: Using Visual Methods with Children." *Visual Anthropology Review* 28 (2): 164–78. https://doi.org/10.1111/j.1548-7458.2012.01122.x.

Johnston, Patrick. 1983. *Native Children and the Child Welfare System*. Canadian Council on Social Development in association with James Lorimer and Company.

Justice, Daniel Heath. 2018. *Why Indigenous Literatures Matter*. Wilfrid Laurier University Press.

Kalua, Fetson. 2009. "Homi Bhabha's Third Space and African Identity." *Journal of African Cultural Studies* 21, no. 1 (June): 23–32. http://www.jstor.org/stable/40647476.

Kärtner, Joscha, Heidi Keller, Bettina Lamm, Monika Abels, Relindis D. Yovsi, and Nandita Chaudhary. 2007. "Manifestations of Autonomy and Relatedness in Mothers' Accounts of Their Ethnotheories Regarding Child Care across Five Cultural Communities." *Journal of Cross-Cultural Psychology* 38, no. 5 (September): 613–28. https://doi.org/10.1177/0022022107305242.

Kellett, Mary. 2010. "Small Shoes, Big Steps! Empowering Children as Active Researchers." *American Journal of Community Psychology* 46 (1–2): 195–203. https://doi.org/10.1007/s10464-010-9324-y.

– 2011. "Empowering Children and Young People as Researchers: Overcoming Barriers and Building Capacity." *Child Indicator Research* 4, no. 2 (April): 205–19. https://doi.org/10.1007/s12187-010-9103-1.

Kierans, Kim. 2003. "Mi'kmaq Craftsman Preserves 'old ways.'" *Halifax Sunday Herald*, C4.

Kim, Chae-Young. 2017. "Participation or Pedagogy? Ambiguities and Tensions Surrounding the Facilitation of Children as Researchers."

Childhood 24, no. 1 (February): 84–98. https://doi.org/10.1177/0907568216643146.

Kimmerer, Robin Wall. 2013. *Braiding Sweetgrass: Indigenous Wisdom, Scientific Knowledge and the Teachings of Plants*. Milkweed Editions.

King, James R. 1999. "Am Not! Are Too! Using Queer Standpoint in Postmodern Critical Ethnography." *International Journal of Qualitative Studies in Education* 12, no. 5 (November): 473–90. https://doi.org/10.1080/095183999235908.

Kohn, Eduardo. 2013. *How Forests Think: Toward an Anthropology Beyond the Human*. University of California Press. https://www.jstor.org/stable/10.1525/j.ctt7zw36z.

– 2015. "Anthropology of Ontologies." *Annual Review of Anthropology* 44: 311–27. https://www.jstor.org/stable/24811667.

Komulainen, Sirkka. 2007. "The Ambiguity of the Child's 'Voice' in Social Research." *Childhood* 14 (1): 11–28. https://doi.org/10.1177/0907568207068561.

Kovach, Margaret. 2021. *Indigenous Methodologies: Characteristics, Conversations, and Contexts*, 2nd ed. University of Toronto Press.

Laclau, Ernesto, and Chantel Mouffe. 1985. *Hegemony and Socialist Strategy: Towards a Radical Democratic Politics*. Verso.

Ladner, Kiera L. 2003. "Governing Within an Ecological Context: Creating an AlterNative Understanding of Blackfoot Governance." *Studies in Political Economy* 70 (1): 125–52. https://doi.org/10.1080/07078552.2003.11827132.

LaFrance, Jean, and Betty Bastien. 2007. "Here Be Dragons! Reconciling Indigenous and Western Knowledge to Improve Aboriginal Child Welfare." *First Peoples Child & Family Review* 3 (1): 105–26. https://id.erudit.org/iderudit/1069530ar.

Lamphere, Louise. 2004. "The Convergence of Applied, Practicing, and Public Anthropology in the 21st Century." *Human Organization* 63, no. 4 (Winter): 431–43. https://www.jstor.org/stable/44127389.

– 2018. "The Transformation of Ethnography: From Malinowski's Tent to the Practice of Collaborative/Activist Anthropology." *Human Organization* 77, no. 1 (Spring): 64–76. https://www.proquest.com/scholarly-journals/transformation-ethnography-malinowkis-tent/docview/2042206518/se-2.

Lancy, David F. 2015. *The Anthropology of Childhood: Cherubs, Chattel, Changelings*. 2nd ed. Cambridge University Press. https://doi.org/10.1017/CBO9781139680530.

"Land Back: A Yellowhead Institute Red Paper." 2019. Yellowhead Institute. https://redpaper.yellowheadinstitute.org.

Lang, Megan, and Becky Shelley. 2021. "Children as Researchers: Wild Things and the Dialogic Imagination." *Childhood* 28 (3): 427–43. https://doi.org/10.1177/09075682211020503.

Lassiter, Luke Eric. 2005. "Collaborative Ethnography and Public Anthropology." *Current Anthropology* 46, no. 1 (February): 83–106. https://doi.org/10.1086/425658.

– 2008. "Moving Past Public Anthropology and Doing Collaborative Research." *NAPA Bulletin* 29, no. 1 (March): 70–86. https://doi.org/10.1111/j.1556-4797.2008.00006.x.

Latour, Bruno. 2014. "From Ontology to Deontology: GAD Distinguished Lecture, 2013." *General Anthropology* 21, no. 1 (Spring): 1–4. https://doi.org/10.1111/j.1939-3466.2014.00001.x.

Latour, Bruno, and Steve Woolgar. 1986. *Laboratory Life: The Construction of Scientific Facts*. Princeton University Press. https://doi.org/10.1515/9781400820412.

Lave, Jean, and Etienne Wegner. 1991. *Situated Learning: Legitimate Peripheral Participation*. Cambridge University Press. https://doi.org/10.1017/CBO9780511815355.

Leon, Lucy, and Rachel Rosen. 2023. "Unaccompanied Migrant Children and Indebted Relations: Weaponizing Safeguarding." *Child & Family Social Work* 28 (4): 1056–65. https://doi.org/10.1111/cfs.13025.

Lewis, Ann. 2010. "Silence in the Context of 'Child Voice'." *Children & Society* 24 (1): 14–23. https://doi.org/10.1111/j.1099-0860.2008.00200.x.

Li, Tania. 2007. *The Will to Improve: Governmentality, Development, and the Practice of Politics*. Duke University Press.

Liabo, Kristin, and Helen Roberts. 2019. "Coproduction and Coproducing Research with Children and Their Parents." *Archives of Disease in Childhood* 104, no. 12 (December): 1134–7. https://doi.org/10.1136/archdischild-2018-316387.

Lien, Sigrid, and Hilde Nielssen, eds. 2021. *Adjusting the Lens: Indigenous Activism, Colonial Legacies, and Photographic Heritage*. UBC Press. https://doi.org/10.59962/9780774866620.

Little Bear, Leroy. 2000. "Jagged Worldviews Colliding." In *Reclaiming Indigenous Voice and Vision*, edited by Marie Battiste, 79–85. UBC Press.

Lonetree, Amy. 2019. "A Heritage of Resilience." *The Public Historian* 41, no. 1 (February): 34–50. https://www.jstor.org/stable/10.2307/26629783.

Longman, Nickita, Emily Riddle, Alex Wilson, and Saima Desai. 2020. "'Land Back' Is More than the Sum of Its Parts." *Briarpatch* 49 (5): 2. https://go.gale.com/ps/i.do?p=AONE&u=anon~7aaf7cc1&id=GALE%7CA636688793&v=2.1&it=r&sid=sitemap&asid=742e01f9.

Loveless, Natalie S. 2015. "Introduction." *RACAR: Revue d'art Canadienne/Canadian Art Review* 40 (1): 41–2. https://www.jstor.org/stable/24327423.

Lowie, Robert H. 1956. *The Crow Indians*. Irvington Publishers.

Lundy, Laura, and Lesley McEvoy. 2011. "Children's Rights and Research Processes: Assisting Children to (in)Formed Views." *Childhood* 19 (1): 129–44. https://doi.org/10.1177/0907568211409078.

Luttrell, Wendy. 2010. "'A Camera Is a Big Responsibility': A Lens for Analysing Children's Visual Voices." *Visual Studies* 25, no. 3: 224–37. https://doi.org/10.1080/1472586X.2010.523274.

Lydon, Jane. 2007. "Pictures Bring Us Messages." *History of Photography* 31 (1): 85–6. https://doi.org/10.1080/03087298.2007.10443506.

– 2010. "Return: The Photographic Archive and Technologies of Indigenous Memory." *Photographies* 3 (2): 173–87. https://doi.org/10.1080/17540763.2010.499610.

– 2019. "Photography and Critical Heritage: Australian Aboriginal Photographic Archives and the Stolen Generations." *The Public Historian* 41, no. 1 (February): 18–33. https://doi.org/10.1525/tph.2019.41.1.18.

Macdonald, Helen. 2014. *H Is for Hawk*. Penguin Random House UK.

Mack, Amy. 2021. "Follow the Memes: On the Construction of Far-right Identities Online." In *Digital Hate*, edited by S. Udupa, P. Henrik, and I. Gagliardone. Indiana University Press.

– 2023. "Defend the Frontier": On Identitarian Activism in the Prairies and Social Media Spaces. In *Global Identitarianism*, edited by J.P. Zúquete. Routledge.

Mack, Amy, and Jan Newberry. 2018. "'It Makes Me Feel Good to Teach People About My Culture:' On Collaborative Research Methods with Indigenous Young People." *Canadian Journal of Family and Youth* 10, no. 2 (April): 85–104. https://doi.org/10.29173/cjfy29392.

– 2020. "Brown Paper Chronicles: Refusal and the Limits of Collaborative Design Work with Indigenous Youth." *Collaborative Anthropologies* 13, no. 1 (Fall): 77–108. https://doi.org/10.1353/cla.2020.0001.

Mack, Amy, Jan Newberry, and Erin Spring. 2021. "Returning to the Trouble." *Entanglements* 4, (1): 28–31.

Malkki, Liisa. 2003. "Children and the Gendered Politics of Globalization: In Remembrance of Sharon Stephens." *American Ethnologist* 30, no. 2 (May): 216–24. https://www.jstor.org/stable/3805373.

Marcus, George E. 1998. *Ethnography Through Thick and Thin*. Princeton University Press. https://doi.org/10.1515/9781400851805.

– 2007. "Ethnography Two Decades after Writing Culture: From the Experimental to the Baroque." *Anthropological Quarterly* 80, no. 4 (Fall): 1127–45. https://doi.org/10.1353/anq.2007.0059.

– 2008. "Collaborative Options and Pedagogical Experiment in Anthropological Research on Experts and Policy Processes." *Anthropology in Action* 15, no. 2 (June): 47–57. https://doi.org/10.3167/aia.2008.150205.

Marcus, George E., and Michael M. J. Fischer. 1986. *Anthropology as Cultural Critique: An Experimental Moment in the Human Sciences*. University of Chicago Press.

Marker, Michael. 1998. "Going Native in the Academy: Choosing the Exotic over the Critical." *Anthropology & Education Quarterly* 29, no. 4 (December): 473–80. https://www.jstor.org/stable/3196292.

– 2000. "Economics and Local Self-Determination: Describing the Clash Zone in First Nations Education." *Canadian Journal of Native Education* 24, no. 1: 30–44. https://www.proquest.com/scholarly-journals/economics-local-self-determination-describing/docview/230306731/se-2.

– 2003. "Indigenous Voice, Community, and Epistemic Violence: The Ethnographer's 'Interests' and What 'Interests' the Ethnographer." *International Journal of Qualitative Studies in Education* 16, no. 3: 361–76. https://doi.org/10.1080/0951839032000086736.

– 2006. "After the Makah Whale Hunt: Indigenous Knowledge and Limits to Multicultural Discourse." *Urban Education* 41, no. 5 (September): 482–505. https://doi.org/10.1177/0042085906291923.

Mason, Jan, and Suzanne Hood. 2011. "Exploring Issues of Children as Actors in Social Research." *Children and Youth Services Review* 33, no. 4 (April): 490–5. https://doi.org/10.1016/j.childyouth.2010.05.011.

Mayall, Berry. 2008. "Conversations with Children: Working with Generational Issues." In *Research with Children: Perspectives and Practices*, edited by Pia Haudrup Christensen and Allison James, 109–24. Routledge.

McGranahan, Carole. 2016a. "Refusal and the Gift of Citizenship." *Cultural Anthropology* 31 (3): 334–41. https://doi.org/10.14506/ca31.3.03.

– 2016b. "Theorizing Refusal: An Introduction." *Cultural Anthropology* 31 (3): 319–25. https://doi.org/10.14506/ca31.3.01.

McKenzie, Holly A., Collene Varcoe, Annette J. Browne, and Linda Day. 2016. "Disrupting the Continuities among Residential Schools, the Sixties Scoop, and Child Welfare: An Analysis of Colonial and Neocolonial Discourses." *International Indigenous Policy Journal* 7 (2): 1–24. https://doi.org/10.18584/iipj.2016.7.2.4.

Mead, Margaret. 1928. *Coming of Age in Samoa: A Psychological Study of Primitive Youth for Western Civilisation*. William Morrow and Company.

Mignolo, Walter D., and Arturo Escobar, eds. 2013. *Globalization and the Decolonial Option*. Routledge. https://doi.org/10.4324/9781315868448.

Milloy, John S. 1999. *A National Crime: The Canadian Government and the Residential School System, 1879 to 1986*. University of Manitoba Press. https://doi.org/10.1515/9780887553035.

Milne, E-J. 2016. "Critiquing Participatory Video: Experiences from around the World." *Area* 48, no. 4 (December): 401–4. https://doi.org/10.1111/area.12271.

Milun, Kathryn. 2001. "Keeping-While-Giving-Back: Computer Imaging and Native American Repatriation." *Political and Legal Anthropology Review* 24, no. 2 (November): 39–57. https://doi.org/10.1525/pol.2001.24.2.39.

Mitchell, Timothy. 2002. *Rule of Experts: Egypt, Techno-Politics, Modernity.* University of California Press. https://doi.org/10.1525/9780520928251.

Mol, Annemarie. 2002. *The Body Multiple: Ontology in Medical Practice.* Duke University Press. https://doi.org/10.1215/9780822384151.

Moore, Henrietta L. 1989. *Feminism and Anthropology.* University of Minnesota Press.

Moreton-Robinson, Aileen. 2009. "Introduction: Critical Indigenous Theory." *Cultural Studies Review* 15, no. 2 (September): 11–12. https://login.uleth.idm.oclc.org/login?url=https://www.proquest.com/scholarly-journals/introduction-critical-indigenous-theory/docview/635921877/se-2.

Murphy, Keith M. 2016. "Design and Anthropology." *Annual Review of Anthropology* 45, no. 1 (November): 433–49. https://doi.org/10.1146/annurev-anthro-102215-100224.

Nandy, Ashis. 1984. "Reconstructing Childhood: A Critique of the Ideology of Adulthood." *Alternatives: Global, Local, Political* 10, no. 3 (July): 359–75. https://doi.org/10.1177/030437548401000303.

Newberry, Jan. 2006. *Back Door Java: State Formation and the Domestic in Working Class Java.* University of Toronto Press.

– 2008. "Women's Ways of Walking: Gender and Urban Space in Java." In *Gender in an Urban World*, edited by Judith DeSena, 77–102. Emerald Group. https://doi.org/10.1016/S1047-0042(07)00004-9.

– 2010. "The Global Child and Non-Governmental Governance of the Family in Post-Suharto Indonesia." *Economy and Society* 39 (3): 403–26. https://doi.org/10.1080/03085147.2010.486217.

– 2012. "Empowering Children, Disempowering Women." *Ethics and Social Welfare* 6 (3): 247–59. https://doi.org/10.1080/17496535.2012.704057.

– 2013. *Back Door Java: Negara, Rumah Tangga dan Kampung di Keluarga Jawa.* Translated by Bernadetta Esti Sumarah. Yayasan Pustaka Obor Indonesia and KITLV-Jakarta.

– 2014. "Women Against Children: Early Childhood Education and the Domestic Community in Post-Suharto Indonesia." *TRaNS: Trans-Regional and -National Studies of Southeast Asia* 2, no. 2 (July): 271–91. https://doi.org/10.1017/trn.2014.7.

– 2017a. "'Anything Can Be Used to Stimulate Child Development': Early Childhood Education and Development in Indonesia as a Durable Assemblage." *Journal of Asian Studies* 76, no. 1 (February): 25–45. https://doi.org/10.1017/S0021911816001650.

– 2017b. "Interiority and Government of the Child: Transparency, Risk, and Good Governance in Indonesia." *Focaal: Journal of Global and Historical Anthropology* 77:76–89.

– 2018. "A Kampung Corner: Infrastructure, Affect, Informality." *Indonesia,* no. 105, 191–206. https://doi.org/10.1353/ind.2018.0008.

– 2021. "Photographic Bundles." *Entanglements* 4 (1): 36–40.

Newberry, Jan, and Makita Mikuliak. 2020. "How Fieldwork in a TBL Classroom Shaped Landscapes of Social Learning." *Learning Communities Journal* 12:65–80.

Newberry, Jan, and Tanya Pace-Crosschild. 2019. "Braiding Sweetgrass Families: A Transmedia Project on Parenting in Blackfoot Territory." *Families, Relationships, and Society* 9(1): 173–80. https://doi.org/10.1332/204674319X15592173807871.

Noble, Brian. 2002. "Niitooii – 'The Same That Is Real': Parallel Practice, Museums, and the Repatriation of Piikani Customary Authority." *Anthropologica* 44 (1): 113–30. https://doi.org/10.2307/25606064.

Nolas, Sevasti-Melissa. 2015. "Children's Participation, Childhood Publics and Social Change: A Review." *Children & Society* 29 (2): 157–67. https://doi.org/10.1111/chso.12108.

Oliver, Mary. 1994. *White Pine*. Harcourt.

Olszewski, Brandon, Deborah Macey, and Lauren Lindstrom. 2006. "The Practical Work of <Coding>: An Ethnomethodological Inquiry." *Human Studies* 29, no. 3 (September): 363–80. https://doi.org/10.1007/s10746-006-9029-2.

Ong, Aihwa, and Stephen J. Collier. 2005. "Global Assemblages Anthropological Problems." In *Global Assemblages: Technology, Politics, and Ethics as Anthropological Problems*. Blackwell.

Association of Social Anthropologists of Aotearoa/New Zealand (ASAA/NZ). 2018. "An Open Letter to the HAU Journal's Board of Trustees." ASAA/NZ website, 18 June. https://www.asaanz.org/blog/2018/6/18/an-open-letter-to-the-hau-journals-board-of-trustees.

Ortner, Sherry. 1995. "Resistance and the Problem of Ethnographic Refusal. Comparative Studies in Society and History." *Comparative Studies in Society and History* 37, no. 1 (January): 173–93. https://doi.org/10.1017/S0010417500019587.

Osterweil, Michal. 2013. "Rethinking Public Anthropology Through Epistemic Politics and Theoretical Practice." *Cultural Anthropology* 28, no. 4 (November): 598–620. https://www.jstor.org/stable/43898499.

Owens, Louis. 2003. "Afterword: Their Shadows Before Them: Photographing Indians." In *Trading Gazes: Euro-American Women Photographers and Native North Americans, 1880–1940*. Rutgers University Press.

Pace-Crosschild, Tanya. 2018. "Decolonising Childrearing and Challenging the Patriarchal Nuclear Family through Indigenous Knowledges: An Opokaa'sin Project." In *Feminism and the Politics of Childhood: Friends or Foes?* edited by Rachel Rosen and Katherine Twamley, 191–97. UCL Press. https://doi.org/10.2307/j.ctt21c4t9k.19.

Pandian, Anand. 2019. *A Possible Anthropology: Methods for Uneasy Times*. Duke University Press. https://doi.org/10.1215/9781478004370.

Pangastuti, Yulida. 2023. "The (Dis-)Appearance of '(M)Others': The Roles of International Development Organizations on the Discourses of Women in Indonesia's Early Childhood Education Programs." In *Education in Indonesia: Critical Perspectives on Equity and Social Justice*, 17–29. Springer Singapore. https://doi.org/10.1007/978-981-99-1878-2_2.

Parreñas, Juno Salazar. 2020. "From Decolonial Indigenous Knowledges to Vernacular Ideas in Southeast Asia." *History and Theory* 59, no. 3 (September): 413–20. https://doi.org/10.1111/hith.12169.

Pateman, Carole. 1989. *The Disorder of Women: Democracy, Feminism and Political Theory*. Stanford University Press.

Pauwel, Luc. 2015. *Reframing Visual Social Science: Towards a More Visual Sociology and Anthropology*. Cambridge University Press. https://doi.org/10.1017/CBO9781139017633.

Pink, Sarah. 2011. "Multimodality, Multisensoriality and Ethnographic Knowing: Social Semiotics and the Phenomenology of Perception." *Qualitative Research* 11, no. 3 (June): 261–76. https://doi.org/10.1177/1468794111399835.

Pole, Christopher, Phillip Mizen, and Angela Bolton. 1999. "Realising Children's Agency in Research: Partners and Participants?" *International Journal of Social Research Methodology* 2 (1): 39–54. https://doi.org/10.1080/136455799295177.

Povinelli, Elizabeth A. 2001. "Radical Worlds: The Anthropology of Incommensurability and Inconceivability." *Annual Review of Anthropology* 30 (October): 319–34. https://doi.org/10.1146/annurev.anthro.30.1.319.

– 2002. *The Cunning of Recognition: Indigenous Alterities and the Making of Australian Multiculturalism*. Duke University Press. https://doi.org/10.2307/j.ctv116895z.

Pratt, Mary Louise. 1991. "Arts of the Contact Zone." *Profession*: 33–40. http://www.jstor.org/stable/25595469.

Pratt, Yvonne Poitras. 2019. *Digital Storytelling in Indigenous Education: A Decolonizing Journey for a Métis Community*. Routledge. https://doi.org/10.4324/9781315265544

Putnam, Robert D. 2000. *Bowling Alone: The Collapse and Revival of American Community*. Simon and Schuster. https://doi.org/10.1145/358916.361990.

Qvortrup, Jens. 2009. "Are Children Human Beings or Human Becomings? A Critical Assessment of Outcome Thinking." *Rivista Internazionale Di Scienze Sociali* 117, no. 2–4 (July–December): 631–53. https://www.jstor.org/stable/41625246.

Rabinow, Paul, George E. Marcus, James D. Faubion, and Tobias Rees. 2008. *Designs for an Anthropology of the Contemporary*. A John Hope Franklin Center Book. Duke University Press. https://doi.org/10.1515/9780822390060.

Rappaport, Joanne. 2008. "Beyond Participant Observation: Collaborative Ethnography as Theoretical Innovation." *Collaborative Anthropologies* 1:1–31. https://doi.org/10.1353/cla.0.0014.

Recollet, Karyn. 2015. "Glyphing Decolonial Love through Urban Flash Mobbing and 'Walking with Our Sisters.'" *Curriculum Inquiry* 45, no. 1 (January): 129–45. http://www.jstor.org/stable/43941689.

Reichman, Daniel. 2011. "Migration and Paraethnography in Honduras." *American Ethnologist* 38 (3): 548–58. https://doi.org/10.1111/j.1548-1425.2011.01322.x.

Reid, Brady. 2020. "Positionality and Research: 'Two-Eyed Seeing' with a Rural Ktaqmkuk Mi'kmaw Community." *International Journal of Qualitative Methods* 19:1–12. https://doi.org/10.1177/1609406920910841.

Riles, Annelise. 2000a. "An Ethnography of Abstractions?" *Cornell Law Faculty Publications*. Paper 781. http://scholarship.law.cornell.edu/facpub/781.

– 2000b. *The Network Inside Out*. University of Michigan Press. https://doi.org/10.3998/mpub.15517.

– 2013. "Market Collaboration: Finance, Culture, and Ethnography after Neoliberalism: Market Collaboration." *American Anthropologist* 115, no. 4 (December): 555–69. https://doi.org/10.1111/aman.12052.

Rollo, Toby. 2018a. "Feral Children: Settler Colonialism, Progress, and the Figure of the Child." *Settler Colonial Studies* 8 (1): 60–79. https://doi.org/10.1080/2201473X.2016.1199826.

– 2018b. "The Color of Childhood: The Role of the Child/Human Binary in the Production of Anti-Black Racism." *Journal of Black Studies* 49, no 4 (May): 307–29. https://doi.org/10.1177/0021934718760769.

Rosen, Rachel. 2023. "Participatory Research in and against Time." *Qualitative Research* 23 (3): 597–613. https://doi.org/10.1177/14687941211041940.

Sabzalian, Leilani. 2018. "Curricular Standpoints and Native Feminist Theories: Why Native Feminist Theories Should Matter to Curriculum Studies." *Curriculum Inquiry* 48 (3): 359–82. https://doi.org/10.1080/03626784.2018.1474710.

– 2019. *Indigenous Children's Survivance in Public Schools*. Routledge. https://doi.org/10.4324/9780429427503.

Sæther, Elin, Ole Kolbjørn Kjørven, Joke Dewilde, and Thor-André Skrefsrud. 2024. "Listening to Young People's Voices: Attempts at Developing Context- and Participant-Sensitive Approaches." *Childhood* 31 (2): 176–91. https://doi.org/10.1177/09075682241246394.

Said, Edward W. 1978. *Orientalism: Western Concepts of the Orient*. Pantheon Books.

Samuels, Jeffrey. 2004. "Breaking the Ethnographer's Frame: Reflections on the Use of Photo Elicitation in Understanding Sri Lankan Monastic Culture." *The American Behavioral Scientist* 47, no. 12 (August): 1528–50. https://doi.org/10.1177/0002764204266238.

Scheper-Hughes, Nancy, and Carolyn Fishel Sargent, eds. 1999. *Small Wars: The Cultural Politics of Childhood*. University of California Press. https://doi.org/10.1525/9780520919266.

Schwartz, Dona. 1989. "Visual Ethnography: Using Photography in Qualitative Research." *Qualitative Sociology* 12 (2): 119–54. https://doi.org/10.1007/BF00988995.

Seesequasis, Paul. 2019. *Blanket Toss Under Midnight Sun: Portraits of Everyday Life in Eight Indigenous Communities.* Knopf Canada.

Shah, Payal. 2015. "Spaces to Speak: Photovoice and the Reimagination of Girls' Education in India." *Comparative Education Review* 59, no. 1 (February): 50–74. https://doi.org/10.1086/678699.

Shankar, Arjun. 2019. "Listening to Images, Participatory Pedagogy, and Anthropological (Re-) Inventions." *American Anthropologist* 121, no. 1 (March): 229–42. https://doi.org/10.1111/aman.13205.

Sharrock, Wes, and Dave Randall. 2004. "Ethnography, Ethnomethodology and the Problem of Generalisation in Design." *European Journal of Information Systems* 13 (3): 186–94. https://doi.org/10.1057/palgrave.ejis.3000502.

Shaw, Patricia A. 2021. "Photo-Elicitation and Photo-Voice: Using Visual Methodological Tools to Engage with Younger Children's Voices about Inclusion in Education." *International Journal of Research & Method in Education* 44 (4): 337–51. https://doi.org/10.1080/1743727X.2020.1755248.

Simeone, Luca. 2010. "Distributed Learning Infrastructures in the Anthropology of Design." *Design Principles and Practices: An International Journal – Annual Review* 4 (2): 95–102. https://doi.org/10.18848/1833-1874/CGP/v04i02/37858.

Simpson, Audra. 2007. "On Ethnographic Refusal: Indigeneity, 'Voice' and Colonial Citizenship." *Junctures* 9:67–80.

– 2014. *Mohawk Interruptus: Political Life Across the Borders of Settler States.* Duke University Press. https://doi.org/10.1515/9780822376781.

– 2016. "Consent's Revenge." *Cultural Anthropology* 31 (3): 326–33. https://doi.org/10.14506/ca31.3.02.

– 2017. "The Ruse of Consent and the Anatomy of 'Refusal': Cases from Indigenous North America and Australia." *Postcolonial Studies* 20 (1): 18–33. https://doi.org/10.1080/13688790.2017.1334283.

Simpson, Leanne Betasamosake. 2014. "Land as Pedagogy: Nishnaabeg Intelligence and Rebellious Transformation." *Decolonization: Indigeneity, Education & Society* 3 (3): 1–25.

– 2016. "Indigenous Resurgence and Co-Resistance." *Critical Ethnic Studies* 2, no. 2 (Fall): 19–34. https://doi.org/10.5749/jcritethnstud.2.2.0019.

– 2017. *As We Have Always Done: Indigenous Freedom through Radical Resistance.* University of Minnesota Press. https://doi.org/10.5749/j.ctt1pwt77c.

– 2022. "Kwe as Resurgent Method." *Feminist Asylum: A Journal of Critical Interventions* 1, no. 1 (October). https://doi.org/10.5195/faci.2022.85.

Singh, Julietta. 2018. *Unthinking Mastery: Dehumanism and Decolonial Entanglements*. Duke University Press.

Skelton, Tracey. 2008. "Research with Children and Young People: Exploring the Tensions between Ethics, Competence and Participation." *Children's Geographies* 6 (1): 21–36. https://doi.org/10.1080/14733280701791876.

Slater, Lisa. 2021. "Learning to Stand with Gyack: A Practice of Thinking with Non-Innocent Care." *Australian Feminist Studies* 36 (108): 200–11. https://doi.org/10.1080/08164649.2021.1998883.

Smith, Dorothy E. 1992. "Sociology from Women's Experience: A Reaffirmation." *Sociological Theory* 10, no. 1 (Spring): 88–98. https://doi.org/10.2307/202020.

Smith, Hinekura. 2019. "Whatuora: Theorizing' 'New' Indigenous Research Methodology from 'Old' Indigenous Weaving Practice." *Art/Research International* 4 (1): 1–27. http://hdl.handle.net/2292/47160.

Smith, Linda Tuhiwai. 1999. *Decolonizing Methodologies: Research and Indigenous Peoples*. Zed Books.

Smith, Linda Tuhiwai, Eve Tuck, and Wayne Yang, eds. 2019. *Indigenous and Decolonizing Studies in Education: Mapping the Long View*. Routledge, Taylor & Francis Group. https://doi.org/10.4324/9780429505010.

Smith, Rachel Charlotte, ed. 2022. "Editorial: Design Anthropology." *Design Studies* 80 (May): 1–6. https://doi.org/10.1016/j.destud.2022.101081.

Solberg, Anne. 1996. "The Challenge in Child Research: From 'Being' to 'Doing.'" In *Children in Families*, edited by Julia Brannen and Margaret O'Brien. Routledge. https://doi.org/10.4324/9780203453803.

Soto, Lourdes Diaz, and Beth Blue Swadener. 2016. *Power and Voice in Research with Children*. Peter Lang.

Spencer, Grace, Hannah Fairbrother, and Jill Thompson. 2020. "Privileges of Power: Authenticity, Representation and the 'Problem' of Children's Voices in Qualitative Health Research." *International Journal of Qualitative Methods* 19 (January): 1609406920958597. https://doi.org/10.1177/1609406920958597.

Spradley, James. 2000. *You Owe Yourself a Drunk: An Ethnography of Urban Nomads*. Waveland Press.

Spring, Erin. 2016. "'Everyone Here Knows a Junior': Blackfoot Children and Their Books." *Bookbird* 54 (1): 55–60. https://doi.org/10.1353/bkb.2016.0018.

Spring, Erin, and Andrea True Joy Fox. 2018. "'I Never Read Anything Like That before': Mapping the Identities of Blackfoot Readers." *Canadian Journal of Family and Youth/Le Journal Canadien de Famille et de La Jeunesse* 10 (2): 51–66. https://doi.org/10.29173/cjfy29389.

Spyrou, Spyros. 2011. "The Limits of Children's Voices: From Authenticity to Critical, Reflexive Representation." *Childhood* 18 (2): 151–65. https://doi.org/10.1177/0907568210387834.

– 2016. "Researching Children's Silences: Exploring the Fullness of Voice in Childhood Research." *Childhood* 23 (1): 7–21. https://doi.org/10.1177/0907568215571618.

Spyrou, Spyros, Rachel Rosen, and Daniel Thomas Cook, eds. 2018. *Reimagining Childhood Studies*. Bloomsbury.

Starn, Orin. 2011. "Here Come the Anthros (Again): The Strange Marriage of Anthropology and Native America." *Cultural Anthropology* 26, no. 2 (May): 179–204. https://www.jstor.org/stable/41238319.

Statistics Canada. 2019. "Census Profile, 2016 Census, Lethbridge." https://www12.statcan.gc.ca/census-recensement/2016/dp-pd/prof/details/page.cfm?Lang=E&Geo1=FED&Code1=48026&Geo2=POPC&Code2=0467&SearchText=Lethbridge&SearchType=Begins&SearchPR=01&B1=Population&TABID=1&type=0.

Stengers, Isabelle. 2011. "Comparison as a Matter of Concern." *Common Knowledge* 17 (1): 48–63. https://doi.org/10.1215/0961754X-7299270.

Stephens, Sharon. 1995. *Children and the Politics of Culture*. Princeton University Press.

Steward, Julian Haynes. 1972. *Theory of Culture Change: The Methodology of Multilinear Evolution*. University of Illinois Press.

Stewart, Georgina. 2017. "The 'Hau' of Research: Mauss Meets Kaupapa Māori." *Journal of World Philosophies* 2, no. 2 (June): 1–11. https://doi.org/10.2979/jourworlphil.2.1.01.

Stewart, Susan C. 2011. "Interpreting Design Thinking." *Design Studies* 32, no. 6 (November): 515–20. https://doi.org/10.1016/j.destud.2011.08.001.

Stirling, Bridget. 2022. "Childhood, Futurity, and Settler Time." *Journal of Childhood Studies* 47, no. 3 (June): 34–46. https://doi.org/10.18357/jcs202219927.

Stocking, George W. Jr. 1983. "The Ethnographer's Magic: Fieldwork in British Anthropology from Tylor to Malinowski." In *Observers Observed: Essays on Ethnographic Fieldwork*. University of Wisconsin Press.

Stoler, Ann. 2001. "Tense and Tender Ties: The Politics of Comparison in North American History and (Post) Colonial Studies." *The Journal of American History* 88, no. 3 (December): 829–65. https://doi.org/10.2307/2700385.

Strathern, Marilyn. 2005. *Kinship, Law and the Unexpected: Relatives Are Always a Surprise*. Cambridge University Press. https://doi.org/10.1017/CBO9780511614514.

– 2018a. "Opening up Relations." In *A World of Many Worlds*, 23–53. Duke University Press. https://doi.org/10.1215/9781478004318-002.

– 2018b. "Relations: An Anthropological Account." In *The Open Encyclopedia of Anthropology*, edited by Felix Stein. Facsimile of the First Edition in The Cambridge Encyclopedia of Anthropology. http://doi.org/10.29164/18relations.

Suchman, Lucy. 2011. "Anthropological Relocations and the Limits of Design." *Annual Review of Anthropology* 40 (October): 1–18. https://doi.org/10.1146/annurev-anthro-041608.105640.

Tallbear, Kim. 2014. "Standing With and Speaking as Faith: A Feminist-Indigenous Approach to Inquiry." *Journal of Research Practice* 10 (2): 1–7. https://jrp.icaap.org/index.php/jrp/article/view/405.html.

Tedlock, Barbara. 1995. "Works and Wives: On the Sexual Division of Textual Labor." In *Women Writing Culture*, 267–86. University of California Press. https://doi.org/10.1525/9780520916814-018.

Thomas, Nigel. 2017. "Turning the Tables: Children as Researchers." In *Research with Children: Perspectives and Practices*, edited by Pia Haudrup Christensen and Allison James, 160–79. Routledge.

Thompson, Jennifer A. 2016. "Urban Youth and Photovoice: Visual Ethnography in Action." *Global Public Health* 11 (5–6): 812–13. https://doi.org/10.1080/17441692.2016.1169308.

Thomson, Pat. 2008. "Children and Young People: Voices in Visual Research." In *Doing Visual Research with Children and Young People*, edited by Pat Thomson, 1–20. Routledge. https://doi.org/10.4324/9780203870525.

Tilley, Helen. 2010. "Global Histories, Vernacular Science, and African Genealogies; Or, Is the History of Science Ready for the World?" *Isis* 101, no. 1 (March): 110–19. https://doi.org/10.1086/652692.

Todd, Zoe. 2016. "An Indigenous Feminist's Take on the Ontological Turn: 'Ontology' Is Just Another Word for Colonialism." *Journal of Historical Sociology* 29, no. 1 (March): 4–22. https://doi.org/10.1111/johs.12124.

– 2018. *Coloniality, Ontology, and the Question of the Posthuman*. Routledge.

Trouillot, Michel-Rolph. 2003. "Anthropology and the Savage Slot: The Poetics and Politics of Otherness." In *Global Transformations: Anthropology and the Modern World*, 7–28. Palgrave Macmillan. https://doi.org/10.1007/978-1-137-04144-9.

Truth and Reconciliation Commission of Canada (TRC). 2015a. *Truth and Reconciliation Commission of Canada: Calls to Action*. https://www.trc.ca.

– 2015b. *Honouring the Truth, Reconciling for the Future: Summary of the Final Report of the Truth and Reconciliation Commission of Canada*. Truth and Reconciliation Commission of Canada. https://publications.gc.ca/collections/collection_2015/trc/IR4-7-2015-eng.pdf.

– 2016. *Canada's Residential Schools: Missing Children and Unmarked Burials: The Final Report of the Truth and Reconciliation Commission of Canada*, vol, 4. McGill-Queen's University Press. https://doi.org/10.2307/j.ctt19rmbnh.

Tsing, Anna. 2005. *Friction: An Ethnography of Global Connection*. Princeton University Press. https://doi.org/10.1515/9780691263526.

– 2012. "Unruly Edges: Mushrooms as Companion Species: For Donna Haraway." *Environmental Humanities* 1, no. 1 (May): 141–54. https://doi.org/10.1215/22011919-3610012.

– 2015. *The Mushroom at the End of the World: On the Possibility of Life in Capitalist Ruins*. Princeton University Press. https://doi.org/10.1515/9781400873548.

Tsing, Anna, Andrew S. Mathews, and Nils Bubandt. 2019. "Patchy Anthropocene: Landscape Structure, Multispecies History, and the Retooling of Anthropology: An Introduction to Supplement 20." *Current Anthropology* 60, no. S20 (August): 186–97. https://doi.org/10.1086/703391.

Tsinhnahjinnie, Hulleah. 2003. "When Is a Picture Worth a Thousand Words." In *Photography's Other Histories*, edited by Christopher Pinney and Nicolas Peterson, 40–52. Duke University Press. https://www.jstor.org/stable/j.ctv125jgs7.7.

Tuck, Eve. 2009. "Suspending Damage: A Letter to Communities." *Harvard Educational Review* 79, no. 3 (September): 409–28. https://doi.org/10.17763/haer.79.3.n0016675661t3n15.

Tuck, Eve, and Rubén A Gaztambide-Fernández. 2013. "Curriculum, Replacement, and Settler Futurity." *Journal of Curriculum Theorizing* 29 (1): 72–89.

Tuck, Eve, Marcia McKenzie, and Kate McCoy. 2014. "Land Education: Indigenous, Post-Colonial, and Decolonizing Perspectives on Place and Environmental Education Research." *Environmental Education Research* 20, no. 1: 1–23. https://doi.org/10.1080/13504622.2013.877708.

Tuck, Eve, Haliehana Stepetin, Rebecca Beaulne-Stuebing, and Jo Billows. 2023. "Visiting as an Indigenous Feminist Practice." *Gender and Education* 35, no. 2: 144–55. https://doi.org/10.1080/09540253.2022.2078796.

Tuck, Eve, and Wayne Yang. 2014a. "R-Words: Refusing Research." In *Humanizing Research: Decolonizing Qualitative Inquiry with Youth and Communities*, 223–48. SAGE. https://doi.org/10.4135/9781544329611.

– 2014b. "Unbecoming Claims: Pedagogies of Refusal in Qualitative Research." *Qualitative Inquiry* 20, no. 6 (July): 811–18. https://doi.org/10.1177/1077800414530265.

– 2014c. *Youth Resistance Research and Theories of Change*. Routledge, Taylor & Francis Group. https://doi.org/10.4324/9780203585078.

–, eds. 2018. *Toward What Justice? Describing Diverse Dreams of Justice in Education*. https://doi.org/10.4324/9781351240932.

Vangkilde, Kasper Tang, and Morten Hulvej Rod. 2015. "Para-Ethnography 2.0: An Experiment with the Distribution of Perspective in Collaborative Fieldwork." Paper for the seminar 'Collaborative Formation of Issues,' 22–23 January, Aarhus, Denmark. The Research Network for Design Anthropology.

Varvantakis, Christos, and Sevasti-Melissa Nolas. 2019. "Metaphors We Experiment with in Multimodal Ethnography." *International Journal of Social Research Methodology* 22 (4): 365–78. https://doi.org/10.1080/13645579.2019.1574953.

Varvantakis, Christos, Sevasti-Melissa Nolas, and Vinnarasan Aruldoss. 2019. "Photography, Politics and Childhood: Exploring Children's Multimodal Relations with the Public Sphere." *Visual Studies* 34 (3): 266–80. https://doi.org/10.1080/1472586X.2019.1691049.

Veracini, Lorenzo. 2015. *The Settler Colonial Present*. Palgrave Macmillan. https://doi.org/10.1057/9781137372475.

Vizenor, Gerald. 2008. *Survivance: Narratives of Native Presence*. University of Nebraska Press.

Wall, John. 2022. "From Childhood Studies to Childism: Reconstructing the Scholarly and Social Imaginations." *Children's Geographies* 20 (3): 257–70. https://doi.org/10.1080/14733285.2019.1668912.

Walley, Christine J. 2015. "Transmedia as Experimental Ethnography: The Exit Zero Project, Deindustrialization, and the Politics of Nostalgia." *American Ethnologist* 42, no. 4 (November): 624–39. https://doi.org/10.1111/amet.12160.

Walter, Maggie, Tahu Kukutai, Stephanie Russo Carroll, and Desi Rodriguez-Lonebear, eds. 2020. *Indigenous Data Sovereignty and Policy*, 1st ed. Routledge. https://doi.org/10.4324/9780429273957.

Walter, Maggie, and Michele Suina. 2019. "Indigenous Data, Indigenous Methodologies and Indigenous Data Sovereignty." *International Journal of Social Research Methodology* 22 (3): 233–43. https://doi.org/10.1080/13645579.2018.1531228.

Wark, Joe, Raymond Neckoway, and Keith Brownlee. 2019. "Interpreting a Cultural Value: An Examination of the Indigenous Concept of Non-Interference in North America." *International Social Work* 62, no. 1 (January): 419–32. https://doi.org/10.1177/0020872817731143.

Warner, Michael. 2002. "Publics and Counterpublics." *Public Culture* 14 (1): 24–90. https://doi.org/10.1215/08992363-14-1-49.

Wasson, Christina. 2000. "Ethnography in the Field of Design." *Human Organization* 59, no. 4 (Winter): 377–88. https://doi.org/10.17730/humo.59.4.h13326628n127516.

Watts, Vanessa. 2016. "Smudge This: Assimilation, State-Favoured Communities and the Denial of Indigenous Spiritual Lives." *International Journal of Child, Youth and Family Studies* 7 (1): 148–70. https://doi.org/10.18357/ijcyfs.71201615676.

Wemigwans, Jennifer. 2016. "A Digital Bundle: Exploring the Impact of Indigenous Knowledge Online through FourDirectionsTeachings.Com." PhD diss., University of Toronto.

White, Richard. 2006. "Creative Misunderstandings and New Understandings." *The William and Mary Quarterly* 63, no. 1 (January): 9–14. https://doi.org/10.2307/3491722.

Williams, Carol. 2003. *Framing the West: Race, Gender, and the Photographic Frontier in the Pacific Northwest*. Oxford University Press. https://doi.org/10.1093/oso/9780195146301.001.0001.

Wilson, Nance, Stefan Dasho, Anna C. Martin, Nina Wallerstein, Caroline C. Wang, and Meredith Minkler. 2007. "Engaging Young Adolescents in Social Action Through Photovoice: The Youth Empowerment Strategies (YES!) Project." *The Journal of Early Adolescence* 27, no. 2 (May): 241–61. https://doi.org/10.1177/0272431606294834.

Wilson, Shawn. 2008. *Research Is Ceremony: Indigenous Research Method.* Fernwood.

Wissler, Clark. 1927. "The Culture-Area Concept in Social Anthropology." *American Journal of Sociology* 32, no. 6 (May): 881–91. https://www.jstor.org/stable/2765396.

Wolf, Eric. 1982. *Europe and the People without History.* University of California Press.

Wolf, Paulette Running, and Julie A. Rickard. 2003. "Talking Circles: A Native American Approach to Experiential Learning." *Journal of Multicultural Counseling and Development* 31, no. 1 (January): 39–43. https://doi.org/10.1002/j.2161-1912.2003.tb00529.x.

Wolfe, Patrick. 2006. "Settler Colonialism and the Elimination of the Native." *Journal of Genocide Research* 8 (2): 387–409. https://doi.org/10.1080/14623520601056240.

Young, Bryanne. 2015. "'Killing the Indian in the Child': Death, Cruelty, and Subject-Formation in the Canadian Indian Residential School System." *Mosaic: An Interdisciplinary Critical Journal* 48, no. 4 (December): 63–76. https://www.jstor.org/stable/44030407.

Young-Bruehl, Elisabeth. 2012. *Childism: Confronting Prejudice against Children.* Yale University Press.

Zaloom, Caitlin. 2004. "The Productive Life of Risk." *Cultural Anthropology* 19, no. 3 (August): 365–91. https://doi.org/10.1525/can.2004.19.3.365.

Zedeño, María Nieves. 2008. "Bundled Worlds: The Roles and Interactions of Complex Objects from the North American Plains." *Journal of Archaeological Method and Theory* 15, no. 4 (December): 362–78. https://doi.org/10.1007/s10816-008-9058-4.

Index

Note: Figures are denoted by the letter *f* following the page number.